Building Boys

Building Boys

Raising Great Guys in a World that Misunderstands Males

Jennifer L. W. Fink

ROWMAN & LITTLEFIELD
Lanham • Boulder • New York • London

Published by Rowman & Littlefield
An imprint of The Rowman & Littlefield Publishing Group, Inc.
4501 Forbes Boulevard, Suite 200, Lanham, Maryland 20706
www.rowman.com

86-90 Paul Street, London EC2A 4NE

Distributed by NATIONAL BOOK NETWORK

British Library Cataloguing in Publication Information Available

Library of Congress Cataloging-in-Publication Data

978-1-5381-5955-2 (cloth)
978-1-5381-5956-9 (electronic)

♾™ The paper used in this publication meets the minimum requirements of American National Standard for Information Sciences—Permanence of Paper for Printed Library Materials, ANSI/NISO Z39.48-1992.

For my four boys: Nathan, Tyler, Adam, and Sam

Contents

Introduction

You know what kind of boy you *don't* want to raise.

You don't want to raise a sexual predator or mass shooter. You do not want to raise a man who takes advantage of others, unleashes his anger and frustration onto innocent victims, or is so enamored with his own talent, success, or perceived "rightful place" in society that he doesn't even realize or admit that his behavior is problematic.

You want to raise a decent human. A boy-turned-man who is kind, steadfast, strong, persistent, and hardworking.

The question is, *how*?

How do we raise confident and secure boys in a world that often paints masculinity in a negative light? How do we teach boys to consider others' needs when their own needs are so often ignored? How do we advocate for our sons when doing so is considered—in some quarters, anyway—an attempt to preserve male dominance?

How do we help our boys navigate evolving gender norms while we adults are still unpacking the ways in which gender influences our lives?

When my sons were born, no one told me about the challenges they'd face in school. No one told me that boys are affected by gender stereotypes and expectations or that male development proceeds at a different pace than female development. Naively, I

1

thought that I could parent a child irrespective of gender. I didn't think that parenting a boy would be significantly different than parenting a girl or nonbinary child. I thought I could raise great guys by letting them play with whatever they wanted (within reason, of course—no unsupervised chainsaw juggling here!) and supporting their growth and development.

If only it were that simple!

I've since learned that ignoring or overlooking a child's gender is as unhelpful as ignoring a child's race because gender, like race, impacts an individual's experience of the world. Gender, like race, affects an individual's self-perception, as well as how other people view and interact with that individual. Neglecting to consider or acknowledge this aspect of a child's experience can result in disconnection and misunderstanding.

Most of you reading this book are probably parents of cisgender boys who were born with a penis and testicles and never questioned their gender. You may believe that boys are biologically predisposed to wrestling and trucks rather than tea parties and dolls, and there's some evidence to suggest that you're right. Some research studies, for instance, have found that male infants prefer to look at moving objects, whereas female infants prefer to gaze at human faces, and other studies have found that male primates are more likely than females to engage in rough-and-tumble play. But other research studies note that the differences between males and females are small and not particularly significant, and careful analyses have found that many of the studies that noted differences included only a small number of subjects.

Frankly, after two decades of parenting boys, I've concluded that it doesn't really matter *why* many boys prefer trucks to tea parties or are more likely than their female counterparts to get in trouble in school. Practically speaking, what matters is the reality that's unfolding before us. Academic discussions of nature versus nurture were not helpful to me when my five-year-old son told me he "hated school" or when my twelve-year-old got in trouble for misbehaving in the boys' bathroom. In-the-trenches parents of boys need information and tools that will help them understand and respond to their sons' behavior and experiences in the world.

That's what this book is: a map and a guide. It introduces you to the landscape you'll be navigating throughout your son's childhood and provide you with guidelines you can use to shepherd his development. You want to raise a great guy; I'm going to show you how.

It's so easy to get lost in the details of parenting. (*What do I do when my son won't stop bickering with his brother? When he refuses to go to school? When he's in danger of failing because he has thirty-two missing assignments?*) It is exhausting to research each problem as it arises and evaluate and select alternatives. *Exhausting.* It is much easier and ultimately more productive to instead use a set of guidelines to direct your parenting choices.

I've distilled twenty-plus years of experience infused by decades of research regarding parenting and gender into ten basic guidelines:

1. Learn the terrain
2. Emphasize emotional intelligence
3. Discuss and demonstrate healthy relationships
4. Let him struggle
5. Help him find and develop his talents
6. Give him time
7. Challenge him with chores and caregiving
8. Keep him close
9. Connect him to the real world
10. Accept him as he is

These guidelines are the backbone of this book. Each guideline is the theme and focus of one chapter, and each chapter shows you how (and why) to apply the guideline to a variety of common parenting challenges. Because these guidelines are broad, they're applicable to boys to all ages and abilities.

Ready? Let's begin.

Here's to building boys!

1

⌘

Learn the Terrain

How dreadful . . . to be caught up in a game and have no idea of
the rules.

—Caroline Stevermer, *Sorcery & Cecelia:*
Or the Enchanted Chocolate Pot

My son had been in school for only a few weeks when I received
The Note.

"Tyler drew a disturbing picture," The Note began.

My brain immediately conjured horrible, violent images: *stick
figure people pointing crude guns at other stick figures who lay bleeding
upon the floor; a person stabbing another, internal organs dripping out of
the gaping hole.*

I brought my attention back to The Note: "of an animal killing a
human," it said. My brain adjusted the images in my head: *A lion,
mauling a helpless person and feasting on their innards. . . .*

Before going any further, I should tell you that I was a Good Girl.
I was (and am) a rule follower and a people pleaser. I got good
grades in school because I followed directions and did what I was
told, and it never occurred to me to do otherwise. Like all good
students, I believed that success in school was necessary for success
in life.

That was BB, before boys. Before I had had four sons who challenged my perceptions and introduced me to the nuances of human behavior. Before I understood that the male experience of the world is very different from the female one. Before I got The Note.

Ashamed and embarrassed by the trouble my son created so soon after starting school, I fired off an email to his teacher: *Thank you for letting me know. I will certainly talk to Tyler.* Then I realized I didn't really know what he'd done. I added one more line to my email: *Can you tell me a little more about the drawing?*

Soon I learned that my son drew an image of a shark attacking a surfer.

A shark. Attacking a surfer. An image that's an integral part of countless movies, TV shows, and news reports. The "disturbing image" created by my son was nothing more than a fantastical depiction of an occasional real-world event. This was cause for a note from a teacher?

Tyler was ten years old at the time. He'd only recently started public school; previously, I homeschooled him and his brothers. We'd pulled his oldest brother out of school halfway through first grade after realizing that school plus homework didn't leave much time for kids to spend with their families or pursue their own interests and passions. Nathan, my oldest, spent most of his first weeks of homeschool tracing pictures of guns from a book about weapons he'd borrowed from the library.

Was I concerned? You bet! Even then, I was acutely aware of the fact that nearly every mass shooting has been committed by young males. Surely an obsession with guns was . . . problematic to say the least.

Yet when I looked more closely, I realized that Nathan's interest in guns was primarily historical and mechanical. He noticed the details that differentiated a gun from the 1850s from one from 1945 and learned to sort weapons into their approximate era based on appearance alone. He grew curious about American wars and devoured books about the Civil War and World War II, and I relaxed a bit. Maybe my child wasn't a school-shooter-in-training. Maybe he was a history buff. A six-year-old who was building his fine motor skills by tracing photographs of weapons instead of writing sentences.

I knew that Nathan could not have followed this path to learning in school. Few (if any) teachers are going to allow a first-grade boy to trace weapons in lieu of practicing his penmanship. Most schools have a zero-tolerance policy for weaponry, and those policies are rooted firmly in educators' desire to protect children.

At the time, though, I didn't realize that zero-tolerance policies and a high level of suspicion for violent thoughts and behavior disproportionately affect young boys. I didn't understand that those policies squelch the development and imagination of many boys and contribute to their hatred of school. I also didn't realize that my sons weren't anomalies. I didn't know then that nearly all parents of boys have received at least one note, phone call, or email about an "upsetting," "disturbing," or "inappropriate" drawing or story their son crafted.

Jayme Kasman was startled when her son's kindergarten teacher shoved a piece of paper in her hand and said, "I think you should see what your son drew." The drawing, scrawled in blue marker on lined loose-leaf paper, featured a phallic-looking shape atop a vaguely heart-shaped, somewhat circular, blob. The tip of the phallic shape was colored in and included a smiley face.

Jayme asked her son to tell her about the picture. His response: "It's a heart man!"

Stacey Hensely's son was also five when she got her first Phone Call—informing her that her five-year-old son used the f-word in class.

"I was shocked because my husband and I had been very careful not to use that word," Stacey says. When she asked her son about the incident, it became clear that he had no idea what the word meant or why everyone was upset.

"They were working on rhyming words at school, and 'duck' was the word he was trying to rhyme. After he went through 'luck' and 'truck,' he started at the beginning of the alphabet and kept going to try to find rhyming words. He got to 'f,' said the word, and moved on. He had no clue why the school called me," Stacey says.

Christine Prescott, an Australia-based mom, was notified that her then-five-year-old son needed to serve a detention because he and a friend were trying to figure out how to spell swear words during art class.

"The boys didn't even really know what the words meant," she says.

Note: in each of these instances, the boys were actively learning. Jayme's son expressed his creativity and basic knowledge of the heart. Stacey's son was engaged fully in his rhyming assignment.

Christine's son and his friend were practicing spelling. And my son, Tyler, the one who drew the "disturbing" image of a shark attacking a surfer? He's always loved big, powerful beasts. At age four, he was obsessed with dinosaurs—T. rexes in particular. For a while, his best friend was an inflatable six-foot dino. Like the rest of our family, he watched a lot of science documentaries. When I asked him about his drawing, he said, "That's what you get for letting me watch Shark Week!"

Of course, I explained to Tyler that "violent" drawings weren't okay in school, just as I'm sure Christine, Stacey, and Jayme explained to their sons that certain words and images aren't welcome in public settings. That's an essential lesson for our sons. But it also strikes me that each of these boys was reprimanded, early in their school career, for creative expression that was misinterpreted and misunderstood by educators. All too often, boys' early school experiences are marked by reprimands, phone calls, and notes about "troublesome" or "inappropriate" behavior rather than by accolades or positive comments.

And it's noteworthy, I think, that even though such phone calls and notes are a nearly universal experience for boys and their families, that fact isn't widely known. No one warns first-time boy parents about the pitfalls our boys often encounter in school and society, so most of us stumble headlong into these issues beside our sons. We then blame ourselves for the challenges we encounter without realizing that there are systemic factors at work. We're so embarrassed and ashamed—because we so want to raise good guys and feel we've failed when our boys fall short of the "great guy" mark—that we don't even realize that other boy parents are struggling with the same issues.

It's time to stop stumbling alone in the dark. I'm here to hand you a map, flashlight, and emergency signaling device.

MAP OF MALE DEVELOPMENT

Biologically speaking, humans of all genders are more alike than different.[1] We all have hearts, brains, and hormones—and even though testosterone is frequently described as a "male hormone" and estrogen as a "female hormone," all humans have a bit of both. Certainly, the proportion of hormones flowing through our bodies varies, as does the overall size and makeup of our adult bodies.

The much-publicized differences between so-called male and female brains haven't held up under closer examination. Yes, the brains of adult males are larger, on average, than the brains of adult females, but that's likely because men are larger, on average, than women.[2]

Male development, though, proceeds at a different pace than female development. At birth, male infants are typically less developed than their female counterparts. According to a seminal 1972 text, newborn baby girls are developmentally similar to four- to six-week-old baby boys.[3] A 2007 study reported that newborn girls are better able to mimic fine motor movements,[4] and multiple studies have revealed that male infants exhibit greater emotional reactivity than female infants.[5] Boy babies tend to be fussier than their female counterparts and need more help than female babies to calm down.[6] In the words of a 2002 academic paper, six-month-old "male infants are less able than females to physiologically regulate frustration."[7]

In plain language, this means that, generally speaking, boy babies require external assistance to settle when their brains and bodies become overwhelmed. That's why holding your baby boy to your chest and swaying back and forth is so effective. With his head against your rib cage, he can hear your heart and feel your breath, and his body gradually adjusts his heart and respiratory rate to match yours. By the time an infant is approximately three months of age, simply sharing a loving look may be sufficient to sync his heartbeat to yours.[8]

But here's the catch: because males are less mature and more emotionally reactive at birth and because generations-old gender norms tell us that boys are "tough," parents are less likely to gaze lovingly at male infants and engage them in "conversation." Which means that boy babies may continue to have a hard time settling down. Continued fussing and crying stresses exhausted and overwhelmed parents, who are then less likely to reply with empathy and understanding—and a vicious cycle of misunderstanding and unmet needs begins.

From the earliest days of life, boys are more likely than girls to need support and assistance and less likely to receive it. This pattern is inadvertently repeated throughout boys' lives. By the time children reach the tween years (approximately ages eight through twelve), boys are about two years behind girls in the development of social sensitivity, or the ability to perceive, understand, and respect the feelings and viewpoints of others.[9] On average, the parts of the brain that handle language—that help children read and write—mature six years later in boys than in girls.[10]

Brain maturation follows the same trajectory in both males and females, but boys' brains take longer to reach the same point of development.

Allan N. Schore, an American psychologist whose research has focused on neuropsychiatry, developmental psychology, infant mental health, and behavioral biology, has written that there are "different maturational rates" in brain growth that "suggests separate norms for each gender. These norms need to reflect normal gender differences in slow-maturing male versus fast-maturing female infants' socioemotional functions."[11]

That, of course, is not the case in modern society. In part because many adults are loath to admit any differences between males and females, boys and girls are held to the same standards throughout childhood. Three- and four-year-old boys and girls are expected to maintain the same levels of attention and self-control in preschool, even though boys are developmentally less able to control and regulate their emotions at that point—which may explain why preschool boys are expelled at a rate of more than four-and-a-half times that of girls.[12]

In elementary school, boys, girls, and nonbinary children are now expected to read and write basic sentences in kindergarten, even though the parts of the brain that handle language are not nearly as mature in five- and six-year-old boys as they are in similarly aged girls. And because boys' emotional control and impulse regulation lag behind girls'—because their brains take longer to reach the same level of maturity—elementary school boys, on average, struggle more in typical classroom settings than their female peers. (A 2018 study found that in almost every public school system, girls came out ahead on reading scores regardless of socioeconomic status or race. In third grade, females outperform males by about half a grade level. By the end of eighth grade, girls are almost a full grade ahead.)

Further complicating matters is the fact that males are also more vulnerable than females to all kinds of physical and psychological stressors, including germs, pollution, and trauma. Boys' slower pace of brain maturation means that their developing brains are vulnerable to harm for a longer period than girls' brains, which can compound boys' disadvantage. In a 2000 paper published in the prestigious medical journal *BMJ*, Sebastian Kraemer, a child and adolescent psychiatrist, writes that "early environmental stressors could lead to disadvantage for boys being 'wired in.'"[13]

Experts believe that this interaction of environment and biology may explain, at least in part, why boys are more likely than girls to exhibit neurodevelopmental disorders such as autism spectrum disorder (ASD) and attention deficit hyperactivity disorder (ADHD).[14] Conditions such as these further inhibit brain development. According to Ryan Wexelblatt (aka ADHD Dude), a licensed clinical social worker who specializes in ADHD, the development of the prefrontal cortex, the part of the brain that manages working memory and executive functioning, lags about 30 percent behind the rest of the brain in children with ADHD.[15] So, a twelve-year-old boy with ADHD may well act and behave like an immature nine-year-old, even if he's sprouted facial hair and looks more like a young man than a young boy.

GENDER STEREOTYPES SET BOUNDARIES FOR BOYS AND LIMIT CONCERN FOR THEIR WELL-BEING

For millennia, the hegemonic myth has shaped human experience.

"The hegemonic myth is essentially the myth that says, 'boys are strong' and 'girls are weak,'" says Robert Blum, MD, MPH, PhD, a professor at Johns Hopkins Bloomberg School of Public Health and the principal investigator of the Global Early Adolescent Study. "That myth is believed in India. It's believed in the Congo. It's believed in New Orleans. It is believed everywhere. It's like someone has written a global script."[16]

That script has been internalized and even written into law in some places. And despite significant advances in gender equality over recent years, the hegemonic myth—that idea that males are and should be strong and dominant—shapes boys' behavior even today.

"Look at automotive fatalities," Dr. Blum says. "Who dies in automotive fatalities? Boys and men die far more than women die. Why? Is this hormonal? Biologic? Absolutely not! It is behavioral. It has a lot to do with our gender norms, and a lot of it has to do with proving that I'm a man."

Dr. Blum tells me that whenever he sees a car speeding down the highway, moving far faster than all the other vehicles on the road, he always looks to see if the driver is a woman or a man. "Almost without exception, it's a man," he says.

A memory from the night before pops into my head: a car full of teenage boys rounding the corner in the high school parking lot. The driver was going too fast and took the corner wide. The car hit the curb. All three males—two passengers and the driver—laughed hysterically. The driver slammed the car into reverse, backing up suddenly, then abruptly jolted the car forward and peeled out of the parking lot.

I was in that parking lot because I was leaving a high school soccer game. The moment stood out because, as a mom of teenage boys, I know that no mother wants to see her son driving like that. It wasn't until my conversation with Dr. Blum that I saw the subtext of the moment: a boy, ashamed and embarrassed in front of his friends, unable to deny evidence suggesting that he's not always a competent driver. But boys—males—are *expected* to be competent; male weakness or vulnerability are not allowed under the hegemonic myth. So the driver responded according to script. He laughed it off as a joke. Took risks. Showed he was "in control" by going fast and acting cool. At that moment, asserting confidence was the only way for the male to save face in front of his peers.

"Is it remarkable, then, that the statistics say that men are more likely to die in vehicular accidents? Is it remarkable that men are more likely to die from guns than are women?" Dr. Blum asks. "This is the natural consequences of our beliefs."

These beliefs, based in society and culture rather than biology, limit our sons' experiences, just as they do girls'. Tony Porter, founder of A Call to Men, popularized the term "man box,"[17] based on the concept of the "act like a man box," which was originated by Paul Kivel, cofounder of the Oakland Men's Project.[18] The "man box" defines the boundaries of acceptable male behavior in most cultures. According to Porter's 2010 TED talk, the "man box" says that men and boys are[19]

- Strong
- Tough
- Athletic
- Courageous

- Heterosexual

   Therefore, they should *not*

- Cry
- Openly express any emotion but anger
- Be "like a girl"
- Ask for help
- Refuse or turn down sex

That list is probably not shocking to you; you've seen these norms in movies, music, advertising, and family interactions throughout your life. You've also almost certainly seen pushback against these standards in recent years—calls from parents and others to allow boys the full range of emotional expression and to steer clear of phrases such as "act like man" and "stop crying." You may know boys who wear fingernail polish and dresses.

And yet . . . parenting author Aaron Gouveia wrote his 2020 book, *Raising Boys to Be Good Men*, after his son was bullied for wearing fingernail polish to kindergarten, and the question of whether it's okay for boys to wear colorful paint on their fingernails or toenails remains a frequent topic of discussion in online parenting groups. (In fact, in 2021, Gouveia's youngest son was *also* criticized for wearing nail polish to kindergarten. Even though the boy opted for blue—which everyone knows is a "boy color.")

A 2018 survey by Plan International USA, an independent development and humanitarian organization that "advances girls' equality and children's rights," reported that one-third of boys believe that society expects them to hide their feelings when they are sad or frightened. Another one-third said that they believe society expects them to "be tough and 'suck it up' when confronted with difficult events and emotions." One in three boys also reported feeling pressure to "dominate or be in charge of others." Eighty-two percent of the boys had heard someone telling a boy he was "acting like girl,"[20] a phrase that is virtually always used in a derogatory manner. Forty percent of heterosexual boys aged fourteen to nineteen said that they feel pressure to "hook up with" a girl, and 62 percent hear sexual comments and jokes about girls at least weekly.[21]

Certainly, progress has been made. Two-thirds of the surveyed boys do not feel pressured to hide their feelings or "suck it up" when the going gets tough. Two-thirds do *not* feel the need to dominate. And yet "you're acting like a girl" remains one of the most offensive charges one can levy against a boy, which clearly implies that (a) boys and girls should act differently and (b) being a girl is much worse than being a boy.

These gender stereotypes get in our heads and shape "boy culture." In many places, boys earn status by adhering to traditional gender norms. That's why the teenage driver who hit the curb laughed and peeled out of the parking lot. If he'd expressed shame, embarrassment, or confusion, his social status might have suffered. He had something to prove.

Gender stereotypes and the "man box" influence our perceptions of boys and men as well. A fascinating study published in the November 2020 edition of the journal *Organizational Behavior and Human Decision Processes* reported an international tendency toward gender bias in moral typecasting—basically, a tendency to assume that males are perpetrators of harm, and females are victims. The researchers presented a variety of scenarios—a senior surgeon bullies a surgical trainee to the point that the trainee develops depression and suicidal tendencies; an animated green triangle pokes an orange triangle, which reacts by whirling away; coworkers are in line for lunch at a professional conference when coworker B drops a fork and bends over to pick it up, at which point coworker A says, "you must get a lot of practice doing that"—to more than three thousand research subjects in the United States, China, and Norway. Researchers deliberately obscured or switched the genders of the actors in each scenario and asked subjects who they perceived as the victim and perpetrator. Across every scenario, participants were more likely to assume that a harmed target was female. They also reported feeling more warmth toward the victims that they perceived as female. Additionally, they desired harsher punishments for male perpetrators and were more willing to forgive female perpetrators.[22]

These findings likely wouldn't surprise young boys who frequently claim that "the teacher likes girls better!"

Child psychologists and authors Michael Thompson and Dan Kindlon highlighted humans' tendency to assume the worst about males in their seminal book *Raising Cain: Protecting the Emotional Life of Boys* more than two decades ago. They wrote, "Whatever else it means to be a boy in our culture, it means that your actions are more likely to be misinterpreted as threatening or disobedient, that you are more likely than the girl next door to be punished or treated harshly."[23]

Yet discussions of gender equity almost universally center women and girls, with little to no attention given to gender-linked harms suffered by boys and men. That, Dr. Blum says, is a mistake.

"There are those in the development community who believe fully that girls and women are vulnerable and need protection. They're right. Girls and women are vulnerable and need protection, but that does not mean that boys and men are not vulnerable and don't need protection," he says. "We have perpetuated this notion that gender equality is about girls' and women's protection, and that's a huge mistake—not because it's wrong but because it's half the story."[24]

In a 2019 commentary published in the *Journal of Adolescent Health*, Dr. Blum and his coauthors note that boys and girls are harmed by gender norms.[25] The evidence, the article states, indicates that "both boys and girls are disadvantaged, some in similar and some in unique ways." The Global Early Adolescent Study pilot data suggest that boys experience as much disadvantage as girls (e.g., fear of being physically hurt, neglected, a victim of sexual or physical violence) and concludes that "To achieve gender equality, we need to redefine the problem as a 'gender,' not a women's and girls', issue," noting that "an abundance of literature shows that males as well as females benefit from a more socially supportive climate."[26]

It is true that being male can be advantageous in some situations. It is not, however, a universal advantage. Gender-linked stereotypes limit boys' opportunities, colors others' perceptions of them, and shape boys' hopes and dreams.

Jim DeVivo's son was about seven years old when he asked his dad, "Why don't they ever say that boys can be anything they want to be?" Jim was startled; he'd grown up in an era in which girls' opportunities were limited and boys (especially white boys) were encouraged to dream big. But he soon recognized the context of his son's question.

"We're big Disney fans and Disney Junior was the TV channel of choice. The boys watched the *Tangled* series and *Sofia the First* and *Elena of Avalor*, and Disney had a 'Dream Big, Princess' campaign. The commercial featured Disney princesses and all these girls in adventurous, active roles—as scientists, explorers, athletes," Jim said.

When Jim and his wife explained to their son that, not so long ago, laws explicitly stated that women and girls were not allowed to do things men and boys could, their son was surprised. His whole life, he'd heard that girls and women could do anything. He saw that truth reflected in his TV shows, commercials, movies, and real-life interactions.

What he hadn't heard, Jim realized, was anyone telling him that boys can do whatever they want.

SPOTLIGHT ON POTENTIAL PITFALLS

I didn't see the many ways in which gender affects boys' lives until—well, until I'd been a "boy mom" for nearly four years.

When my first son was born, I didn't know that boys were falling behind girls academically or that male students are far more likely than their female counterparts to be suspended or expelled. I didn't realize that the tween years are a time of tremendous transition (and stress!) for boys and their families, and I definitely did not know that boys' brains do not fully mature until they're in their twenties.

I didn't realize that massive misunderstandings regarding boys' needs and developmental trajectory underpinned most of their socialization.

If I'd known any of that, I might have been more prepared when my bright son started telling me he "hated school" at age five. I probably wouldn't have spent so much time crying as we navigated the tween years, and I would have proactively prepared for my boys' teen years. Instead, like most parents, I stumbled, unaware, into entirely predictable pitfalls.

I don't want you to be as unprepared as I was, so I'm going to shine a light on the potential pitfalls that lie ahead.

Starting School

According to the sixth annual American Family Survey, 63 percent of parents think the United States' education systems caters well to girls, whereas 55 percent think it serves boys well.[27]

There's plenty of data to back up parents' perceptions that modern institutional education is, on the whole, more girl friendly than boy friendly. Boys make up about half of all preschool classes but account for approximately 80 percent of preschool suspensions.[28] As early as elementary school, boys are more likely than girls to be held back a grade,[29] and boys are far more likely than girls to be identified by teachers as reading disabled.[30] Although those stats may seem reasonable—after all, why wouldn't a school hold back elementary students who struggled with reading?—they obscure two important contributing factors: (1) teacher bias and (2) the slower pace of male development.

A 2012 report[31] from the Organisation for Economic Cooperation and Development (OECD) found that girls are more likely to receive better grades in school than boys in most countries and economies, *even when boys and girls have similar reading performance and learning habits.* The report further noted that many teachers "reward class cooperation and penalize disruptiveness and disciplinary problems"[32]—which, again, may seem reasonable until you learn that additional research[33] has shown that many teachers are prone to categorizing boys as disruptive and uncooperative.

Lynn A. Barnett, PhD, an associate professor in the Department of Recreation, Sport and Tourism at the University of Illinois at Urbana-Champaign, followed 278 children (boys and girls) from kindergarten to third grade and identified degrees of playfulness among the children, while also noting student and teacher perceptions of individual students. She found that playful boys were regarded by kindergarten teachers as rebellious and intrusive. The boys were labeled "class clowns" and considered to have poor social skills. Although their classmates initially considered the playful boys "fun" and "appealing" playmates, they sensed their teachers' disapproval and by third grade avoided the "class clowns."

Boys internalize these negative messages as well, and by third grade, many come to believe that school is "not for them." Not helping matters is the fact that many young boys struggle to read and write (and sit still!) because their brains and fine motor skills are not as mature as most females' at ages five and six. Developmentally, most young boys are asked (and required) to do things at school that their minds and bodies aren't mature enough to master.

Boys whose early school experiences are marred by feelings of failure and frustration are not likely to become enthusiastic students. That's why I urge parents to carefully plan and monitor their sons' transitions to school and act quickly if problems emerge. Here's how.

- *Avoid academically oriented preschools and elementary schools.*
  Sounds crazy, right? After all, isn't academics the *point* of
  school? Unfortunately, that's the message we've been sold and
  the consistent emphasis on standardized tests and scholastic
  achievement means that most schools do indeed emphasize
  academics, often at the expense of free play, even though reams
  of data (and millennia of anecdotal experience) show that boys
  (and girls and gender nonconforming children, for that matter)
  learn best via active exploration.

  Teacher-led instruction is not the most effective means of
  learning for young children; kids learn best via active exploration. So look for a play-based, child-led learning environment
  and steer clear of preschools and elementary schools that rely
  heavily on worksheets or screen-based instruction. Forest or
  nature schools, which utilize outside spaces and allow children
  to learn via their interaction with the natural environment, are
  a great alternative. (Search online for "forest school," "nature
  school," or "outdoor school.") In fact, kids who struggle the
  most in traditional schools—wiggly kids who can't sit still or
  focus—often do well in nature.

- *Ask about recess.* Recess time has been dwindling for decades,
  and although there have been concentrated efforts in some
  parts of the country to restore and protect recess (since numerous studies have shown that recess benefits kids academically,
  socially, and physically), only 64.8 percent of US school districts
  require that elementary schools offer regularly scheduled recess, according to the 2016 School Health Policies and Practices
  Study.[34] Just 52 percent of districts prohibit or actively discourage schools from excluding students from all or part of recess as
  punishment for inappropriate behavior or failure to complete
  classwork, which means that many boys miss much-needed
  recess time.[35] Look for a school that prioritizes recess, encourages free play, and doesn't consider recess a privilege that must
  be earned.

- *Consider delaying your son's school entrance.* Remember: boys'
  brains take longer to mature than girls' brains. Data also shows
  that kids who are comparatively young at school entrance
  may not fare as well as children who are a bit older. A study
  published in *the New England Journal of Medicine* in 2018 found
  that children with August birthdays were significantly more

likely to be diagnosed with ADHD than kids with September birthdays in states that require children to be five years old by September 1 for enrollment in kindergarten.[36] The rate of ADHD diagnosis was 34 percent higher for children with August birthdays, who are often nearly a full year younger than many of their same-grade peers. Giving your son an additional year or so to mature may be one of the best gifts you ever give him. (We'll talk more about the gift of time in chapter 6.)

The Tween Years

Did you know that male puberty can start at age nine?

Many parents of boys don't (I didn't!), which is one reason so many parents are overwhelmed, confused, and frustrated during their sons' tween years. Our sons' transition from sweet-little-boy-who-loves-you-more-than-you-thought-possible to mercurial-human-being-who-is-annoyed-by-your-mere-presence can happen seemingly overnight.

The tween years aren't easy for our sons either. External pressure to live up to sexist stereotypes intensifies around puberty. According to a 2020 report by Promundo and the Kering Foundation, boys ages ten to twelve report feeling increased pressure to fit masculine stereotypes. Parents of boys see and sense their sons' struggles: approximately 60 percent said they recognize the social pressures boys face to be physically strong, show interest in sports, and fit in. Forty-five percent said boys still face pressure to not cry, and 41 percent said boys are expected to have a girlfriend or to like girls romantically.[37]

Exposure to pornography is all but guaranteed. (Yes, even if you use internet filters and install parental controls.) A lackadaisical attitude toward school and formal education is de rigueur for tween boys; academic effort is frowned upon in many social circles. Peer pressure increases, and boys will be exposed to vaping, alcohol, and drugs. Even if your son resists peer pressure, he may be affected by substance use. According to a 2021 *Washington Post* article by Jessica Lahey, author of *The Addiction Inoculation*, 29 percent of twelve- to fourteen-year-olds say they have close friends who use substances.[38]

If you know that your son may pull away and show flashes of moodiness around age ten, you'll be much better prepared to navigate your son's tween years than most parents of boys. Expect some choppy waters during this stage of the journey. You won't be able to completely avoid the rapids and rocks, but you and your son have the best chance of coming through relatively unscathed if you:

- *Pick your battles.* Tween boys' brains are still developing. Your son's executive functioning—the cognitive skills used to assess risk, prioritize, and organize—won't mature until he's in his twenties. Tween boys are messy and disorganized because they're still developing self-control. And because their priorities are not the same as yours.

- *Welcome his friends.* It's natural and normal for tween boys to want to spend more time with friends than family. So, as often as possible, say yes when he asks if his friends can come over. Stock up on snacks, and keep your mouth shut when the boys crowd around one screen to watch a YouTuber play a video game. Continue to welcome his female friends too. Mixed-gender friendships help tweens see one another as unique humans rather than potential sexual conquests.

- *Prioritize mental health—and stop stressing about school.* According to Dr. Michele Borba, author of *Thrivers: The Surprising Reasons Why Some Kids Struggle and Others Shine,* many boys are secretly stressed. The boys don't want to share their discomfort because they "don't want to disappoint their parents," who often have emphasized academics and achievement, she says.

  Body dysmorphia—dissatisfaction with one's body, sometimes accompanied by an eating disorder or compulsion to exercise—can develop during the tween years. Chiseled and muscular is in—and absolutely ubiquitous on TikTok, Instagram, and youth-oriented TV shows. By age six, most boys have internalized a desire to be muscular, and by the time males reach adolescence, nearly one-third of boys are trying to gain weight or bulk up.

  An overemphasis on academic and athletic achievement—and underemphasis on mental health—is one reason why the suicide rate for boys ages ten to fourteen more than doubled from 2007 to 2018 (from 1.2 percent to 3.7 percent).[39] You can—and should—encourage your son in school but nagging your son about homework, grades, weight, or his athletic performance is often counterproductive. Focus on your son's mental health, not his achievements.

Adolescence

Teen boys are more likely to be feared than protected. As Australia's "boy champion," Maggie Dent wrote in a 2020 *Guardian* article, "teen boys are a universally maligned group, frequently seen as a scourge to orderly society. Yet underneath the often hard-to-chat-to, forgetful, restless, accident-prone boy is a big heart yearning to be understood and valued."[40]

Dr. Warren Farrell, coauthor of *The Boy Crisis: Why Our Boys Are Struggling and What We Can Do about It*, also has commented on the near-ubiquitous societal tendency to ignore the needs of male adolescents. In a 2020 *Newsweek* article, Farrell said that society cares "less about boys, and the closer they get to becoming men, the less we care."[41]

Teen boys sense this lack of care. They know that society views them as potential predators. They know that males are blamed for much of the inequality in the world today. They know that males historically have perpetuated inequality, but they're also acutely aware of the fact that they personally didn't cause any of the harms of the past. Many teenage boys feel prejudged, which makes them feel angry, because more than anything, they want reassurance that they're okay.

You can help your son survive the turbulence of adolescence by consistently demonstrating unconditional love and acceptance. Focus on his strengths, not his weaknesses. Your son will thrive—and your home will be more peaceful—if you frequently notice what's going *right*, instead of fixating on what's wrong.[42]

Of course, that's easier said than done because it's easy for teen boys to get into trouble. Biologically, they're predisposed to making some unwise choices. Teenagers typically weigh the potential rewards of an activity more heavily than potential risks, and the presence of peers further skews their assessment.[43] Social status is critical to boys' safety and well-being, so when he's with a group of guys, your son may do things he'd never do alone.

Parents who expect some heartache and pain during their sons' teenage years and view challenges as normal, natural waves to be surfed will fare better than those who consider any trouble a sign of failure. Their sons will too.

You and your son may be able to avoid some serious pitfalls if you:

- *Support healthy risk taking.* Risk involves engaging in behavior with an uncertain outcome. Risky activities require us to move past fear and test our capabilities and problem-solving skills. Teenagers worldwide exhibit a heightened attraction to novel and exciting experiences despite their evident risk, and researchers believe this innate attraction to risk helps adolescents test and refine their burgeoning capabilities.[44]

  You can support your son's development—and perhaps prevent or limit his engagement in unhealthy risky activities such as substance use, reckless driving, and crime—by encouraging healthy risk taking. Entertain your son's "crazy ideas." If he wants to build a bike ramp in the backyard or attempt a triathlon or solo backpacking trip, don't immediately say no. Listen. Discuss. Help him figure out how to attain the skills and supplies he'll need. Whether he ultimately completes his quest or not, he'll learn a lot—including the fact that you trust him and support his ambitions.

- *Let him make choices—and experience consequences.* A big part of parenting teenage boys is standing back and holding your tongue while they make (questionable) decisions and experience the consequences.[45] We parents may have a wealth of experience and wisdom to share, but our children, like us and our parents before us, don't want to hear most of it. Humans learn best from experience. So practice listening. Don't offer your thoughts or opinions unless asked.

  As Deborah Reber, founder of TiLT Parenting, wrote in a 2021 article published in *ADDitude* magazine, teens "may fall on their face from time to time—fail a class, make bad social choices—which can be painful to watch, but learning from those experiences will prepare them for the future better than a reward or bribe."[46]

- *Give him opportunities to contribute.* In years past, teenage boys were integral parts of their communities. They worked on farms and in factories and defended freedom and liberty via service in the armed forces. Today, they are rarely viewed as assets. That's a shame because most boys desperately want to contribute to the well-being of the world. Find ways for your son to meaningfully contribute to your family. Remember, he wants to test his skills, so it may be time for him to graduate from emptying the dishwasher to meal planning and grocery shopping. Or let him tackle a landscaping or building project. Help your son identify ways to serve within the community as well. A boy who loves to fish may want to lead a local river cleanup or volunteer to teach younger children how to fish.

HELP! (OR, DON'T BE AFRAID TO SEND OUT A DISTRESS CALL)

Parenting boys is the most challenging thing I have ever done. I inadvertently made it harder by keeping many of our struggles to myself. I was afraid to disclose our all-too-normal problems to anyone else because, at the time, I didn't realize our problems were common. I assumed that my boys were getting in trouble at school because we were doing something wrong. When my oldest son raged during his tween years, I was positive that my inability to manage his moods meant that I was an ineffective mother.

I didn't reach out for help because I feared I'd be seen as a bad mom. I also didn't realize that help was available.

Since then, I've learned that it's far better to share your struggles. You are *not* the only parent who feels like you're failing your son. You're not the only one getting notes from school or the only one who's got a boy who's convinced he doesn't need school because he's going to make big money streaming video games.

You need a community of "boy parents" who can validate your experiences and share wisdom and encouragement. You can begin developing an informal network of parents by connecting with the parents of your son's friends, classmates, and teammates. Take a chance: the next time you're on the sidelines during one of your son's games, for instance, casually mention an issue you're currently experiencing with your son. Odds are good that another parent is dealing with the same thing. When we speak honestly and frankly about our challenges, we tacitly give permission for others to do the same—and when we parents of boys share our stories, we begin to see commonalities. Then we can share information and support.

Can't find support locally? Look online. My Building Boys Facebook group is a global community of parents of boys. Our cross-cultural connections have helped us see that boys around the world face many of the same challenges. There are lots of online parenting groups for moms of boys, as well as groups focused on specific ages or physical and emotional challenges. (Groups for dads of boys are harder to find. Start one if you can't find what you need.)

Reach out to, connect with, and support local and national organizations that help boys and their families. (See the appendix.) Most of these organizations offer free information about boys and their well-being on their websites, and many also host educational events for parents and boys. Some also offer professional development to educators and coaches, so they can more effectively help the boys in their charge.

Don't be afraid to seek professional support either. A counselor can help you unpack your worries and fears, and parenting coaches can teach you how to more effectively handle everyday interactions with your son. You can easily find parenting coaches online, but don't hire just anyone. Ask about their experience with boys; you want a coach who has either raised or worked with boys *and* has successfully helped families connect with male children. Get references and speak to one or more of their clients before you decide to work together.

NAVIGATING A WORLD THAT MISUNDERSTANDS MALES

My first reaction to The Note—the one informing me about my son's "disturbing" drawing—was shame.

Years later, I realized my reaction was misguided. And unhelpful. There's nothing inherently wrong about an image of a shark attaching a surfer. Interactions between sharks and people have long fascinated humans. Steven Spielberg made a movie out of the 1974 novel *Jaws because* shark attacks are visually dramatic.

Instead of ingratiating myself to Tyler's teacher by sending an email that implied I'd take care of my son's errant behavior, I should have simply responded, "Thanks for letting me know." Then, after I talked to my son, I should have made it absolutely clear to him that there was nothing wrong with his drawing. And then I should have had another conversation with his teacher. I should have asked why the image was considered problematic and asked for more guidance regarding which subjects are allowed for visual or creative interpretation.

If that sounds over the top to you—I mean, we're talking about a ten-year-old's drawing!—well, maybe it is. But in the years since I received The Note, I've learned that many teachers misunderstand males because they've never been taught about male development. I've learned that many people—women especially—are quick to assume violent intent in boys' drawings, stories, and play. I've seen boys gradually realize that their interests aren't welcome in school and society, and I've seen their subsequent emotional withdrawal from school and society.

In a world that misunderstands males, parents must affirm and support their sons. In the next chapters, I'll show you how.

To build boys:

- *Reflect on which of your current parenting challenges may result from a mismatch between school or societal expectations and your son's current developmental level.*
- *Connect with a community of "boy parents," either locally or online.*
- *Befriend a parent with sons older than yours. Watch and learn!*

2

⌐∞⌐

Emphasize Emotional Intelligence

When a boy is cut off from being aware of his own feelings, he is less able to relate to others. . . . Unconstrained by empathy, he is more capable of hurting others.

—Michael C. Reichert, *How to Raise a Boy*

When my boys were young, fighting was an everyday occurrence.

Bouts of roughhousing and wrestling occurred on the regular. Rolling around on the floor with their dad, they reminded me of baby lion cubs grappling with the king of the jungle. They flailed, jumped, and screamed, but their little boy strength and strategy were no match for their father. So the boys turned toward each other, practicing their moves and jockeying for power.

A lot of moms would have intervened and put a stop to the "violent" behavior, which, admittedly, sometimes (okay—*often*) ended in tears. And I'll be honest: the constant bickering, verbal one-upmanship, and physical fighting bothered me. I wrote in my journal, *Peaceful play is alien to them; fighting, second nature.*

I planned to raise boys who appropriately manage emotions and respect others' thoughts, opinions, possessions, and personal space, so the constant fighting—daily evidence of my *failure* to instill respect and teach my boys emotional control, as I saw it—got on my nerves.

I was convinced that I needed to put a stop to what I viewed as antisocial behavior, so I tried to intervene. "*Stop that!*" I'd say, or "*Enough!*"

It didn't work, at least not long term. The boys would stop and separate for a moment, but within a few hours, they were back at it. Bicker. Fight. Wrestle. Repeat.

What I didn't realize then is that my boys were honing their emotional intelligence via wrestling, roughhousing, and bickering.

"If you watch two boys wrestling, most of the time they are paying such close attention to one another's bodies and facial expressions," says Tom Hobson, aka "Teacher Tom," a preschool teacher at Woodland Park Cooperative Schools in Seattle, Washington. "Half the time, they're looking into each other's eyes as they're wrestling. It's a beautiful thing to see."[1]

Deep in the parenting trenches and ignorant, at the time, of traditional male approaches to emotional development, I tried to smother my boys' inclination to fight. I didn't see beauty; I saw little boys in danger of becoming violent men.

Many people make the same mistake.

"One of the things some female teachers struggle with, compared to male teachers, is that they see boys' physical-ness as violence. It is not violence; it is the opposite," Teacher Tom says. "When boys start wrestling around, that's an act of love."[2]

WHY EMOTIONAL INTELLIGENCE MATTERS

The Oxford English Dictionary defines emotional intelligence as "The capacity to be aware of, control, and express one's emotions, and to handle interpersonal relationships judiciously and empathetically."[3]

That's what I want for my boys. And yours.

Think about it: You *don't* want your son to be violent; to sexually harass, assault, or intimidate others; to experience loneliness or despair. You *do* want him to experience intimacy, connection, and contentment. Emotional intelligence is at the root of it all.

According to research by Dr. Jean Greaves and Dr. Travis Bradberry, authors of *Emotional Intelligence 2.0*, 90 percent of top career performers scored high in emotional intelligence, and those with a high degree of emotional intelligence earned an average of $29,000 more annually than those with a low degree of emotional intelligence.[4] Children with strong socio-emotional skills, including perseverance, impulse control, and the ability to delay gratification earn higher grades, stay in school longer, and make healthier choices than children with weaker socio-emotional skills.[5] Emotional intelligence is also linked to mental health: children who learn how to identify and manage emotions, feel and show empathy, and establish and maintain supportive relationships are less likely to suffer from anxiety and depression.[6]

Lack of attention to male emotional development contributes to sky-high suicide rates (in 2019, the suicide rate among males was 3.7 times higher than among females, according to the National Institute of Mental Health)[7] and may contribute to domestic violence, sexual assault, and crime, including school shootings and mass murder. A 2017 study[8] examining twenty-nine school shootings committed between 1995 and 2005 found that most school shooters were the targets of bullying, which triggered feelings of shame and humiliation. More than half of the shooters had recently experienced female rejection, and most struggled with anger control. Lacking effective means to deal with shame, humiliation, and rejection, these boys turned their anger outward with devastating results.

OBSTACLES TO EMOTIONAL INTELLIGENCE[9]

The ability to express one's emotions and respond empathetically hasn't always been valued.

For generations, boys and men were expected to be stoic, and that expectation influenced (and still influences) parenting norms. As Andrew Reiner, author of *Better Boys, Better Men*, wrote in a June 2021 *NBC News* article, "We fear that giving boys access to the full range of their deeper emotional lives will make them less successful in a harshly competitive world."[10]

Which brings us to . . .

Obstacle 1: Shifting Gender Norms

Culturally, we are *just now* entering an era where it may be safe—and advantageous—for males to share their emotions. Not that long ago, emotional vulnerability was a luxury not afforded to most males. Enslaved Black men were not permitted tears when their wives were raped and their children sold. Subsistence farmers focused solely on survival, and soldiers under orders continued to fight despite the horrors swirling around them. Valued primarily for their bodies and brawn, males locked away their emotions and did what must be done.

The "strong and stoic" model of masculinity is increasingly out of sync with modern society. To succeed in the twenty-first century, children of all genders need to develop self-awareness, self-restraint, emotional resiliency, tolerance, and empathy, as well as strong collaboration and communication skills.

And yet male self-restraint, tolerance, and empathy aren't necessarily prized or rewarded. Donald Trump was not elected president of the United States in 2016—or ranked thirteenth in a 2021 world's most admired men survey[11]—because he demonstrates self-awareness, restraint, or empathy. Vladimir Putin, Russia's president from 2000 to 2008 and 2012 to the present (and #9 on the same list) is known as a "strongman"; bare-chested photos of him atop a horse and holding a gun are widely circulated on the internet. In 2018, Barry Diller, chairperson of IAC, an American media company, said that Microsoft cofounder Bill Gates (#2) "had the emotional quotient of a snail" when the duo first met.[12]

At the top of the 2021 list of the world's most admired men, Barack Obama *is* recognized for self-restraint, empathy, and interpersonal communication skills—as are a number of the other men on the list, including Pope Francis (#16) and Bollywood actor Amitabh Bachchan (#15). But the inclusion of so many men who adhere to the strong and stoic model of masculinity points to a global truth: male strength and power is still respected and rewarded. Underscoring that truth is the fact that one-quarter of the list—one in four "most admired men"—is professional athletes.

Despite a societal push toward a more well-rounded version of masculinity, athleticism and physical and mental strength still give boys and men status. Displays of kindness, emotion, and understanding may not. That fact creates a conundrum: parents want their boys to experience the joy, freedom, and potential benefits of emotional expression, but they don't want their sons to face harm in the here and now. Dads, especially, know that boys who are perceived as "weak" become targets, so even progressive fathers (and mothers) sometimes struggle with boys' tears. As writer Rebecca Ruiz observed in her 2020 *Mashable* article, "How to Raise Boys So They're Comfortable with Their Emotions," "Parents want to raise emotionally intelligent boys who can be their true selves, but none of them want to see their child bullied, ostracized, or beaten as a result."[13]

Some people currently are working to expand the "man box"; others are fighting to maintain the status quo. Trying to raise an emotionally intelligent son in an environment that doesn't consistently value male emotion is a challenge.

Obstacle 2: Dismissal of Traditional Male Responses

Stoicism as defined in popular culture—the endurance of pain or hardship without the display of feelings and without complaint—has gotten a bad rep. It's been linked with so-called toxic masculinity and blamed, in part, for high rates of male suicide and self-harm. (Stoic philosophy, on the other hand, is enjoying a bit of a resurgence.)

But the human ability to function despite physical and emotional pain has helped humanity persist. It's not healthy to continually suppress emotion, yet, at times, it's expedient and necessary to do so. Similarly, males' tendency to connect with others via physical activity rather than intimate conversation is considered by some to be part of a "traditional masculinity ideology" that "discourages men from being intimate with others and is the primary reason men tend to have fewer close friends than women," according to the 2018 "APA Guidelines for Psychological Practice with Boys and Men." However, connection via mutual activity is an effective means of literal and metaphoric community building, with the American Psychological Association also noting that "the majority of boys and men indicate that they have close male friends with whom they share secrets [and] are emotionally intimate."[14]

Many well-intentioned parents, teachers, and even counselors dismiss traditional male responses as inadequate or subpar. They assume that boys (and men) who do not cry, weep, emote, or discuss openly after experiencing a loss are emotionally deficient. But the truth, says therapist Tom Golden, is that many males use activity to cope with strong emotion.

He recalls a mother who brought her teenage son to him after the boy's father died.[15]

"She was all upset because her son hadn't talked about his father since his death. He hadn't cried about his father," says Golden, author of *Swallowed by a Snake: The Gift of the Masculine Side of Healing*. "'All he's been doing,' his mother said, 'is playing basketball.'"

Golden advised her to shoot hoops with her son the next time she saw him playing in the backyard. She did.

"She went out and played with him, and it was magic," Golden says. "The first thing he said was, 'Mom, you suck. You can't play like Dad could.' And then tears started coming down his face. He told his mom that his father always wanted him to make a three-pointer. He'd tried and tried but had never done it. He was out there working to make that shot. And when he finally made it, he said, 'Dad, I did it' and crumbled in tears."

Traditional and indigenous people "almost always give men a task after a death," Golden says, citing cross-cultural anthropological research. The task moves men to action, and physical activity, biology has shown, improves mood and stabilizes emotions.[16] Studies in mice have even found that physical activity increases activity in the part of the brain that processes emotions.

Golden suspects that males' traditional tendency toward action may be a socio-biological adaptation to differing physiology. Testosterone, the so-called male hormone that's present in large quantities in men and boys, inhibits crying, whereas prolactin, a hormone that's present in larger quantities in women, may promote crying. Women's tear ducts are also smaller than men's, so they're more likely to shed tears and experience the release of oxytocin and other feel-good endorphins that occurs after a good cry.[17] Males can't as easily access that biochemical relief via tears, but physical activity also releases endorphins.[18]

"If you feel sadness and don't have the physical release of tears, activity is another way to release," Golden says.

In our eagerness to expand boys' opportunities, we must be careful to not belittle or dismiss traditional male responses. It's okay for boys to cry. And it's okay for boys to *not* cry. Connection via conversation is great, so is connecting via a game of hoops.

Obstacle 3: Ignorance of Physical Approaches to Emotional Development

Human beings are driven to control and harness their emotions. None of us likes to feel out of control, and none of us likes to experience unpleasant emotions.

Like many well-meaning adults, I didn't initially realize that things like roughhousing, wrestling, adventure, and risky play are venues for the development of emotional intelligence. Because of my social conditioning, I didn't see the potential benefits of these activities; I saw only the potential for hurt and harm. So I attempted to steer my sons toward more socially acceptable forms of play.

That was a mistake.

According to a 2017 article published in *Behavioral Neuroscience*, rough-and-tumble play "is thought to both require and entrain emotional regulation and empathy."[19] Wrestling and play fighting often involve tickling, poking, and tumbling—behaviors that the article's authors note "would be hostile in many circumstances." In the context of play, however, these actions are welcome. Mammals of many different species indulge in rough play, and researchers have found that this style of play aids in brain maturation and the development of social competence.

THE DAD DIFFERENCE

Human fathers engage in more rough-and-tumble play with their sons than with their daughters—a finding that may be linked to socialization, to dads' exposure to elevated levels of testosterone before birth, and to the fathers' responsiveness to their sons' cues.[20]

In contrast, dads whistle and sing more often with daughters than sons, leading researchers to the "intriguing hypothesis" that "there are multiple routes for the augmenting the development of empathy and emotional regulation."[21]

⌒∞⌒

Roughhousing is a unique kind of reciprocal play that requires exquisite attention to interpersonal cues, including facial expressions, body language, and vocal tone. Participants carefully watch and listen to one another to determine if another tickle or poke is welcome or not. The game is over when one participant starts crying, gets hurt, or opts out.

Because play fighting involves some of the same gestures that occur during real fights—and a slight risk of harm—most schools and childcare centers do not allow roughhousing or rough-and-tumble play.

Parents who are determined to raise kind, well-rounded men may even prohibit play fighting at home because they fear that allowing "aggression" will nurture additional aggression. It's easy to understand this point of view: at first glance, allowing your son to leap off the couch and tackle his brother seems like, well, tacit approval of an unprovoked assault, and unprovoked assaults are exactly what most parents of boys are hoping to avoid. But researchers have found that play fighting may teach participants "to keep calm when confronting unexpected, potentially dangerous situations."[22] What looks like violence to you may be a child's way of developing attention, impulse control, and emotional regulation.

Similarly, adventurous and sensation-seeking play—activities like jumping off a moving swing and climbing to the very top of the monkey bars—teaches children about uncertainty, coping, and emotional arousal.[23] Adults who hope to avoid child injury often limit such play, which may inhibit child development by depriving children of opportunities to manage their emotions and test their physical capabilities. Some researchers even hypothesize that engaging in adventurous play may decrease a child's risk of developing chronic anxiety.[24]

Boys do not have to engage in rough-and-tumble, adventurous, or risky play to develop emotional intelligence, but we adults must be aware of the ways in which we may be unconsciously limiting child development. There is zero evidence that play fighting leads to increased real-world violence, but a mountain of evidence suggests that mammals of many species use rough-and-tumble play to develop social awareness and internal regulation. Remember that fact the next time you see a boy wrestling with his siblings or friends.

BUILDING BOYS' EMOTIONAL INTELLIGENCE

By age four or five, many boys "suddenly start walling off their emotions," says Teacher Tom. Surrounded by mass media images of superheroes, they know it's far better to be the hero than to need help. Many have been told, multiple times, to "stop crying," so they begin stuffing their tears.

You can't stop the torrent of mixed messages boys receive regarding masculinity, but you *can* help them build emotional intelligence. Here's how.

Hone Your Emotional Regulation Skills

Maggie Dent, Australia's "boy champion" and author of *From Boys to Men: Guiding Our Teen Boys to Grow into Happy, Healthy Men*, once said that "Our main job as grown-ups, especially as parents, is to be the big safe people that our children need to lean on during times of stress and uncertainty."[25]

That's easier said than done because most of us still struggle with emotional reactivity. No one taught me how to recognize or process my emotions as I was growing up. In fact, emotions were mostly unacknowledged in my family of origin. I couldn't count on others to share my excitement, happiness, or pride, and feelings like sadness, anger, or disappointment were ignored or dismissed, so I learned to avoid conflict and keep my emotions to myself. These lessons didn't prepare me to teach my boys how to effectively manage emotions. They didn't prepare me well for adult relationships, either, and they did not teach me how to constructively respond to a screaming toddler or a sullen tween.

Early in my parenting career, I frequently viewed my toddlers' screams (and my tweens' moodiness) as disrespect. I felt that "disrespect" in every fiber of my being—my heart rate increased, my breathing became shallow, and my muscles clenched. In hindsight, I can see that I was experiencing a classic "fight-or-flight" response. My brain and body, wired by the lessons I learned in my childhood, responded to a stressful stimulus by dumping a load of adrenaline into my bloodstream so I'd be ready to fight or flee. My child didn't need me to battle or run, but with adrenaline running through my veins, I frequently yelled and made rash, impulsive decisions. I might swiftly and not-at-all tenderly pick up the crying toddler and deposit him, none too gently, in his room before closing the door harder than necessary. I might stomp away from the tween while muttering angry, hurtful words not quite under my breath.

In the peace and quiet of this page, you can probably clearly see exactly how unhelpful those responses were. I was frustrated and overwhelmed—and responded with an emotional outburst. I inadvertently modeled the exact behavior I wanted my boys to avoid.

DEPRESSED? GET HELP

Parents who are depressed find it more difficult to feel empathy for their own children.[26] Depressed parents are also more likely to engage in indifferent or hostile parenting practices—and parental depression can negatively affect a child's physical, social, and psychological development.[27]

One study found that women who give birth to boys are 70 percent more likely to experience postpartum depression,[28] and other studies have found that male infants are more vulnerable to negative effects of parental depression.[29]

Eventually, I realized that I couldn't expect my boys to manage their emotions effectively when my emotional management techniques were limited to "ignore" or "explode." So I started seeing a certified mental health counselor, who helped me untangle my family history and learn to reframe thoughts and feelings. I began journaling regularly, which helped me identify and process my emotions. I learned positive parenting techniques, including empathizing, and realized that building my emotional intelligence was the absolute best way to boost my boys' emotional intelligence quotient, or EQ.

Adults who parent or work with boys must get comfortable with uncomfortable emotions. We must learn to tolerate unpleasant emotions and learn how to regulate our emotional temperature when faced with anger, fear, frustration, and loneliness. Many women find male anger, fear, and sadness scary and threatening, even when expressed by young boys—often because we've experienced emotional or physical abuse at the hands of males. It is absolutely critical to unpack your emotional baggage so you can respond to each boy as a unique, vulnerable human being, rather than yet another male who may hurt you.

Fathers and other men who work with boys may struggle with their own emotional upbringing, as most did not grow up in families or environments that allowed free emotional expression. Many guys instinctively respond to boys' tears with stock phrases such as "don't cry," "man up," or "want me to give you something to cry about?" because that's what they heard growing up. It takes deliberate effort (and time) to break ingrained habits.

Couples may be able to support one another as they learn healthier ways of expressing and responding to emotion. Be prepared for some conflict, though.

"My husband used to tell our boys, 'Don't cry!'" says Gemma Gaudette, an Idaho mom of two sons. "I took him aside and said, 'Don't you ever tell them not to cry. If they want to cry, they can cry.' He struggled to accept that concept. The sounds of the boys' crying triggered an intense emotional reaction inside him, and he wasn't at all sure that allowing boys to cry freely was a good idea.

Because the sound of their boys crying drove her husband "crazy," Gaudette suggested he ask their sons to move to another room, if needed. Together, Gaudette and her husband discussed their goals for their sons. Both want to raise emotionally healthy, socially adept men who treat others with respect, so they are working on their own emotional regulation skills and attempting to make space for their boys' emotions.

Professional counseling can help you identify and heal emotional wounds, if needed. If counseling is not an option for you, you may find journaling, making art, or talking with friends helpful.

Self-care practices, including a consistent sleep schedule, regular physical activity, and time engaging in activities you love help you manage stress and make it easier for you to respond calmly and deliberately, rather than reactively, to life's challenges. Modeling self-care also increases the chances that your son will engage in healthy self-care activities throughout his life.

Honing your emotional regulation skills is a lifelong practice. There are no quick fixes, but here's one tip you can immediately implement: pause and breathe. When your kid (or anyone!) says or does something that bothers you, pause and take a deep breath before doing anything else.

Notice and Name Emotions

"One of the most helpful things parents can do to help their sons retain the innate emotional vulnerability with which they are born is to teach them how to put a name to what they're feeling," said Dr. Cara Natterson, author of *Decoding Boys: New Science behind the Subtle Art of Raising Sons.*[30]

You can begin by role modeling. Say you get disappointing news at work or via an email or phone call. Feel free to say, aloud and within your child's earshot, "Ugh. This is so disappointing." If the washing machine breaks, instead of cursing or hiding your emotions, try saying something like, "This is so frustrating! I'm really busy this week and I'm upset and overwhelmed because I'm not sure how I'll find the time to deal with this." Or "Ugh! I was saving money for a vacation, and now I'm sad and disappointed that we have to spend some of it to fix the washing machine."[31] Your son will learn the names and characteristics of various emotions *and* understand that feelings are a normal, natural part of life.

You can do the same thing when your child expresses emotions. If he starts screaming or throwing things because he can't get his shoes on, you can say something like, "Wow, honey, you seem frustrated and angry right now." (You can also reiterate any applicable family rules, such as "no name-calling" or "treat other people's possessions with respect.")

Tanisha Henderson, a mom of five in North Carolina, uses a Feelings Wheel developed by psychotherapist Gloria Willcox[32] to expand her boys' emotional vocabulary. A rainbow-hued, emotion-based version of the color wheel, the Feelings Wheel is composed of three concentric circles. At the center are six basic emotions: sad, mad, scared, joyful, peaceful, and powerful. The next circle contains more specific words—hurt, hostile, rage, and hateful, for example, are in the circle outside "mad." The outermost circle suggests other variations, such as "jealous" for "hurt." The wheel is arranged so that complementary emotions—sad and joyful, for instance—are opposite one another. (You can find the Feelings Wheel online by searching for "Gloria Willcox Feelings Wheel.")

When Tanisha noticed her ten-year-old son crying, she said, "I can see this is causing you stress. I'm hoping I can help," and pointed him to the Feelings Wheel, which she'd previously introduced to her family.

"Can you find a word on here that describes what you're feeling?" she asked.

Her son scanned the wheel then pointed to "confused." Tanisha showed him that "confused" is part of "scared" and then directed her son's attention to the opposite side of the wheel. "'Peaceful' is opposite 'scared,'" she said. "I wonder what we can do so you can feel peaceful and relaxed?"

Her son paused and took a few deep breaths. His body relaxed.

"It was beautiful to experience," Tanisha says. "My son felt heard, supported, and empowered, and we broadened his emotional vocabulary. I've now got copies of this wheel in every room of my house and in the car because I'm determined to raise emotionally intelligent men."

The Henderson family also use the wheel to play what she calls "emotions charades."

"I'll have one child pick a word and then act it out," she says. "The rest of us can look at the Feelings Wheel and try to figure out what word, what emotion that person is acting out." Learning to recognize and name emotions from nonverbal signals is a helpful life skill for all children, and little effort historically has been devoted to helping boys develop this skill.

Ian Thomas, a former elementary schoolteacher in Australia, noticed that his male students "would often return to class from breaks, upset and overwhelmed by emotionally charged playground experiences," he says. "These incidents frequently impacted the boys' abilities to take part in teaching and learning activities throughout the rest of the day. But because the boys didn't have the vocabulary to express themselves, it was a serious challenge to determine what had actually happened."[33]

So he created handmade cushions with different facial expressions (which he dubbed Moohsuns) to help his students learn to recognize and name emotions. Boys who don't yet have the words to describe their feelings and experiences can point to or grasp the "moody cushion" that represents their emotional state.

When my sons were teens, my family received a free Kimochis Mixed Bag of Feelings—a cloth sack of tiny stuffed pillows labeled with various emotions and corresponding facial expressions—from Ellen Dodge, a speech-language pathologist who serves as education director and curriculum author for Kimochis. My boys were too old for emotional education via soft, stuffed objects, I thought, so I simply dumped the pillows into a small basket in our family room, expecting little to no emotional growth or learning. But the pillows caught my boys' eyes and a few days later, I noticed that they *were* using them to express and discuss emotions. One picked up "frustrated" and tossed it at his brother after losing a game; another rummaged through the basket and suggested "embarrassed" might be a better choice. A few weeks later, I discovered that one of my boys wrote "horny" on one of the included Make-Your-Own-Feelings pillows—a feeling that's certainly relevant in the world of teenage boys.

Such lighthearted approaches are a wonderful way to help boys explore emotions. (Trust me, "Let's sit and talk about feelings" rarely works.) If you have a Nerf gun in the house, you can use a washable marker to write "feelings words" (happy, mad, scared, proud, frustrated, etc.) on a white board (or wall of your shower) and then ask your son to "shoot" the one that best represents his feeling. A boy who's reluctant to talk about his feelings may be happy to "shoot" them.

⚭

MUSIC BOOSTS EMPATHY

Making music together can boost boys' empathy. Tapping in rhythm to music increases social bonds between young children—and the likelihood that they'll help one another.

According to Joan Koenig, author of *The Musical Child: Using the Power of Music to Raise Children Who Are Happy, Healthy, and Whole*, "Learning to make music together is also learning to listen to others, which leads to the ability to 'read' that other person and anticipate their actions and intentions."[34]

Role Model Resilience

Noticing and naming emotions isn't enough. Boys also need to develop the ability to endure unpleasant feelings. They need to know that it's possible to bounce back from disappointments—and they need to learn *how* to survive tough times.

Resilience is "the process of adapting well in the face of adversity, trauma, tragedy, threats, or significant sources of stress," according to the American Psychological Association (APA).[35] Boys who are not resilient are at increased risk of suicide and substance abuse. In fact, researchers have suggested that higher suicide rates in males "may be partially related to a 'male depressive syndrome' which includes low stress tolerance, acting out behavior, [and] poor impulse control" (in addition to substance abuse and a family history of dependency, alcoholism, and suicidal behavior).[36]

Katey McPherson, an Arizona-based educator and suicide prevention activist, has noticed that many boys "crumble and think it's the end of the world when their sport ends or they're injured."[37] At least one boy she knew died of suicide when he lost his athletic scholarship after being caught with marijuana.

A boy's ability to tolerate and recover from frustration, rejection, and disappointment is crucial to his safety and well-being—and to that of society in general. (Remember: research has found that many mass shooters experienced rejection and humiliation.) You can boost your son's "bounce-back ability" by modeling resilience.

If you respond to everyday frustrations—spilled milk, the driver who cut you off on the highway—with a string of choice words delivered in an angry tone, your son eventually will follow your lead. If a friend accidently bumps your son's block tower, your son may be more likely to hit his friend or deliberately destroy his friend's creation than to calmly repair or rebuild his own structure. On the other hand, if you muster your inner strength to respond to challenges, your son gradually will learn resilience.

Consider this. You just lost out on a job promotion. You're feeling sad, disappointed, angry, and a bit jealous of the colleague who got the gig. You can either (A) hide your feelings from your child (which may leak out anyway via a sharp tone and short temper) or (B) share your experience in age-appropriate language.

You might tell an elementary-aged child: "I was really excited about something, but I found out I won't get to do it and I'm kinda sad." (With a teen or tween, you can share more detail: "You know that job I wanted? The boss gave it to someone else. I'm pretty disappointed.") It may be helpful to talk about how you plan to deal with your unpleasant feelings: "I'm sad, so I'm going to [go outside for a bit/go for a run/talk to friend]. That usually helps me feel better."

Your actions over the next few days and weeks matter too. It's normal to feel overwhelmed after a big disappointment, and it's okay to move more slowly than usual for a while. Ideally, though, you'll also start to act. You might journal or exercise to process your pain; mentioning your self-care activities within earshot of your son will teach him that it's normal and natural to use coping techniques during times of stress. It may also help your son to see you deliberately engage in a few moments of fun; kids need to learn that it's possible to feel joy even during times of stress.

Too many adults, in an effort to protect kids from life's hardships, hide the tough stuff. We don't talk about disappointments unless absolutely necessary, and when challenges occur in our lives, we hide our tears and frustration because we don't want our children to feel unsettled.

Our intentions are good. Kids draw their emotional cues from the adults around them, so it's smart to project an overall attitude of calm and competence. But when adults go to great lengths to hide their emotions from children—retreating to the bedroom, for instance, to cry about Grandma's cancer diagnosis or refusing to acknowledge the sadness and fear that accompanies a job loss—kids learn that emotions aren't welcome. They learn that grownups "suck it up," which increases the likelihood that they'll bottle up their feelings. According to psychotherapist Lisa Damour, psychological health is not about being free from emotional discomfort; in part, it's about being able to bear unpleasant feelings.[38]

It can be hard to admit fear or let your child see you cry, especially if you never saw adults doing such things when you were growing up. But allowing children to see you experience various emotions empowers them to feel and express what's on their minds and in their hearts, which (A) boosts their emotional intelligence, (B) gives them opportunities to offer love and support, and (C) teaches them that adults have feelings too.

A quick caveat: it's perfectly okay—wonderful, even!—for children to offer grown-ups sweet expressions of support, such as a hug, a kiss, or a simple "I love you. It'll be okay." Children should not, however, be the sole or primary source of emotional support for an adult. It is all right for your child to see you cry but save the details of Grandma's diagnosis (as well as the complicated feelings resulting from your conflicted relationship with your mother) for therapy or conversations with friends.

Allow Boys to Experience Their Emotions

Many adults inadvertently short-circuit boys' emotions.

Because their tears, anger, or fear make us feel uncomfortable, we shut them down. We tell boys, directly and nonverbally, that their emotions aren't welcome.

But think about it: Does abruptly cutting off your tears resolve sadness? Does keeping your fear inside eliminate or lessen the anxiety you feel when you learn a loved one has been injured in an accident? Personally, I don't feel any better when I hide my fears; if anything, my thoughts start to go 'round and 'round and I find it difficult to focus on anything else. And if someone says or implies that I shouldn't worry—well, I feel angry, resentful, and not at all supported. I might even mentally label that someone a Person Not to Be Trusted and resolve to not share anything of significance with that person in the future.

Our boys aren't so different. Like all humans, they fare better when they're allowed to fully experience their emotions, and they do best when they are safe and supported while doing so. Yet all too often, we inadvertently deny boys this opportunity.

While researching her 2020 book, *Boys & Sex: Young Men on Hookups, Love, Porn, Consent, and Navigating the New Masculinity,* journalist Peggy Orenstein was struck by some teenage boys' reported inability to cry. A college sophomore told her he resorted to watching back-to-back movies about the Holocaust one weekend because he desperately wanted and needed to cry; his parents had divorced, and years of social conditioning made it next to impossible for him to cry.

"I didn't initially understand this," Orenstein wrote in an article about her reporting experience, noting that she, "by virtue of [her] sex, has always had permission to weep."

In contrast, the boys she interviewed "routinely confided that they felt denied—by male peers, girlfriends, the media, teachers, coaches, and especially their fathers—the full spectrum of human expression."[39]

You can reverse that trend. Give your boys implicit and explicit permission to feel their emotions. Gemma Gaudette, the Ohio mom of two boys, has told her sons many times, "You can be angry with me. That is 100 percent fine. You cannot be disrespectful."

Allowing emotions does not mean tolerating abuse or disrespect. Note Gaudette's approach: an openness to emotions coupled with boundaries and limits. Her boys can feel whatever they feel; however, they are not allowed to verbally abuse or physically harm other people or property. If they choose to do so, the boys know they will face consequences, which may include removal from the situation, loss of privileges, and apologizing or making restitution. Allowing emotions does not mean tolerating abuse or disrespect.

As "inconvenient" as emotions may seem, Teacher Tom has learned that giving children space and time to experience emotions is more productive than suppressing emotional outbursts.

"Emotions have a beginning, a middle, and an end," Teacher Tom says. "When we threaten punishments or distract kids, we stop them from experiencing the full arc of the emotion—and then they don't learn that they're capable to coming out on the other side on their own."

Even though it is vitally important for boys to learn that they can survive unpleasant emotions, many adults try to eliminate children's discomfort. Parents hate to see their children suffer physical or emotional pain—in part because most moms and dads feel their children's pain acutely—so they often jump straight to solutions.

"We parents are so quick to try to fix or intervene, or, worse, minimize or dismiss," says McPherson, the educator and suicide prevention activist, "but it's not your job to carry them out of the proverbial ditch. We actually do our kids a disservice when we throw them over our shoulder and walk up the ladder because then they never learn how to grow and stretch through pain."

Teacher Tom no longer distracts crying children with an enticing activity; instead, he sits with kids while they finish their cry. He doesn't hurry or rush distressed students, and he doesn't gloss over students' joy or celebrations either.

"My job," he says, "is not to make things better. My job is to be with them when they're crying and when they're cheering or speaking truth, to create space for them to feel exactly how they feel for as long as they need to feel it."

Boys rarely find this kind of openness in the classroom, community, or among their peers, so it is vitally important for parents and family members to create a climate of openness at home. Having a safe space to experience emotions can help boys develop self-awareness, resilience, and coping skills.

Unpack the Link between Emotions and Energy

Emotions affect our energy. When we're scared or angry, our heart rates increase and blood flows to our limbs, preparing us for physical action. When we're sad, our energy wanes. Almost instinctively, we're drawn to rest. We want to curl up in a ball or crawl under the covers.

Explicitly discussing the link between emotions and energy can help boys understand their bodies' reactions to strong feelings. It also allows you to broach an important topic: what to *do* with emotional energy.

Without direction, many angry boys smash or throw things. Smashing and tossing aren't inherently problematic, of course. As long as your son is smashing, say, an empty cardboard box and not his brother's face or your living room wall, things are fine. In fact, a burst of physical activity and a bit of benign destruction can be quite therapeutic.

It's next to impossible, though, to redirect a raging fifteen-year-old (or a determined four-year-old). You can't effectively discuss boundaries with a person whose brain is in the middle of an emotional storm. So you need to establish ground rules before strong emotions hijack rational thinking (yours or your child's!).

It's best to talk about emotions during calm moments. Ellen Dodge, the speech language pathologist who develops curriculum for Kimochis suggests saying something like, "We all get to be mad at each other sometimes. How are we going to do our mad? What are we allowed to do with our mad, and what are we not allowed to do?"

Teacher Tom uses a similar approach in the classroom. Before students engage in rough-and-tumble play, the group discusses what will and will not be allowed.

"We sit down together, and I ask, 'okay, what are our agree-ments around this?'" Hobson says. (Note the use of the word "agreements," rather than "rules." Even very young children know that an agreement is something two or more people have decided together, whereas "rules" are often imposed by others and linked to punishment.)

If needed, Hobson kicks off the conversation: "Does anyone want their eyes poked?" He watches his students' reactions and listens to their comments. Hobson helps the children streamline their agreements—"no eye poking" and "no hair pulling," for instance, becomes "we'll keep our hands off people's heads."

You can do the same thing in your home or classroom. Talk about "mad," "sad," and "jealous" and how members of your family or class can safely express the energy that accompanies those emotions. You may be surprised by some of the boys' suggestions! Keep an open mind and say yes to their ideas as often as you can, even if their propositions seem outlandish.

I never would have thought about releasing my anger on an old metal storage container, but one of my boys did. He dragged the empty three-foot cube home one day after discovering it on a neighbor's curb awaiting trash pickup. For years afterward, when he was really angry, he'd go outside and kick, throw, or bash the cube with a baseball bat.

Note: the more ownership you give your boys over this process, the better your chances of gaining their cooperation. Also, it likely will take multiple conversations and reminders from you and oth-ers, both during and after emotional outbursts, for boys to remem-ber your agreements in heated moments. It takes time to learn and adopt new habits.

You should also discuss (and demonstrate) how to manage emotions that negatively affect mental and physical energy. Sadness and disappointment, for instance, sap energy. Talk about how you handle lower-than-normal energy levels (Do you binge-watch your favorite TV shows? Give yourself permission to take a nap? Throw a private, impromptu dance party to boost your spirits and energy?) and ask your boys to brainstorm ways to manage energy-sapping moods.

These conversations can (and should) unfold over time. Keep emotions on the agenda and watch to see how your boys' emotional intelligence evolves over time.

⌒⧜⌒

CAN VIDEO GAMES BUILD BOYS'
EMOTIONAL REGULATION SKILLS?

If you've ever watched (or heard!) a boy having an emotional outburst while playing *Fortnite*, you may think that video games negatively affect emotional control. But research has found that some
gamers use video games to regulate their emotions, and a few video
game designers have created games intended to boost emotional
regulation—and studies have shown they're effective.[40]

Do boys need clinically validated games to develop emotional
control? Absolutely not. They can develop emotional regulation
skills offline or by playing video games with friends.

⌒⧜⌒

To build boys:

- *Reflect on how you feel when your son is angry, happy, or sad and
  how you respond to his tears and anger.*
- *Introduce (or say "yes") to rough-and-tumble play.*
- *Begin naming emotions.*
- *Develop your emotional regulation skills. Prioritize sleep and self-
  care. Get professional help if needed.*

3

⌒∞⌒

Discuss and Demonstrate Healthy Relationships

A loving relationship is one in which the loved one is free to be himself—to laugh with me, but never at me; to cry with me, but never because of me; to love life, to love himself, to love being loved.

—Leo F. Buscaglia

Nathan was seventeen years old when he walked out of a school assembly aimed at preventing gender-based violence.

It was 2015, nearly two full years before sexual misconduct allegations against Oscar award–winning Hollywood producer Harvey Weinstein sparked the #MeToo movement and global conversations about sexual harassment, coercion, and rape. Two years before societal interest in how we raise our boys spiked due to our collective desire to *not* raise creeps and predators.

The high school assembly Nathan abruptly exited was delivered by a man whose nineteen-year-old daughter was sexually assaulted and brutally murdered by a male "friend." According to material sent home before the assembly, the presentation would contain a "call to action to raise awareness, examine our culture, and ultimately *end* male violence against women." And that, according to Nathan and others who attended, is exactly what the assembly delivered: a call to end male violence against women.

"The overall idea was that we, as men, need to fight the violent, felonistic ways inside of us," Nathan says.

That's a powerful, incomplete, skewed, and potentially alienating message. Powerful and incomplete because *all* humans should resist violent and dangerous impulses. Skewed and potentially alienating because it implies that men and boys are potential predators, without addressing the fact that males can be victims of abuse and sexual violence as well.

According to data compiled by the US Centers for Disease Control and Prevention (CDC), approximately one in five women in the United States has experienced rape or attempted rape in their lifetime, and approximately one in fifteen men has been forced to penetrate someone at some point during their lives.[1] Definitive statistics are difficult to obtain, largely because sexual abuse (particularly sexual abuse of males) is underreported, but research suggests that at least one in twenty-five boys (and perhaps as many as one in six) will be a victim of sexual abuse before age eighteen.[2]

The National Coalition against Domestic Violence reports that nearly 21 percent of female high school students and 13.4 percent of male high school students have been physically or sexually abused by a dating partner,[3] and studies have found that approximately one in three young people will be in an abusive or unhealthy relationship. Data from the most recent Youth Risk Behavior Surveillance Survey revealed that more eleventh grade males than eleventh grade females report being hit, slapped, or physically hurt on purpose by their boyfriend or girlfriend.[4]

None of this information was included in the assembly.

It is vitally important to teach our boys about healthy relationships—and incredibly challenging to do so. How can we teach our boys about healthy relationships when most adults don't know how to initiate, sustain, or even recognize a healthy relationship? In a culture that's far more likely to see boys as potential predators than humans in need of care, compassion, and instruction?

Efforts that center the experiences of girls and women without acknowledging the experiences of boys and men can backfire. Boys who detect bias in conversations about relationships, sex, and consent may stop listening. Boys who suspect that our "concern" for them is driven primarily by a desire to protect females from male harm will quickly shut down—or walk out, as Nathan did. They won't seek adult guidance as they navigate romantic and sexual relationships; instead, they will take their cues from other boys and young men who feel similarly alienated by a society that has yet to prioritize their need for protection and connection.

All too often, when parents and teachers talk to boys about relationships, we focus on sexual interactions. We project our worst fears onto our boys and tell them not to rape or sexually harass women and girls. We share scary facts about sexually transmitted infections and unplanned pregnancy—and completely ignore the *relationship* part of sexual relationships.

We're making things more difficult than they need to be.

The "work of preparing boys for healthy relationships often has nothing to do with sex at all," notes Emma Brown, author of *To Raise a Boy: Classrooms, Locker Rooms, Bedrooms, and the Hidden Struggles of American Boyhood*.[5]

Brown, an investigative reporter for the *Washington Post*, gave birth to a son just weeks before the Harvey Weinstein scandal broke. As the #MeToo movement gathered steam, she—like so many other parents of boys—wondered, *How will I raise my son to be different?*

Initially, she "thought we needed to raise our sons differently in order to protect our daughters," Brown said. But after "spending time in the world of boys," she realized that "we also need to raise our sons differently for their own sakes. . . . We simply have not given boys what they need to build healthy relationships with themselves, with other boys and men, and with girls and women."[6]

RELATIONSHIP EDUCATION BEGINS AT HOME

Boys begin learning about relationships at birth. They learn via our interactions with them (do we routinely respond when they cry, or do we ignore their calls for attention?) and by seeing, hearing, feeling, and experiencing our interactions with others. Even before they can speak, most children are incredibly adept at detecting the emotional temperature of a room. By preschool age, many know which adults (and children) to approach and which to avoid. They may not be able to explain their preference for one person over another, but they've learned to discern who they can trust and who cannot be trusted.

We tend to forget that we are our children's first and most influential role models. Yes, our boys will be influenced by the music they hear and the storylines they see play out in video games and movies. Their behavior will be swayed by their peers and the influencers they follow on social media. Don't get distracted, though. It's all too easy to watch the news, panic, and focus our attention on changing our boys' behavior so they behave appropriately in future relationships.

A better, more effective approach is to shift your attention and . . .

Look at Your Relationships

Are you in healthy relationships? Which of your relationships include a good balance of give and take and which are skewed? How are your conflict resolution skills? Do you maintain and respect personal boundaries? Do you clearly communicate your thoughts and desires, or do you guilt-trip others into doing what you want?

According to information provided by the Hennepin County Medical Center, healthy relationships involve respect and equality.[7] A healthy relationship is characterized by open and respectful communication, respect for personal boundaries, trust, honesty, shared decision making, and ample time for each individual to enjoy personal hobbies and friendships. In contrast, unhealthy relationships may include hurtful, threatening communication; insults and demeaning comments; disrespect; blame; an imbalance of power; physical or emotional abuse; isolation from others; and control, intimidation, or force.

Most relationships, of course—including romantic relationships, workplace relationships, and friendships—fall somewhere on the spectrum between healthy and unhealthy. Almost all relationships include moments of disrespect, blame, and poor communication. What matters most is how the individuals in relationships manage disagreements and unhealthy behaviors. Do they (do you?) accept responsibility as needed, apologize, make things right, and do things differently in the future? Or do you repeatedly engage in (or tolerate) unhealthy behavior?

Role Model Respect

We realistically cannot expect our boys to behave respectfully if they are surrounded by disrespect. We cannot expect them to resolve conflicts peacefully if our disagreements erupt into yelling, fighting, or passive-aggressive behavior. We can't expect them to ask for consent if we repeatedly ignore their personal boundaries or allow others to violate our boundaries.

Treat your boys the way you'd like them to treat others.

Refine Your Communication and Conflict Resolution Skills

Many of us grew up in families that were dysfunctional because our parents didn't learn healthy relationship strategies from *their* parents. You may need to unlearn relational patterns and develop new communication and conflict resolution strategies. Some of the strategies and communication techniques you learned as a child may have kept you physically or emotionally safe then, but shutting down or leaving the room when there is conflict, for instance, may limit your ability to connect with others now. If you learn and begin using healthier communication and conflict resolution strategies, your son will learn them too.

Amy Paturel Bieber and her husband, Brandon, do their best to model respect, kindness, and consideration—and they allow their boys to see them disagree and make up.

"We consciously have chosen not to do the 'fighting behind closed doors' thing," Amy says. "When we have an argument, we have it in front of them."

Handling disagreements in front (or within earshot) of their sons reminds Amy and Brandon to keep their language and tone respectful—something they hope their boys will notice and eventually do regularly as well. They stay on topic and stick to facts, instead of bringing up past hurts and failures. And they work to find mutually acceptable solutions.

"If we disagree about how to handle a situation—even on something like which punishment or consequence is most appropriate for one of the boys—we'll discuss it in front of the kids," Amy says. "We'll consider options, talk through what each alternative might achieve."

If tension arises, Amy and Brandon take a break and revisit the topic later. If one (or both) of them lose their cool and yell, they later apologize—again, in front of their boys.

Of course, some topics should be handled privately. However, allowing children to see and hear some conflicts shows them that two (or more) people can have differing ideas and priorities and still find a path forward. Respectfully resolving differences via conversation and negotiation can teach your son healthy conflict resolution skills—and show him that relationships can (and do) survive conflict.

Improve and Strengthen Your Relationships

Children who experience healthy relationships in childhood are more likely to avoid (or extricate themselves from) unhealthy relationships in adolescence and adulthood.

If you are in an unhealthy relationship—or engaging in unhealthy relationship behaviors—taking steps to improve your relationship is one of the best things you can do for your boy. You may want to consider professional assistance; a licensed counselor or therapist can help you understand your current relationships, unpack family dysfunction, and learn new coping strategies and communication techniques. If your relationship is affected by substance use (or you grew up in a family affected by alcoholism or substance abuse), you may benefit from Al-Anon meetings; they're free. (Go to https://al-anon.org to find a meeting near you.) There are also dozens of excellent self-help books. A few highly recommended titles include *The Seven Principles for Making Marriage Work: A Practical Guide from the Country's Foremost Relationship Expert*, by John Gottman and Nan Silver; *Not Nice: Stop People Pleasing, Staying Silent & Feeling Guilty . . . and Start Speaking Up, Saying No, Acting Boldly, and Unapologetically Being Yourself*, by Dr. Aziz Gazipura; *Adult Children of Emotionally Immature Parents*, by Lindsay C. Gibson; and *Daring Greatly: How the Courage to Be Vulnerable Transforms the Way We Live, Love, Parent, and Lead*, by Brene Brown.

If you think you may be in an abusive relationship or are unsafe, call the National Domestic Violence Hotline at 1-800-799-SAFE or text START to 88788.[8]

⸜∞⸝

INTRODUCE "EVERYDAY CONSENT"

Sexuality educator Al Vernacchio teaches students that consent is required any time you're going to interact with someone else's body, property, or reputation.

"Help boys first understand consent in a low-risk, not-fraught situation," says Vernacchio, author of *For Goodness Sex: Changing the Way We Talk to Teens about Sexuality, Values, and Health.* "The more practice they get at everyday consent, the better they'll do when things are more intense."[9]

Demonstrate everyday consent by knocking on your son's door before entering and asking for permission before swooping in for a hug.

SIBLING RELATIONSHIPS AND RIVALRY

"Sibling relationships—like the third rail on a subway track that carries the electrical current—are powerful and intense, driving development forward, but presenting dangers as well."[10]

Those words are from a 2012 study that examined the connections between sibling relationships and mental and behavioral health. They're also immediately understandable to any parent of more than one child.

Approximately 80 percent of kids in the United States have at least one sibling, and research has found that children spend more out-of-school time with their siblings than with anyone else.[11] For most children, sibling relationships are an important "arena for developing and practicing relationship skills."[12]

In my home, that arena often looked like a battle royale—or epic rap battle, sans the clever rhymes. My boys spit insults at one another with the precision gained by knowing one's target well. Like all siblings, they fought for attention and access to resources. (Who gets the last piece of leftover pizza? Who has to share a room, and who can claim space in the garage?) The bickering, as you learned in the last chapter, was nearly constant and crazy making. And yet, my boys help one another when needed. As teens and young adult, they (mostly) enjoy each other's company.

You can't avoid sibling conflict, especially if you have boys. (Serious academic research has found that sibling relationships that include a brother "may be more conflictual."[13]) Approximately 85 percent of siblings are verbally aggressive to one another and nearly three-quarters of families report physical aggression (including pushing and shoving) between siblings.[14] More than 40 percent of children with a sibling were kicked, bitten, or punched by a sibling within a one-year period.[15] Researchers who have observed siblings in action have documented "the occurrence of sibling conflict at a rate of up to 8 times per hour."[16] Do the math: that's one incident of sibling conflict every seven and a half minutes. No wonder you feel like a full-time referee sometimes!

Fighting and arguing between siblings is not an indication of poor parenting or "a sign of siblings not getting along. It is *how* they get along," according to *Psychology Today*. Children use "conflict to test their power, establish differences, and vent emotions."[17]

Sibling relationships are a practice field for interpersonal relationships. With brothers and sisters (or cousins, friends, and neighborhood kids, in the case of only children), boys can experiment with different ways of expressing needs, setting boundaries, and letting others know their boundaries have been violated. Children learn via trial and error, and their earliest attempts at boundary setting and conflict negotiation aren't very elegant. You are far more likely to hear "Hey, that's mine!" and "Give it back!" accompanied, perhaps, by tears and tussling than you are to hear, "Excuse me. That's my truck. I'd like to play with it now. Please give it back."

As messy, loud, and annoying as sibling conflict can be, it's an opportunity for children to hone essential relationship skills.

"Without a degree of challenge, we can't develop new skills— whether it's a basic skill such as matching shapes or an emotional skill like perseverance," Mona Delahooke, PhD, says in her book, *Brain-Body Parenting: How to Stop Managing Behavior and Start Raising Joyful, Resilient Kids*.[18] She recommends waiting before intervening in sibling squabbles. "If you immediately tell your child what to say to a sibling he's struggling with," she says, "he won't have the opportunity to solve problems on his own, in the process practicing and seeing what works and doesn't work."

Tanisha Henderson, a North Carolina mom of five, gives her children some space when they start fighting but monitors their activity from a distance. "I'm listening to hear, are they going to be able to work this out? Or is this where I need to step in and help with conflict resolution?"

That's a good approach. When siblings are completely "left to sort out problems on their own, they're likely to continue fighting—and that unresolved conflict can intensify, potentially leading to sibling bullying or aggression," according to an article in *Monitor on Psychology*, the official journal of the American Psychological Association.[19] Allowing children to persist with ineffective, immature, and unhealthy conflict resolution strategies can crystallize bad habits. A boy who learns that he can get what he wants by intimidating or hitting a sibling is likely to continue that behavior, which may carry over into his friendships, work life, and future romantic relationships.

You can decrease the intensity of sibling squabbles—and teach your son healthy relationship skills—by proactively coaching young children. When you hear or see sibling interactions going off the rails, step in. Reiterate your family expectations: *Whoa! We don't hit in this family.* Help each child find a way to express their needs ("I want the truck because I want to haul some sand" or "You've been playing with the truck all morning and I want a turn") and then encourage and support the siblings as they brainstorm possible solutions.

Yes, moderating sibling conflict is time consuming. But time you spend helping your four- or seven-year-old navigate sibling fights helps him to develop the skills he'll eventually need to navigate romantic challenges.

Note: what looks (and sounds) like fighting to you may actually be brotherly bonding—and important relational skill development. Name-calling between siblings is not necessarily cause for alarm, as many boys (and men) use insults and sarcasm to express familiarity and cement relationships. (One academic researcher noted that "the language process of insulting is important in the production of, and innovation in, a local masculine order."[20]) Learning to deflect and handle insults, in fact, is a key social skill for boys. A young boy who responds cleverly to an insult delivered by his older brother is demonstrating mastery of his ability to manage verbal abuse without resorting to violent behavior, utilizing a technique that is respected in masculine communities. It is a strategy males use to de-escalate conflict while preserving social status—a strategy that will likely come in handy on the playground and in locker rooms.

You can certainly forbid the use of offensive language in your home—and please, speak up when you hear boys use terms like "ho" or "simp" (a pejorative term for a boy who is "overly" submissive to a girl). Don't get too worked up, though, over terms like "stupid head" or "idiot."

Similarly, wrestling among siblings doesn't necessarily signal conflict or physical aggression. Roughhousing help boys (and girls) expel excess energy, test their strength, and, occasionally, settle disagreements. Don't assume that younger, smaller siblings are at a disadvantage and swoop in to save them. Many a younger sibling has figured out innovative ways to triumph over stronger, more experienced siblings.

Roughhousing is also a great vehicle for teaching consent. Writer and mom Janelle Randazza notes that "Part of rough and tumble play is learning to stop. . . . [Kids] learn in a real and relatable situation what 'stop' and 'no' means."[21] Again, keep an eye and ear on the action. If you hear laughing and exertion giving way to anger and frustration, step in. If things aren't yet critical—no injuries, no serious attempts to cause injury—you can say something like, "It doesn't sound like you two are having fun anymore," and suggest time to regroup. If one child seems intent on hurting the other, separate the children immediately. After everyone has calmed down, revisit the incident. Discuss signs that might signal one child's desire to stop—tears, a change in vocal tone, verbal request to stop. These lessons lay the groundwork for later, more explicit discussions of consent, which is after all the notion that we should respect one another's boundaries to be safe and build healthy relationships.[22]

⌐∞⌐

WHAT IF MY SON IS AN ONLY CHILD?

Boys don't need siblings to develop healthy relationship skills. Research has confirmed that adult only children are just as socially competent as adults who grew up with siblings.[23]

Only children may not have as many built-in opportunities for conflict (and conflict resolution), but they can develop their skills by fighting and playing with friends, cousins, and other kids at school or daycare.

cᢒᢙᢒᵓ

FRIENDSHIPS MATTER FOR BOYS TOO

"One of our chief jobs as parents," says Lydia Denworth, author of *Friendship: The Evolution, Biology and Extraordinary Power of Life's Fundamental Bond*, is to encourage our children "to make and maintain strong friendships."[24]

The ability to make and keep friends is vital to human well-being.[25] Friends provide companionship, of course, as well as essential feedback and emotional support. Having friends is also associated with increased happiness, self-confidence, and sense of purpose—all of which may contribute to improved physical and mental health. Youthful experiences with friendship are important because "what we learn about friendship in our formative years helps define our relationships for the rest of our lives," Denworth says.

Boys are at a disadvantage for a number of reasons. First, long-standing masculine norms (and homophobia) discourage intimate relationships between males (and yes, most boys are well aware of this unspoken pressure by ten years of age). Second, more boys than girls have attention deficit hyperactivity disorder (ADHD) and autism, two conditions that may make it more challenging to control impulses and recognize and respond to social cues.[26] Third, existing gender norms still celebrate "stand-alone" men—guys who handle even massive challenges, like saving the world, without assistance; we don't see nearly as many movies with male protagonists eating ice cream with their friends after a breakup as we do movies with female protagonists doing so. Finally, many adults simply don't understand male patterns of interaction and may unconsciously interrupt and discount boys' friendship activities.

These challenges may explain why boys and men typically have fewer close friends and feel lonelier than girls and women. Although young boys often have vibrant, exuberant friendships, their friendships tend to wane in number and intensity as they age.

"The sweet intimacy of young boys sort of gets killed as they get older, and that's unfortunate," says Jo Langford, a therapist, sex educator, and dad. Little boys, he notes, are physically affectionate with one another and will tell each other, "I love you." His son and his son's best friend used to spend hours entangled on the couch, torsos touching, while watching movies or playing video games. But at some point, Jo says, "it stops. It's society, I think, that tells them to do that."[27]

By middle school, boys are twice as likely to be friendless as girls.[28] By adulthood, one in five men say they don't have any close friends.[29] Twenty-three percent of men report feeling lonely "often" or "all of the time," compared to 20 percent of women.[30]

Boosting boys' friendships is good for their physical and emotional well-being—and for the rest of us. In friendships, boys are better able to resist the boy code, that strict set of unspoken guidelines that outline what boys "can" and "cannot" do, says Michael Reichert, founding director of the Center for the Study of Boys' and Girls' Lives, and Niobe Way, a developmental psychologist and author of *Deep Secrets: Boys' Friendships and the Crisis of Connection*.[31] It's hard to be the only boy in your class who wears a tutu to school; it's easier if your friends also wear tutus (or at least welcome and accept you as enthusiastically when you're wearing a tutu as they do when you wear blue jeans).

Friendships also help boys (and girls) build essential social skills, including companionship, trust, loyalty, and reconciliation. These skills, Denworth says, "are muscles they need to strengthen for adulthood."[32]

Yet we adults often de-emphasize friendship, focusing instead on our boys' academic or athletic achievement. That is a mistake. "Having and being a good friend counts for as much or more than many other achievements," Denworth says.

Imagine how different society might be if we prioritized their relationships over their achievements. If we spent as much time helping boys develop their social skills as we do practicing math facts or playing catch.

MOMS OFTEN MISUNDERSTAND (AND UNDERESTIMATE) MALE FRIENDSHIPS

It's easy—particularly for moms (and female teachers)—to miss the bonding that occurs in boys' friendships because their friendship interactions often don't resemble what we picture when we think "friendship bonding."

Boys' relationships are typically forged via presence and shared interests. The *what* of their interactions matters less than the fact that they are spending time together—and that's a nearly universal truth that's easy to miss in the busyness of everyday life. After all, when you're focused on bills, grades, behavior, and worrying about how to prepare your son for a world that's shifting faster than you can adapt, a bunch o' boys playing video games looks like a waste of time, talent, and energy.

It's so easy to nitpick and denigrate our boys' choices, and, frankly, much of the world encourages us to do so. You've certainly seen (and heard) countless articles and news stories blaming screen time and video games for everything from school shootings to males' declining participation in the workforce.

Ironically, Denworth, the author of a book about the power of friendships, didn't initially see the value of the hours her teenage son spent gaming with his friends.

When she returned home from a reporting trip and found her son and his friend gaming on the couch, she was frustrated.

"It felt as if they had not moved while I was away. . . . [T]he video games were driving me crazy: They are violent, they objectify women, and they cast an unbreakable spell over our children. They are also annoying. Listening to the roar of the fake crowd on *FIFA*—again—makes me roar myself, and not in celebration," Denworth wrote in an extremely relatable *New York Times* essay.[33]

Then she realized that the boys were doing something valuable.

Days earlier, Denworth was in Puerto Rico, learning about the socialization and bonding behaviors of rhesus macaques, a type of monkey. And something about the scene on her couch suddenly seemed eerily familiar.

The boys "were sitting close together and doing the human equivalent of grooming—laughing and talking, strengthening their bond before they left home for different colleges," she says. "Even I, who was spending my days thinking about friendship, had nearly missed that. I was so focused on the video game I didn't see the visceral connection."

Many parents—especially moms—don't make the connection between boys' seemingly purposeless activities and friendship bonding. Our boys' interactions can appear so common and shallow that it's easy to assume that we're witnessing meaningless interplay. But boys and men often use shared activities to establish and solidify relationships.

Some researchers, in fact, have proposed a more gender-neutral definition of intimacy, suggesting "emotional closeness."[34] Those same researchers also noted that girls tend to "take a disclosure path to emotional closeness"—sharing secrets and information—while boys are more likely to get there via "shared experience." As far back as 1953, some academics argued that "one learns as much about a friend from behaviors and responses observed in shared experience contexts" as they do from deep conversation.[35]

Think about it: boys learn a lot about potential friends' communication patterns, anger management strategies, problem-solving ability, cooperation, and conflict resolution skills while gaming (or fishing, playing basketball, or doing dozens of other activities) with friends. They learn who's loyal and team oriented and who's self-centered. Video games are now a "critical form of socializing," for boys, as nearly 97 percent of boys game.[36] Approximately three-quarters of video game–playing teens use voice connections to engage with other players.[37]

Boys definitely need opportunities to socialize and connect in person, but it's a mistake to dismiss the value of online interactions. Nora Gross, a visiting assistant professor of sociology at Boston College who's studied Black teen boys' responses to the deaths of friends and classmates, found that they "talk vividly about their pain, their grief [and] their love for their friends."[38] Many of these conversations, she notes, occur online, out of sight of adults.[39] The boys reminisce together and support one another.

HELPING BOYS BECOME BETTER FRIENDS

Some boys are naturally social. Others struggle in social interactions. Gifted boys often prefer the company of adults and find it hard to engage with same-age peers. Boys with social anxiety or autism may need extra support connecting with their peers.

Just as you can coach boys toward healthier sibling interactions, you can help boys become better, more attractive friends. Research suggests that making friends depends on skills that children can develop with practice: conversational skills, interpersonal skills, and emotional self-control.[40] You can develop these abilities at home.

Before a playdate, for instance, talk to your son about which toys and possessions he's willing to share with his friend; put away anything he's not yet ready to share. Brainstorm activities he and his friend might do together. Encourage (or prompt) your son to ask his friend what he'd like to do—and teach him that good hosts typically try to accommodate their guests' wishes as long as the suggested activities are safe and don't violate house rules.

Talk about and teach perspective-taking, which ADHD Dude Ryan Wexelblatt defines as the ability to mentally step into someone else's shoes and think about their thoughts, including their thoughts about you. Wexelblatt helps boys develop social skills by explicitly explaining to them that how they treat (and behave around) other people influences their interactions. He tells them that "the thoughts other kids have about you influence how they treat you." These thoughts, explained in boy friendly terms, fall into three categories: (1) "cringey" (weird and uncomfortable), (2) neutral, or (3) "clutch" (good).[41]

"If we don't like how people are treating us," Wexelblatt says, "sometimes we have to look at our behavior and say, 'are we giving them cringey thoughts about me?' And if I am, 'how do I use my brain coach so they have better thoughts about me?'"[42] (The "brain coach," Wexelblatt teaches his clients, is the "voice in your brain you use to talk to yourself.")

This kind of self-reflection lays the groundwork for the self-awareness that's necessary to adapt behavior to fit various situations. Frankly, this kind of awareness, self-reflection, and adjustment has been noticeably lacking in the behavior of many powerful men. Teaching boys this skill may decrease the chances that they'll prey on others or fail to consider how their actions affect others.

Talking to boys about the characteristics of a good friend is another way to build their relational skills—and teach them the difference between healthy and unhealthy relationships. You can start by asking your son to describe the qualities of a good friend. Reinforce positive friendship skills, such as loyalty, honesty, respect, and appreciation of personal interests. Then, talk about friendship deal-breakers. Ask boys to think about who they're comfortable—and not comfortable—around. Ask them why.[43]

Encourage your son to consider his behavior in friendships as well. "Friendships shouldn't be lopsided," Denworth says.

"Ask him, 'when was the last time you did something nice for your friend?'"

These conversations will make it easier for you to address friendship challenges when they arise. Boys also experience exclusion and bullying, and by the time they reach their tween years, they do *not* want you to intervene. (And forget forbidding friendship with certain individuals. That almost never works. In fact, your disapproval may make the forbidden friend more enticing.) Instead, ask open-ended questions that inspire reflection and action: "How do you feel when you're around this friend? What do you think about the way they talk to you? How do they treat other people?"[44] You can also teach your son the skills he'll need to handle relationship challenges. Child and adolescent psychotherapist Kate Hurley recommends teaching boys to identify and verbalize the problem; brainstorm three possible solutions; and evaluate each possible solution for obstacles before choosing one and proceeding. Later, she says, you can check in with him "to see what worked and what didn't."[45]

Do not discourage mixed-gender relationships. Children who are encouraged to play with friends of other genders learn better problem-solving and communication skills, perhaps because boys and girls often deal with disagreement in different ways.[46] Boys who have friendships with girls are also less likely to think of girls and women as sexual conquests.

TEACH BOYS HOW TO HANDLE REJECTION

According to Eileen Kennedy-Moore, author of *Growing Friendships: A Kids' Guide to Making and Keeping Friends*, "even well-liked [preschoolers] get rejected about one out of four times they approach another child to play."[47]

You may want to share this stat with your son to underscore the fact that all people experience rejection—and that rejection isn't a referendum on a person's inherent worth.

Boys also need to learn that "friends don't belong to you," says Maggie Dent.[48] A friend has the right to spent time with other people and can choose to end a friendship at any time, for any reason. Helping boys understand this fact "may even reduce the potential in adulthood for stalking, harassment, and physical violence towards those who have chosen to end a relationship," Dent says.

⌒∞⌒

LET'S TALK ABOUT LOVE, BABY

In Norway, South Korea, New Zealand, and parts of Australia, some form of relationship education is compulsory. In the United States and many other countries, it is not. And all too often, parents and educators skip or gloss over this important topic. As noted in a 2017 report by Making Caring Common, "we do remarkably little to prepare [young people] specifically for the focused, tender, generous work of learning how to love and be loved."[49]

Contrary to what many adults think, kids are hungry for relationship education. Of the more than three thousand young adults surveyed by Making Caring Common, 70 percent said they wished they'd received more information from their parents about the emotional aspects of romantic relationships. Kids want to know how to begin and end relationships, how to avoid getting hurt, and how to develop mature relationships.

Boys may experience (or be the object of) romantic interest as early as age ten, with first crushes often occurring between ages ten and thirteen.[50] Because boys typically mature more slowly than girls, tween boys may not be as interested in romance as tween girls. They may, in fact, be bewildered by their female classmates' sudden interest in them.

Do not pressure or push your son (or anyone!) to engage in a romantic relationship. Don't assume he'll have a girlfriend, either. Use nongendered language when discussing relationships, such as "sweetheart" or "someone special" instead of "boyfriend or "girlfriend."

Continue to point out and discuss indicators of healthy relationships, including mutual trust, honesty, and support, as well as time and freedom to pursue individual interests. Call out unhealthy and abusive behaviors—controlling, micromanaging, name-calling, physical abuse, intimidation—when you see them in TV shows, movies, and real life. The tween and teen years are also a great time to discuss the complexity of relationships. Help your boy understand that relationships are rarely either healthy or unhealthy; rather, most relationships exist on a spectrum between healthy and unhealthy. Understanding this distinction can empower boys to remove themselves from relationships that may be fun and loving at times but also hurtful.

DISCUSS DIGITAL DATING ABUSE

Nearly one in three teenage boys have experienced digital dating abuse.[51]

Digital dating abuse can include:[52]

- Threats sent via text or social media
- Constant unwanted calls or texts
- Controlling or wanting control of a partner's device, email, or social media
- Posting private images without consent
- Posting content to threaten or embarrass

Controlling, harassing, hurting, or intimidating someone electronically is not okay, and an expectation of near-constant digital connection is unreasonable and unhealthy.

Teenage boys are more interested in meaningful relationships than sexual adventures, contrary to popular belief. Researchers who interviewed fourteen- to sixteen-year-old boys about their early romantic relationships report that the boys "emphasized a desire for closeness, intimacy and trust" and wanted "a meaningful friendship with potential partners, whether or not sex was part of the relationship."[53] And when researchers asked a group of eighteen- to twenty-five-year-old males to pick their ideal Friday night from a list of activities—"sex in a serious relationship," "sex with a friend," sex with a stranger," "hooking up (but not sex)," "going on date or spending time with a romantic partner," "hanging out with friends," "spending time alone," or "something else"—84 percent chose an option that didn't involve sex or reported wanting to have sex in a serious relationship.[54]

You can help boys understand love by asking questions such as:

- What's the difference between attraction, infatuation, and love?[55]
- Why do you think people are sometimes attracted to people who don't like us or who are unhealthy for us?[56]
- How do your friends/people in your class show they like someone?
- How do you know if you're in love?
- What do you think are reasonable expectations for a relationship? How does that compare to the relationships you see?
- What do you think are some characteristics of meaningful, gratifying relationships?[57]
- How do you think romantic relationships enhance or detract from the individuals' lives?

There are no right or wrong answers to these questions, of course. (And you can't interrogate your boy with these questions. Trust me, it won't work well!) These are topics to ponder and discuss over time when opportunities arise.

PREPARE BOYS TO RESIST SEXUAL PRESSURE

Because puberty starts earlier in girls, females experience hormonal surges and the accompanying sexual urges before similarly aged boys. Add into the mix our highly sexualized culture that awards status to sexually desirable women, and it's not surprising to learn that some girls actively pursue sexual interaction in middle school.

Boys, of course, also experience sexual urges, and they're constantly bombarded by media messages that suggest that "real men" want and have sex every chance they get. Boys of all sexual orientations need to know that's it's okay to say no, even if another person *offers* nude photos or sexual activity.

According to a 2015 study published in *Psychology of Men and Masculinity*, 43 percent of surveyed high school boys and college-aged men experienced sexual coercion, or the use of words, seduction, substances, or physical force to get them to engage in sexual activity. Verbal coercion was most common (experienced by approximately one third of the males), followed by seduction (experienced by about one quarter of the males) and physical coercion (experienced by nearly one in five guys). Ninety-five percent of the respondents reported females as perpetrators.[58]

Teen boys may find themselves the object of strong sexual attention. Some boys will welcome this attention. Some will not. Our job is to help boys learn how to handle this interest. Here's how.

Step 1: Make Sure They Know It's Okay to Say No

Boys need to know that people of all genders have the right (and responsibility) to say no to sexual activity if they are uninterested or not ready.

Comedian and actor Michael Ian Black told his son, "Don't go through with it because you feel bad or you feel like it's expected of you, or you feel like somehow you will be less of a man if you do not. Just as a woman's body is hers to control, your body is yours to do with what you choose."[59]

Step 2: Talk about Reasons to Have Sex

Adults spend a lot of time telling kids why they shouldn't have sex. We also need to talk about reasons *to* have sex. Good reasons do not include "because she wanted to" or "because my friend did" or "everyone will laugh at me if they find out I said no."

In his book, *A Better Man: A (Mostly Serious) Letter to My Son*, Black reminds boys that "It's okay to want an emotional connection with somebody before you have sex with them. It's an obvious thing to say, but we tend to think of placing emotional intimacy before physical intimacy as a 'girl thing' instead of a 'human thing.'"[60]

Step 3: Talk about Sexual Aggression and Pressure

Talk about the difference between flirting and sexual aggression. Point out examples on TV and in movies and videos. Reality shows and popular TV series and songs include all kinds of examples of sexual aggression. Comment on those scenes. Ask your boys what they think. Ask about their friends' experiences (a less direct way to discover what may be going on in your own son's life): Have any of them experienced sexual or romantic pressure? How did they react?

Step 4: Introduce White Lies

Give boys some "outs" they can use in case of unwanted sexual attention. Tell them it's okay to say, "I don't want to"—but it's also okay to say, "I got to go now. My dad will go crazy if I'm not home in ten minutes" or "I gotta keep my strength up for the game." Help the boys in your life brainstorm some possible responses now, because it's a lot easier to think straight when you're not in a sexual situation.

Boys, like all humans, fare best if they wait until they are physically and psychologically ready to engage in sexual activity.[61]

⁂

YOU CAN'T IGNORE PORN

Most boys (and girls) discover porn by age eleven.[62]

A developmentally appropriate search for "boobs" or "sex" can turn up some seriously explicit material. So use parental controls and internet filters to manage internet access, and talk to boys about porn. They need to know that what they see online is *not* representative of most sexual relationships.

⁂

SEIZE TEACHABLE MOMENTS TO TALK ABOUT CONSENT

An email from my son's school turned into a lesson about consent.

According to the email (which was labeled "Bathroom Incident"), my then-twelve-year-old son pulled down his pants to urinate and then, with pants still down, turned around and poked another student in the stomach.

When I spoke with my son, I learned that he'd been pretty confident in his audience. Most of the boys in the bathroom at the time were his friends, and he was sure they'd find his behavior funny.

Clearly, someone did not.

"That's the tricky thing," I told him. "It's hard to read other people sometimes. Sometimes, you think they're up for something, but they're not. The only way to know for sure is to ask."[63]

I then took the conversation a bit further: "Sometimes," I said, "you might think that someone wants you to kiss them or wants to have sex with you, but the only way to know is to ask."

TV, music, and real life offer many opportunities to discuss consent. The Making Care Common report notes that "Media images of love . . . may be more harmful than media images of violence," in part "because we are not taught to view them as aberrant."[64] In many movies, for instance, continual pursuit of romance or sexual activity after an initial "no" is portrayed as romantic. Our boys are inundated with these messages—and told that persistence is the key to success to nearly every other pursuit in life. We must counter these messages.

That's exactly what one woman did when her teenage nephew told her a girl turned him down after he asked her out. According to a viral 2018 tweet, the woman asked her nephew, "you know what to do now, right?" and he replied, "I know. Keep trying."

"No," the aunt responded. "Leave. Her. Alone. She gave you an answer."[65]

You can also use news stories to talk about both the moral and legal requirements of consent. Together, review the federal definition of rape, sexual assault, aggravated sexual contact, and abusive sexual contact. (You can find them by searching online for "federal definition of rape, sexual assault.") Check your state laws as well; some states consider any sexual activity involving a minor a crime, whereas some allow consensual sex between close-in-age minors.

Reiterate and reemphasize the need to tune into others' verbal and nonverbal signals. Just as a switch from smiles and laughter to tears or angry words means it's time to stop roughhousing, a switch from smiles and comfort to tension signals *stop* (regardless of the words being spoken). Teach your son to err on the side of caution: a verbal "no" (or variation of "no," such as "not now," or "not tonight") always means no. Nonverbal signs of discomfort should also be considered a bright, flashing stoplight. Sexual activity should occur only when there is mutual enthusiasm. A blank or neutral face, silence, or absence of the word "no" does not imply consent.

Be specific! Teenage boys need (and want) detailed information. Andrew Smiler, author of *Dating and Sex: A Guide for the 21st Century Teenage Boy*, teaches the three-second rule and advises boys to wait three seconds after putting their hand somewhere to see if the other person acts or reciprocates.[66] If the person moves away or says no, stop. If there's no response, stop and ask directly what they'd like to do. Listen and proceed accordingly.

Emphasize the fact that it is a very bad idea to engage in sexual activity while under the influence of drugs or alcohol and illegal to have sex with someone who is under the influence, as he or she cannot properly consent.

Make sure your son knows that anyone can withdraw consent; he or his partner has the right to change their mind at any time. He or his partner can choose to stop in the middle of sexual activity. Continuing when one person has withdrawn consent is always a bad idea (and likely illegal). He also needs to know that sexual boundaries should be discussed and respected. Consent to engage in oral sex does not mean consent to engage in sexual activity involving penis insertion.

Yes, these conversations are uncomfortable. Teenage boys generally don't like to discuss sexual activity with their parents. But despite their discomfort and eye-rolling, they *want* to know the rules. And if you don't have these conversations with them, they'll likely take their cues from porn—which rarely shows mutually respectful interactions.

Boys want, need, and deserve close, caring relationships. It's time to move beyond a danger-focused approach to sexuality education and violence prevention. It's time to acknowledge boys' desire for intimacy and time to equip them with the skills they need to develop and sustain healthy relationships.

⚭

To build boys:

- *Reflect on whether your primary relationships are healthy ones.*
- *Role model respect.*
- *Introduce "everyday consent."*
- *Support your son's friendships.*
- *Discuss the characteristics of healthy, caring relationships.*

4

❧

Let Him Struggle

We don't develop courage by being happy every day. We develop it by surviving difficult times and challenging adversity.

—Barbara de Angelis

Within hours of seeing a Facebook Marketplace ad for a 2002 Audi A4, fifteen-year-old Adam purchased the sixteen-year-old car.

He and a slightly older friend, Ethan, met the seller, a dude in his twenties, at a parking lot approximately sixty miles from our home. The seller wanted $1,300 for the car. Adam paid $1,200. Ethan drove the car home because Adam didn't yet have a driver's license. And because Adam didn't know how to drive a vehicle with a manual transmission.

(Reader, if you're thinking, *this is a bad idea*. . . . I thought so too.)

The boys knew the car needed some work—it had a couple dents and dings and the seller told them the rear struts needed to be replaced—but they were confident. They'd already completed a few repairs on Ethan's car, and they regularly serviced dirt bikes and snowmobiles. The duo started work on the car almost immediately.

But after a few days, Adam realized he was in over his head. He took the car to a local mechanic, who put the car on a lift, revealing a cracked bell housing. Adam's $1,200 car needed a new transmission. Estimate cost for a used transmission: $2,800.

Are you surprised? Probably not. You're an adult, so you probably know that it's not smart to buy a used car without first having it inspected by someone who knows cars. You know that purchasing a vehicle you can't drive is a questionable decision, at best, and that used cars that are older than you aren't usually reliable vehicles.

I knew that too. When Adam first told me, "Ethan and I are going to look at a car," I wondered if I should allow the boys to go alone. But I remembered one important fact about teenagers: they find a way to do what they want to do, regardless of what you "allow." I kept my doubts, hesitation, and advice to myself.

When Adam told me how much it would cost to get his car in drivable condition, my heart sank. I knew how excited he'd been to buy this car and how hard he'd worked to earn the $1,200 he spent to buy it. I could only imagine how he felt.

"Ouch," I said. "That sucks."

He nodded. "Yep."

Adam soon realized that sinking nearly three grand into a sixteen-year-old Audi was not a good investment. One month after purchasing it, Adam sold the car for $800. He was $400 in the hole and still didn't have a vehicle.

As parents, we're eager to save our kids from heartbreak and expensive lessons. We want them to succeed and are willing to do almost anything to help them achieve their goals. But our children don't necessarily want—or need—our input. In fact, our efforts to pave the way for our sons can inhibit their development. As uncomfortable as it may be, struggle helps humans discover and refine their strengths. Struggle teaches us the power of perseverance and shows us that we're far more competent than we once thought.

Boys need to struggle and make mistakes. And we need to let them. As Debbie Reber, founder of TiLT Parenting and the author of *Differently Wired: Raising an Exceptional Child in a Conventional World*, told parenting writer Sharon Holbrook in a 2021 Capable Kids Q&A, "it's critical that our kids have many opportunities to struggle and, yes, fail" because that is how children develop the skills and confidence necessary to surmount challenges and live independent lives.[1]

As difficult as it was, I trusted Adam to independently handle his first vehicle purchase. I didn't alert him to the red flags I saw because his words and actions told me that he didn't want help.

When he suffered the consequences of his ill-advised purchase, I didn't shame, berate, or criticize him. I listened, empathized, and served as a sounding board as he explored his options and selected his next steps. I didn't rescue him, and he learned from his experience. Adam bought a 1992 Dodge Stealth (I *know*! An even *older* vehicle!) after selling the Audi and has since repainted and revamped the car. He also enrolled in an automotive program at our local technical college.

WHY STRUGGLE IS IMPORTANT FOR BOYS

"Safeguarding children from disappointment, removing all obstacles in their way, and providing external incentives—in other words, shielding and controlling—is a short-term strategy," says Gail Cornwall. A parent who does so, she says, "may protect the bodies of their progeny and even win (or buy) admission to a school like Stanford, but the approach can deprive kids of the chance to develop the resilience, resourcefulness, and inner compass to navigate life independently."[2]

Just as muscles need stress and strain to grow, so too do we (and our boys). I'd personally prefer to experience all the benefits of exercise—increased endurance, strength, stamina, and flexibility—without the associated sweatiness, shortness of breath, fatigue, and sore muscles, but that's not possible. I've learned to persist through the uncomfortable moments of my workouts because experience has taught me that those moments don't last. They pass, and I realize that my body and brain are more capable than I thought. I almost always feel better after a workout, despite the discomfort I experience during exercise.

The temporary discomfort our boys experience during struggle helps them realize the full capability of their brains and bodies. Without struggle, they won't have opportunities to practice self-regulation and problem-solving skills. They won't experiment with different strategies and solutions. I have watched my youngest son, Sam, wrestle with the same mechanical problem for hours. Days, even. And I have seen extreme pride and satisfaction on his face when he finds a workable solution.

Sam purchased a used 2001 snowmobile when he was fifteen years old. (I know—what *is* it with my guys and vehicles that are older than they are?). The machine was in great shape for its age and "just needed a carb clean," according to Sam. You can probably see where this is going. . . .

Sam didn't, though, and was despondent when the engine didn't work even after he thoroughly cleaned the carburetor.

"The night I realized that the engine needed a whole rebuild, I just laid on the floor of my room with the lights off for like an hour and a half," he says.

Sam was frustrated and not at all looking forward to putting *more* time and money into the sled. But he wanted the machine to run more than he wanted to quit—after all, he'd have next-to-nothing to show for his efforts if he simply gave up—so he kept going. Over the next days, weeks, and months, Sam considered potential problems. Consulted YouTube videos and fellow snowmobile fanatics in online groups. He asked his coworkers at a local motorsport shop for advice and assistance. And over a period of about nine months, he completely rebuilt the engine.

One night shortly before his sixteenth birthday, Sam stayed up working on his sled 'til nearly 3:00 a.m. It was a school night, but he was *so close* to finishing and determined to test-drive his sled before bed. I let him continue, despite the cost to his body. I also let him sleep in and miss his first hour shop class the next morning. (Send him short on sleep or allow him to sleep an extra hour after hours of mechanical learning the night before? The choice, to me, was obvious.)

That weekend, Sam took his fully functional snowmobile on a trip with his father. The machine worked beautifully, and Sam glowed with pride and pleasure when he returned home.

A week later, Sam entered his first-ever snowmobile race—and took third place. His self-confidence skyrocketed, appropriately. Sam's trophy was quite literally the result of his sweat and struggle.

Research tells us that engaging in productive struggle can build boys' confidence, competence, and emotional intelligence. When children are allowed to experiment, make mistakes, and try again, they discover their preferred learning strategies. They learn about their emotional reactions to stress—and they learn how to manage those reactions, because they eventually realize that it's virtually impossible to successfully problem solve when in a heightened emotional state like fear or anger.

Of course, none of this is neat or easy. A boy who is on the way to discovering that it's impossible to problem solve while in a heightened emotional state may look like a little boy having a meltdown over a math worksheet. He may look a teenager, storming out of the room and loudly proclaiming, "You never do anything for me!"

Struggle, for most of us, isn't a one-and-done thing. We humans often need to experience the same frustration multiple times before we find the path forward. (Think about it: How many times, even as an adult, have you had to relearn a lesson?)

Your boy may need to grapple with the same problem many times before he finds a workable solution. He may make the same mistake many times, and he'll almost certainly try things that you know won't work.

"HELPING" ISN'T HELPFUL

The adult instinct to protect children from harm can drive us to swoop in—sometimes even *before* boys start to struggle. With our years of experience, we can perceive threats from a distance, so we may jump into action as soon as we sense potential danger. I was leery of Adam's Audi deal from the get-go; part of me wanted to say, *No! You can't go buy a car without adult supervision.* If I'd done so, though, Adam wouldn't have learned nearly as much about negotiation or what to consider when buying a used car. He wouldn't have stretched his brain and problem-solving skills in quite the same way and may not have the confidence he has now. Because of his experience, he was a far more competent car buyer by age eighteen than I am, well, right now.

Adults who leap into action before (or as soon as) boys experience struggle send a powerful, often unintended message: *I don't think you can handle this situation.* To a boy, that can sound like, *I don't trust you to find a solution.*

Boys—even very young ones—perceive these unspoken messages and adjust their behavior accordingly. A boy who thinks you don't trust him to find solutions may come to distrust himself. Instead of leaning into his ideas, he'll question them from all angles, looking for possible flaws. He may come to believe his ideas are subpar, because why else would you always jump in with solutions?

Our boys live in a world that is quick to point out their shortcomings. Many of them already doubt their capabilities. (Tween and teen boys are especially vulnerable to shaky self-confidence and low self-esteem.) They look to us for reassurance that they're on the right track. Just as toddlers glance at their parents immediately after a fall or injury to determine if they're okay, boys are constantly monitoring our reactions to see if they're all right. Whether they state it or not (and believe me, tween and teen boys probably won't), they trust our judgment. And just as a toddler who sees tears or fear on his parent's face after he falls will likely collapse and begin screaming—because he concludes, based on his parent's reaction, that something must be horribly wrong—a boy who senses adult unease with his activity may collapse, metaphorically speaking. He may quit whatever he's doing because he can tell that you don't fully support his action.

If I'd micromanaged Sam's spending (of his own money) during his engine rebuild, I would have signaled distrust and displeasure with his actions. If I'd repeatedly suggested taking the snowmobile to a mechanic or other expert, Sam would have assumed that I didn't believe he was capable of fixing the machine—even if my motivation was to spare him some stress and give him more time to sleep. And if I'd forbidden Adam from going with a friend to look at the Audi that day because I feared he might be an easy mark for someone who wanted to take advantage of him—well, he might not be the confident negotiator and mechanic he is today.

Boys need to hone their judgment and skills. When they bump into obstacles and experience the resulting frustration, they have an opportunity to practice their self-regulation and problem-solving skills. If you consistently deprive a child of opportunities to test their abilities, you'll end up with a child—and then, an adult—with underdeveloped judgment and problem-solving skills.

RESISTING THE URGE TO STEP IN

In a 2019 NBC news article about the ill effects of helicopter and bulldozer parenting—parenting styles in which parents eliminate obstacles to their children's success and achievement—writer (and mom of five) Meagan Francis notes, "we live in a culture that pressures us to take on these behaviors even as we criticize them."[3]

Recognize that truth and your desire to protect your boy from harm. Remind yourself of the benefits of struggle. Take a deep breath when the urge the interfere strikes. And apologize when you step in and take over. (It takes time to learn new ways of reacting!)

⌀

ADDRESSING "MALE PRIVILEGE"

You've probably already encountered the term "male privilege," the idea that existing as a male in the world gives a human some unearned advantages. Your son will encounter it as well; in fact, if he's in middle school or beyond, he's almost certainly heard or read the term before, as it's used to explain the continued predominance of males in positions of power in both business and politics.

The word privilege, of course, conveys advantage, which is almost the exact opposite of struggle. That's one reason why some men and boys—people who have overcome challenges and worked hard to achieve their goals—resist the term.

It's important to help boys understand that so-called male privilege does not mean an absence of obstacles. Boys and men of all colors, creeds, and socioeconomic classes face plenty of challenges in daily life, and anyone who denies or glosses over that reality loses credibility in the eyes of most males.

Today's boys are generally unaware of the degree to which sexism limited females in the recent past (and continues to affect women today). They can't imagine the financial struggles of a single woman in the early 1970s, when banks could refuse to issue credit cards to unmarried women and employers could legally fire pregnant people. They don't realize that some employers are still reluctant to hire women because they fear females will want or need time off to care for children—even though men father and parent children as well.

Mothers of sons are particularly well-positioned to talk with boys about the ways in which gender can hinder (and help) humans in society. Moms can share their personal stories and gender-related struggles. Remembering their own frustrations, moms can listen with empathy as their sons share ways in which gender contributes to the struggles their boys experience.

Don't shy away from discussions of male privilege. Help your boys unpack the term. Ask them what they think it means. Ask them if it reflects their reality. Share your experience, stories, and observations, and listen carefully and respectfully to theirs.

GRIT, GROWTH MINDSET, AND GROWING GREAT GUYS

Grit, as defined by Angela Duckworth, the psychologist and researcher who first popularized the term, is "perseverance and passion for long-term goals."[4] It involves "working strenuously towards challenges, maintaining effort and interest over years despite failure, adversity, and plateaus in progress." Olympic athletes have grit; they devote years of their lives toward their athletic goals, despite unavoidable plateaus and sometimes even public failures. Parents demonstrate a lot of grit too. If raising a decent human isn't a long-term goal, I don't know what is! And if any endeavor includes a lot of adversity and plateaus, it's child-rearing.

Duckworth and others started studying grit because they wanted to know what separated achievers from languishers. Why, they wondered, might two people from relatively similar backgrounds end up with such different results? They discovered that grit mattered more than intelligence or inherent ability. An athlete who is willing to keep training, despite setbacks and injury, may achieve more in the long run than a more naturally talented athlete who quits at the first sign of failure.

Intriguingly, researchers have found correlations between grit and gender. Multiple psychology studies have reported higher levels of grit in female subjects than males. There may be multiple explanations for this gender-related difference in grittiness. Among them is the fact that boys are more likely to attribute their successes and achievement to innate internal traits, whereas girls are more likely to credit persistence and hard work.

That's where "growth mindset" comes in. In the early 2000s, psychologist Carol Dweck identified two distinct mindsets: "growth mindset" and "fixed mindset." Individuals who have a growth mindset believe that their skills and abilities can be developed through effort and training. Those who have a fixed mindset believe that their abilities are "fixed" and innate. A person with a fixed mindset may say, "I'm just not any good at math" or "I don't have a math brain," whereas someone who has a growth mindset might say, "If I work at this math problem, I'll make progress" or "I'm not good at multiplication yet, but with practice, I'll get better."

It's pretty easy to see the advantages of a growth mindset: if I believe I can get better at something with practice, I'm more likely to persist at, say, skiing, than if I think I'm either naturally good at the sport or not good at it. Those who believe that competence and skill are linked to innate ability are much less likely to persist past frustration. Why would I go through all the trouble of bundling up, strapping on skis, and heading out into the cold, only to fall again and again, if there's no hope of real improvement—if I'll never be any good at it anyway?

Interestingly, Chathurika Kannangara, a professor of psychology, has found that mindset may explain why some people with dyslexia, a learning disability characterized by difficulty reading, thrive while others languish. Her research has found that "languishing dyslexics" are anxious about facing challenges, so they tend to avoid reading and writing. They focus on their weaknesses, so they are hyperaware of obstacles and likely to give up when criticized. In contrast, "thriving dyslexics" focus on their strengths and use them to overcome challenges. They persevere and consider criticism to see if they can learn anything from it.[5]

Sounds great, right? Now consider most boys' experiences in schools (and in the world). Parents and teachers often focus on boys' weaknesses rather than their strengths. Adults criticize little boys' inability to sit still and rarely compliment their creative, energetic problem-solving skills. Mistakes are framed as something to be avoided rather than embraced. Carol Dweck herself has noted that "many parents . . . endorse a growth mindset, but react to their children's mistakes as though they are problematic or harmful, rather than helpful."[6]

Struggle and mistakes are a necessary part of the learning process. Grit and a growth mindset will help boys endure struggle and persist past mistakes. So how do we nurture grit? And how can we promote a growth mindset?

A 2021 study published in *New Ideas in Psychology* suggests a possible path. The study explored gender differences in passion, grit, and mindset. Researchers used psychological tests to measure the grit, passion, and mindset of 917 participants ranging in age from fourteen to seventy-seven and found a significant correlation between passion—which has been defined as "a strong inclination toward . . . activity that one likes (or even loves), finds important, and in which one invests time and energy"—and grit *in males only*. The authors conclude that "Boys have more possibility to focus on area/theme/skill they are interested in. "[7]

That observation matches my anecdotal experience. Sam spent hours in the garage working on his snowmobile because *it mattered to him*. He is passionate about snowmobiles and dirt bikes and has invested thousands of hours into research, reading, and hands-on learning to help him achieve his goals. Trust me, Sam is far more likely to spend hours working on his sled than on his civics homework because he's passionate about snowmobiles; he's not passionate about government or social studies.

Here's the great thing about struggle, grit, and growth mindset, though: the content of the struggle isn't nearly as important as the process. Sam developed his critical thinking, problem-solving skills, and persistence while working on a snowmobile, but those skills are transferrable to other aspects in his life. His hours in the garage honed his growth mindset, which he now applies to school, work, and relationship challenges.

If you want your son to learn how to persist past challenges, allow them to tackle problems and projects that matter *to him*. Tap into his passions. (We'll touch on this more in chapter 5.) Whenever possible, say yes rather than no to his crazy ideas. Supply space and supplies, if you can—or encourage the boys to figure out ways to gather the supplies and support necessary to achieve their goals.

When eleven-year-old Walter asked his mom for a $400 Meta Quest virtual reality headset from Oculus, she didn't immediately say "No" or "Are you kidding?" or "Do you have any idea how expensive those things are?" She didn't suggest he add it to his birthday or holiday gift list either. But she didn't dismiss his request. Instead, she asked him, "What is the best way to get $400?" Walter, who'd recently raised funds to cover his Boy Scout camp fees by purchasing pocketknives wholesale and then selling them to adults and other Boy Scouts, immediately started brainstorming.

"Oh!" he said. "We need to set up an online store!"

Brittany, Walter's mom, didn't belittle his idea. Instead, she said, "That's a great idea!" She told Walter about a family friend who's a successful online entrepreneur and suggested her son contact the friend with questions.

Walter may not follow through, but because his mom refused to take on his "problem" and instead returned it to him, Walter can decide how much time, attention, and energy he wants to devote toward his desire. His answer will likely depend on how much he really wants an Oculus—and that's a great lesson to learn at age eleven.

WHAT ABOUT BOYS WHO AVOID STRUGGLE?

Young males are more likely to respond defensively to criticism and suggestions for improvement than young females, according to research by Jack Zenger and Joseph Folkman, two leadership development consultants.[8] This resistance can look like arrogance and overconfidence, but Zenger and Folkman discovered that it's often related to a *lack* of confidence.[9]

Boys who avoid struggle may be extremely low in self-confidence. Try giving them opportunities to succeed. Look for (and seize) opportunities to praise their efforts. Normalize mistakes and let them experience (and survive) a few of their own.

HOW TO SUPPORT BOYS DURING STRUGGLE

It's one thing to say we should let boys struggle, and another to watch them experience frustration. In the hypothetical, it all seems so easy: boy confronts problem, struggles, and eventually experiences success! His confidence and capabilities grow!

In practice, it can be heart wrenching to see a boy you care about bump (or slam!) into obstacles and make mistakes. And it can be hard to know what to *do* while said boy struggles. Do you do nothing? Offer advice? Support him? *How?*

The answers to those questions, of course, must be tailored to the boy's age, personality, and specific struggle, as well as to *your* availability and personality. Here are some ideas to get you started.

Offer Support

There's no need to allow your boy to struggle all alone—unless that's his preference. (You'll often be able to tell by his words and actions. If he says, "Go away!" "Leave me alone!" "I don't want your help!" or "I want to figure it out myself!" go and away and give him time. Similarly, if he merely grunts in response to your inquiries or refuses to make eye contact, it's probably best to back away for a bit. Some boys work best alone.)

When you see signs of struggle, simply ask, "How can I support you?" This question puts the metaphorical ball in his court; he can ask for your help or not. The phrasing of the question indicates that you trust him to handle the problem but are available should he need or desire assistance.

Verbally expressing your support is helpful too. Comments like, "I believe in you," "I think you can do it," or "I've seen you handle hard stuff before" signals confidence in his abilities—and our boys need to borrow our confidence more than we know!

As a child, Chathurika Kannangara, the psychology professor who studies thriving and languishing dyslexics, couldn't read. She didn't do well in school, and neither she nor her teachers expected that to ever change. Until one teacher "started believing in her," she said in her 2016 Tedx talk, "Success in Failure."[10]

"No matter what the outcome was, [my] effort was appreciated . . . and that really started changing [my] life," Kannangara said. She began investing more time in her strengths, eventually earned a doctoral degree, and now serves as an associate teaching professor and early career researcher in psychology at the University of Bolton in the England.

Note: it's okay to privately doubt your boys' ability and approach. Most of us do at one point or another! You can share your concerns with your friends or partner but do not let your son overhear these conversations. Be cautious, because boys' ears are more alert for mentions of their names than you may think.

Support His Attempts

It can be *so difficult* to watch our struggling boys try things we know won't work. But the process of problem-solving is important, and an unsuccessful attempt may reveal tidbits of information that help your boy come at the problem from another angle.

Watch for signs of productive struggle: determination, focus, and continued attempts at problem-solving. If he has not asked for help and continues to work the problem, simply support his attempts; you can say something like, "Wow! I can see you're really working hard!" or "I'm impressed with the effort you're putting into this." Do not attempt to interfere or redirect him, even if you're 99 percent sure that your approach would save him time.

Remember: different people have different ways of solving the same problem. Your boy may surprise you by finding a solution you hadn't even considered!

Don't Dismiss His Struggle

It's okay—and important, even—to acknowledge the difficulties and challenges a boy is facing. Pat reassurances ("It's going to be all right," "I know you'll figure it out in the long run") aren't very reassuring if the person issuing them doesn't seem to see or under-stand the size or impact of the problem. It's far more helpful to share accurate observations with empathy: "Wow. That looks really hard" or "This isn't easy."

Your recognition of your son's struggle shows him that you care. It also validates his experience. If you instead ignore, dismiss, or minimize his struggle, he may doubt his perception of reality—as well as his own judgment and capabilities. He'll also be more likely to hide future challenges from you, since, in his view, sharing his challenges would be pointless and may expose him to criticism and a lack of emotional support.

Emphasize the Importance of Rest

Sometimes our best ideas come during periods of rest—when we're *not* actively working on solving a problem.

The importance of rest can be difficult to convey to a boy growing up in a culture that values activity far more than rest and rejuvenation, but we're all better problem solvers when we're adequately rested.

As Shawn Achor, author of *The Happiness Advantage*, and Michelle Gielan, author of *Broadcasting Happiness*, wrote in a 2016 *Harvard Business Review* article, "We often take a militaristic, 'tough' approach to resilience and grit." (That's especially true for those of us who are raising boys, I think.) "We imagine a Marine slogging through the mud, a boxer going one more round, or a football player picking himself off the turf for one more play. We believe that the longer we tough it out, the tougher we are, and therefore the more successful we will be."[11]

Many of our boys believe the same thing. After all, they've seen many of the same movies we have. They know—because our culture has told them, again and again—that pushing on is preferred. They know that some people view the need to sleep as a weakness, even though sleep is a human imperative and physiologic necessity for good health.

Maintaining bedtime and naptime routines for young boys will help them get the rest they need to manage the struggles of daily life. With older boys, it can be helpful to explicitly discuss the benefits of rest. Role modeling is essential as well. Let your son see you taking a break when a problem frustrates you. Talk about how a walk around the block helped you clear your head and consider new approaches to your problem. Remind your son that the "the key to resilience," as outlined by Achor and Gielan, "is trying really hard, then stopping, recovering, and then trying again."[12]

Obviously, I haven't always been successful in conveying this message to my sons. Sam, after all, stayed up until nearly 3:00 a.m. to work on his snowmobile, and my boys have seen me working well into the night on this book. We're all learning to take breaks and refuel as needed.

Teach Him the Power of "Yet"

"Yet," author Jessica Lahey says, is a "magical word." In those three letters are the essence of the growth mindset, the idea that humans can build their capability and capacity via sustained effort.

A kid who says, "I can't do it!" is frustrated. Whatever he's attempting is beyond his current skill set and, in the moment, may feel so difficult that he doesn't even see the point of persisting. Why waste valuable time and energy trying to do something impossible anyway?

But *yet*, Lahey reminds us, is "all about the promise of next time." Something that seems impossible today may be within reach tomorrow or next week, particularly if we take action. So if your son is struggling to read an assigned text or frustrated because he can't consistently make a left-handed layup, remind him that he can't read the book (or make the layup) *yet*. Together, brainstorm what he can do today so that tomorrow he'll be a bit closer to his goal.

SHOULD I LET HIM QUIT?

The short answer: yes.

The slightly longer answer: it depends.

No one needs to continue a sport, activity, or hobby indefinitely. But some kids are quick to quit when the going gets rough and may benefit from learning to push past the tough stuff. Encourage him to stick it out if:

- He's having a bad day.
- The natural end of the activity (end of the season, for instance) is near.

Let him quit if:

- He consistently resists the activity.
- His interest has shifted to something else.
- He's being abused, bullied, or injured.

WHEN *NOT* TO LET A BOY STRUGGLE

There are times adults must step in. As Deborah Farmer Kris, founder of Parenthood 365 wrote in a 2020 article, "Like any other parenting conundrum, the desire to avoid becoming a 'helicopter parent' can be taken to extremes. When teens are in distress, sometimes parents think, 'I need to step away from you. You have to figure it out by yourself.'"[13]

That's particularly true for parents (as well as teacher and coaches) of boys, who have often subconsciously bought into the strong-and-stoic model of masculinity. Boys, we believe, must figure things out alone. But some problems are beyond boys' current problem-solving abilities. Some require professional assistance.

Don't ignore any of these red flags, which signal a need for immediate action.

Drastic Changes in Behavior

Pay attention if your formerly social son starts spending tons of time alone in his room. Or if your sports lover suddenly wants nothing to do with sports. Boys' interests and behavior certainly change as they grow but get curious about any big changes. Don't interrogate your son; first, simply and calmly state your observation: "I notice you've been spending a lot of time in your room lately," "You haven't been spending as much time with friends," or "Sports used to be your life." Pause and give him an opportunity to respond. Listen carefully to his answers; dig a bit deeper if he seems open to continuing the discussion. ("Huh. Baseball isn't as fun as it used to be?")

You may want to talk with his friends, teachers, or coaches to gain additional insight. Caution: if you have preteen or teenage son, it's a good idea to let him know in advance that you plan to talk with his coach or teacher; otherwise, he may feel ambushed or betrayed, which means he'll be less likely to turn to you for support or assistance in the future.

Persistent Mood Changes

Mood swings are normal during adolescence. But persistent mood changes and shifts in behavior can also signal anxiety, depression, relationship issues, or suicidal thinking.

Don't ignore notable or persistent mood changes—and if you are worried that your son (or another child) may be considering suicide, *ask*. There is no evidence that asking about suicidal thoughts or intent to self-harm increases the risk of suicide; not asking, however, may be a fatal mistake. You can reach the US National Suicide

Prevention Lifeline by calling or texting 988. A trained crisis coun-selor will answer and provide support, information, and connection to local resources, as needed.

Your son's primary care provider or school counselor can provide information and context and help you access resources within your community. When it comes to mental health, it's almost always bet-ter to err on the side of caution.

Self-Harm

Contact a healthcare provider or licensed mental health provider immediately if you see evidence of self-harm, including unex-plained scars or fresh cuts, burns, or bruises; a sudden or recent insistence on wearing long sleeves and pants regardless of the weather; unexplained weight loss or gain; restrictive eating; or compulsive exercise.

These symptoms may indicate the presence of anxiety, depres-sion, or an eating disorder, and professional assistance can help you help your son.

Unsafe or Illegal Behavior

Many children and teens—especially teenage boys—experiment with drugs, alcohol, and many engage in an illegal activity like vandalism or reckless driving at least once. Trying drugs or alcohol or spray-painting an exterior school wall doesn't mean your son is a bad kid; most boys learn from their experiences, especially if allowed to contend with the natural consequences of their actions, including monetary fines, restriction from school activities, and legal penalties.

However, if your son regularly engages in unsafe or illegal behavior, get support. Share your concerns with your son's health-care provider, who can help you connect with local resources. Schedule an appointment—for yourself!—with a counselor or other mental healthcare provider who can help you process your emo-tions, bolster your coping strategies, and set boundaries. Check out Al-Anon, which provides support to family members and friends of people with alcohol and drug addiction. You can also call the Substance Abuse and Mental Health Services Administration's

National Hotline at 1-800-662-HELP (4357) for free, confidential information and treatment referrals.

Your Gut Says Something's Not Right

Trust your intuition! If you're worried about your son's physical health, emotional adjustment, schooling, or relationships, and a voice deep inside you keeps whispering, "something's wrong," keep pushing, even if so-called experts have already dismissed your concerns. Parental intuition is powerful, so seek a second (or third or fourth) opinion.

To build boys:

- *Reflect on when you are most likely to "rescue" your son and why you intervene.*
- *Ask your son what he thinks "male privilege" means.*
- *Give your son a chance to solve problems. Support his efforts.*
- *Let your son make (and learn from) mistakes.*

5

⌒∞⌒

Help Him Find and Develop His Talents

The person born with a talent they are meant to use will find their greatest happiness in using it.

—Johann Wolfgang von Goethe

Max loved to dance.

At age four, he asked his mother if he could stop playing rugby and focus on dance instead. His mom—a thoroughly modern mother who'd exposed her young son to Legos, Barbies, rugby, and ballet—enrolled him at a local dance school.

Max looked forward to his lessons and often danced at home, but his enthusiasm waned after an older boy told him that if he dances, he must be a girl. Or gay.

"He was the only boy in his class, so when he got that message and looked around—everybody else in their pink tutus and he, the only one in shorts and a t-shirt—he assumed he didn't belong," says Max's mom, Sassy Harvey.[1]

Max dropped out of dance class; his mom jumped into action. A dancer herself, Harvey knew that dance is universal. And as an avid feminist, she knew that gender-based limitations are ridiculous and outdated. After realizing the extent to which rigid gender norms still restrict boys' experience, Harvey launched My Boy Can, a United

Kingdom–based organization that supports and encourages boys who don't adhere to the traditional rules of masculinity.

"There are so many people who will say 'no, you can't' or 'you shouldn't because you're a boy' to boys who dance, love mermaids, or like to wear makeup," says Harvey, noting that some of these objections arise from parental concern that a child might be bullied for stepping beyond traditional gender norms. "But as soon as you say, 'no, you can't,' a wall comes up. Boys internalize those messages."

Without guidance and support, a boy whose interests are met with derision, anger, or fear assumes that *he* is a bad person or misguided, at least. Unfortunately, boys' interests and activities are under attack from all directions. Boys like Max, who love dance and mermaids, are routinely ridiculed by those who believe males should be tough, strong, and stoic. Boys who love to wrestle and take physical risks are regularly reminded to "settle down!" and boys who enjoy target shooting and hunting are viewed as potential mass murderers.

Girls today are regularly reminded that they can do anything, even if the realities don't always deliver on that promise. Boys face criticism from all corners even before they try. Identifying, embracing, and developing our sons' talents will help them flourish—and may make the world a better place.

WHY IT'S SO IMPORTANT TO
HELP BOYS DEVELOP THEIR TALENTS

Kids come into the world preloaded with gifts and talents. But unlike, say, a box of cereal, children don't come with ingredient labels. We parents gaze upon our babes with wonder and fantasize about who they are and what they might become—often unconsciously projecting our hopes and dreams on a child who can't even yet roll over.

As helpful as it might be, we don't get notes that clue us in to the person our child is meant to become. (Can you imagine? *"Deep emotional thinker with a penchant for stories. Writer in the making." "Strong sense of justice. Adept at arguing. Might make a good lawyer."*)

Instead, our children gradually reveal themselves to us, and it is on us to recognize and encourage the growth of their talents.

Some boys' talents are evident from an early age, especially in hindsight. Milwaukee mom and writer Jeanette Hurt says that her son Quinn "liked to move from the time he was in my womb."

"When I was pregnant, we'd play a game in which I'd tap my belly and he would kick and punch exactly where I tapped," Hurt says. At ten months, her son was running. By age nine years old, Quinn was a competitive gymnast.

Kodi Lee, a 2019 *America's Got Talent* (AGT) contestant who is blind and autistic, demonstrated an early interest in music. Before his jaw-dropping, Golden Buzzer performance of "A Song for You," his mother Tina told the judges that when young Kodi listened to music, "his eyes just went huge and he started singing." That, Tina said, was when she realized he was an entertainer.

As Kodi grew, his mother focused on his interest rather than his challenges. She didn't let blindness and autism keep her son from the piano or performing. Instead, she provided him with the tools and support necessary to pursue his passion. Kodi flourished.

"Through music and performing, he was able to withstand living in the world," Tina said. "It actually saved his life, playing music."

When Kodi opened his mouth to sing on the AGT stage, revealing a soulful voice and soaring falsetto, he opened hearts and minds as well. Where people first saw a white cane, unfocused eyes, and funny facial expressions, they soon saw beauty. Kodi's AGT audition earned a standing ovation from the crowd. Two days after his performance, the video of his audition was the top trending video on YouTube, with more than twelve million views. Kodi was ultimately crowned the 2019 AGT champion.

When we nurture our children's talents, we help them discover their purpose in the world. We deepen our connection with our children as well. When we meet their expressed interests with enthusiasm and support, they feel safe, secure, and whole. If we instead react with hesitation, fear, or disgust, our children interpret our negative reaction as a sign that something must be wrong with their natural inclinations—with them.

Some boys diminish and downplay their interests in response to a lack of support. Some push down their natural inclinations and pursue parent- and socially approved activities instead. Others simply decide not to care about anything. They disengage and do as little as possible to get by.

Unfortunately, disengaged boys may grow into unsatisfied, depressed, anxious, or even suicidal men. According to the Centers for Disease Control and Prevention, males are approximately four times more likely to die of suicide than females.[2]

It's not always easy to identify or embrace our boys' talents. But we may protect our boys' spirits—and lives—if we do.

Unfortunately, boys and their parents face a few obstacles.

Social Expectations Still Limit Boys' Growth

For generations, social expectations slotted boys into assigned roles: *Provider. Protector. Husband. Father. Warrior. Worker.* Today, strict adherence to gender roles is, for the most part, a thing of the past. We're even questioning the very concept of gender. But boys still face tremendous pressure to behave and act "manly." The "man box"—that set of expectations that defines how a boy or man should behave—is alive and well. We're well into the twenty-first century, but it's still common to hear baseball coaches tell young boys to "man up!" or "stop crying" if they get hit by a ball. Parents still debate whether dolls are appropriate toys for boys, and teen boys are surrounded by billboards and ads that suggest ideal men have six-pack abs, bulging biceps, and hot girlfriends.

The National Science Foundation has invested at least $270 million dollars since 2001 into initiatives supporting women in the sciences,[3] but there's been no similar effort undertaken to increase the number of men in nursing, early education, and domestic roles. In fact, a 2019 study published in the *Journal of Experimental Social Psychology* found that people consistently support social action to correct the gender imbalance in male-dominated fields but are unwilling to commit funding to promote gender balance in traditionally female-dominated fields.[4]

It's not easy for boys and their families to acknowledge and nurture talents that go beyond what's socially acceptable within your community. Many schools and communities have football teams—even for five-year-olds—so it's easy for boys who love football to find friends on the playground. Not so for boys like Max who love dance. When I asked a group of parents in 2019 which activities their sons enjoy but have a hard time pursuing due to outside pressure, five out ten respondents said "dance." (One parent said, "He loved it when he was younger but had an adult make too many negative comments, so he gave up.") Other answers included baking, singing, and acting.

Notice a theme?

Adults Devalue Boys' Interests

Unwittingly, many adults attempt to channel boys toward socially acceptable, "worthwhile" interests. In the process, however, we may be neglecting our boys' innate gifts.

Consider a boy with a deep interest in video games. Do you encourage his passion or try to persuade him to do something useful? If you're like most parents, you've probably spent plenty of time attempting to redirect your son toward something you consider more worthy of his time and effort. His gaming habit may even have become a point of conflict between you.

But what if video gaming is his *thing*? When we were kids in the '80s, one of my brothers spent the bulk of his time playing sports and video games. Even on gorgeous summer days, it wasn't unusual for him to devote hours to Atari and ColecoVision in our darkened basement. That brother eventually became a video game designer who spent the first part of his career creating sports video games, including the 2K baseball and basketball series. (He once directed a motion capture session with LeBron James.) Today, he teaches video game design to high school students.

What looked like a waste of time at first glance—hours spent staring at a screen, maneuvering pixels—was actually a boy feeding his imagination. Those hours of gameplay gave my brother a deep understanding of game structure and storytelling, and that understanding is what allowed him to create compelling games.

Boys who express traditionally accepted interests are sometimes shut down as well. Whereas it was once commonplace for boys to play cops and robbers on the playground, complete with weapons fashioned from sticks, boys today who draw pictures of guns (or sharks attacking humans, for that matter) may be suspended from school or referred to the school psychologist. As a result, many boys are faced with an impossible conundrum: follow their instincts and risk punishment and disapproval or suppress their natural inclinations in hopes of garnering adult approval. It's a no-win situation that ultimately causes boys to distrust their intuition and creates distance between boys and the adults who care for them.

"I'm a big proponent of boys' need for limits, but not limits in the way we typically think of them," says Michael C. Reichert, founding director of the Center for the Study of Boys' and Girls' Lives and author of *How to Raise a Boy: The Power of Connection to Build Good Men*. "If a boy is being destructive in some way or endangering himself in ways that he doesn't perceive, it really is the adult's job to exercise independent judgment, but it's really important that the way we do that isn't to invalidate the boy's judgment or undercut his independent exercise of initiative."[5]

You can offset some of this negative societal pressure by validating your son's instincts and nurturing his talents.

HOW TO NURTURE YOUR SON'S TALENT

Supporting your son's interests will help him discover and develop his talents—and confidence in his abilities. Here are seven ways you can nurture your son's talent.

SEVEN STRATEGIES TO HELP BOYS DEVELOP THEIR TALENTS

1. Encourage their obsessions
2. Expose them to the world
3. Provide resources
4. Connect them to mentors
5. Don't instantly go to "no"
6. Protect their interests
7. Give them control

ENCOURAGE HIS OBSESSIONS

Approximately one in three young children develops what psychologists call an "intense interest," typically before age five. My Tyler was obsessed with dinosaurs from around age two to age four—at which point he became fascinated with butterflies.

According to a 2007 article in *Developmental Psychology*, intense interests are much more common in boys than girls.[6] Psychologists suggest that this proclivity for obsession may be related to the surge of testosterone male fetuses receive in utero; prenatal exposure to testosterone has been linked to an increased ability to "systemize," or understand and organize the parts of a whole. Of course, culture likely plays a part as well.

Whatever the root cause of our sons' obsessions, it's worthwhile to encourage them. Deep, intense interests in the preschool years are related to increased knowledge and persistence, heightened attention, and deep processing and understanding—skills that will benefit our children in school and in the future.

If you've got a boy who's obsessed with dinos, head to your local library and check out books about dinosaurs. (Don't restrict yourself to the children's section either. One of my son's favorite books was a hardcover illustrated dino book aimed at adults.) Watch documentaries about dinosaurs. Buy or borrow some plastic dinosaur figurines and follow your son's lead as he incorporates dinos into his play. For a while, my son's best friend was the six-foot-tall inflatable dinosaur his godfather gave him as a birthday present.

Aim to follow, rather than direct, your son. "Too often, parents impose their own expectations and desires onto their kids," says Jeanette Hurt, the mother of competitive gymnast Quinn. "How do you help your kids discover their veins of gold, and their special gifts and talents, if you don't let them follow their interests?"

EXPOSE HIM TO THE WORLD

Research has found that intense interests are most likely to emerge when parents provide plenty of time for undirected play. In other words, trying to predict and channel your son's talents by enrolling him in classes and clubs early on may not be nearly as effective as simply giving him space and time to follow his natural instincts.

Of course, balance is needed. A child's world is typically only as large as we allow, and the more you can expose your son to novel experiences and people, the more likely it is that he'll find something that resonates with him. So take your son to interesting places—museums, craft shows, parks, forests, and farms. Let him try new activities.

"Every kid should do something they really love, but how do they find what that is unless they take classes, go to the library, and research things?" says Quinn's mom Jeanette. She enrolled him in his first gymnastics class at age two—partly out of desperation.

"It was January in Wisconsin. What are you going to do with an active two-year-old in January?" she says. Jeanette, a reporter by trade, did an internet search for "gymnastics two-year-old Milwaukee" and discovered the Diaper Dinosaurs class at Swiss Turners Gymnastics Academy. Quinn loved it—and tried a lot of other activities over the years as well. He cycled through swimming lessons, baseball, golf, violin, and competitive diving before deciding to devote the bulk of his time to gymnastics.

PROVIDE RESOURCES

Ben Garner was drawn to crafting at an early age, so his parents supplied him with paper, tape, cardboard, and—reluctantly—a glue gun. ("I thought he was going to burn himself," says his mom, Liesl. "He did.")

Ben used the bits of paper and cardboard to create wearable Iron Man costumes. Then he started building cardboard guitars and ukuleles. "The whole house was covered in little shreds and pieces of cardboard," Liesl says. When it became clear that Ben needed more space to work, the family cleaned out a section of their barn and created a workshop for him. Within a few weeks, Ben created an Iron Man costume from scrap metal. He was six years old.

Without access to tools and materials, Ben's interest in crafting may have withered. Instead, his parents provided supplies as well as time and space for him to hone his talents.

It's not easy to trust our boys with dangerous tools. As parents, our minds jump to the harm that could occur if, say, a saw slips. But what harm might we be inflicting on our sons if we keep them from the tools necessary to develop their skills?

Ohio mom Judi Ketteler has spent a lot of time pondering that question. Her son Maxx developed a passion for Gtramp, an extreme sport that involves doing crazy flips and tricks on backyard trampolines. Judi, a former competitive gymnast, knows well the risks of the stunts her son wanted to try.

"I tried to forbid it," Judi says. "I don't want him to get hurt. I don't want that at all. I was terrified."

But when Judi saw the deep desire for mastery in her son's eyes—and learned more about Gtramp—she relented. Their backyard now contains multiple trampolines, mattresses, and a fifteen-foot-tall wooden bounce tower. (Leaping onto the trampoline from the tower allows kids to get more bounce, a necessity for some tricks.)

"I work with him to be as safe as we can," Judi says. "I try to find that balance between what do I forbid, and how do I just let him be who he is?"

The Garner family does the same thing. When Ben wants to work with a new-to-him tool, his father shows him how to operate it; then Ben uses it under supervision. When his parents are confident that he understands how to safely use and store the tool, he's allowed to use it independently.

Of course, we don't all have access to power tools, barns, or spacious backyards. That's okay. Start small. Shop secondhand stores and garage sales. Dig through your recycling bin. Borrow equipment. Check your local library; some libraries have makerspaces that are open to the public. Ask your school for access to materials that they may already have but keep aside. Search local freecycle initiatives. Give your child gifts related to his interest for birthdays and holidays and encourage other relatives to do the same. (A couple of my sons love fishing and have received fishing gear as gifts over the years, including lures, fishing poles, an ice auger, and chest-high waders.)

Make space where you can. My dining table has been pushed to the edge of the room for years now, first to make room for indoor basketball and then to accommodate the many supplies my oldest son accumulated as he launched his all-in-one fishing kit business. Does my dining room look like a magazine spread? No. But the truth is that I rarely host dinners and I'd rather nurture my sons' talents than worry about the appearance of a seldom-used room.

CONNECT HIM TO MENTORS

Historically, boys learned alongside skilled men. In the distant past, boys learned to hunt from their fathers and village elders. In the Middle Ages, many boys were formally apprenticed to tradesmen around age ten.

Formal and informal mentorships remain a great way to help boys develop their talents. When then-thirteen-year old Luke Thill expressed a desire to build a tiny house in his parents' backyard, his parents knew that their son didn't possess all the skills he'd need to construct a house from scratch. Nor did they.

"Right off the bat, we tried to teach Luke to talk to other people that had the skills he needed to learn," says Luke's father, Greg. Whenever possible, his parents facilitated introductions, but they also trusted Luke to make connections.

Luke reached out to several of his past Boy Scout leaders, including one who works as a carpet layer and one who is a mechanic. He also asked his neighbor, an electrician, for help.

"I cleaned out his garage and in return, he helped me wire the house," Luke says.

When a child connects with an adult or older child who shares his passion, he learns new skills and discovers that others share his interest. That affirmation can be tremendously validating for a young boy who may feel isolated among his same-age peers. For many boys, it's also exciting to find another human being who can discuss their interest in detail. (I try to keep up with my boys' fishing conversations, but it is blatantly obvious that I don't know—or care to know— the difference between a topwater bait and a Texas rig.)

The best way to find a mentor for your son is through personal connections. Think about everyone you know—family members, friends, coworkers, neighbors, teachers, coaches. Ask around; you just might learn that one of your coworkers fishes bass tournaments on the weekend or collects antique fans. You can also reach out to clubs and special interest groups. Got a boy who's obsessed with trains? Look for a model railroad club.

HOW TO FIND A MENTOR

1. *Check local mentoring organizations.* Some communities have Boys to Men Mentoring programs; others have Big Brothers. Ask around or search online for "boys men mentoring." Some local faith communities also have mentoring programs.
2. *Look for local special interest clubs and activities.* Got a kid who's into gardening? Check out your local Master Gardner program. Have an avid angler? Spend some time at the next local fishing expo or tournament.
3. *Ask around.* You might be surprised to discover that a work colleague or neighbor shares a common interest with your son. Passionate people typically love sharing their interests with others, so there's no harm in asking.

Of course, it's crucial to vet anyone your son spends time with. Meet any potential mentors in person. Ask questions. Consider a background check. Don't leave your son alone with a mentor unless you're comfortable with the situation—and even then, make sure your son knows how to contact you if anything seems "off." Let your son know that it's okay to leave at any time.

Caution is certainly necessary, but please don't let your fear of what might happen keep your son from connecting with skilled, like-minded human beings. The risk of harm to your child is small compared to the odds of great growth, and there's a lot you can do to mitigate the risk.

Maxx Ketteler, the Ohio boy interested in Gtramp, discovered the sport online and learned from videos shared on YouTube and Instagram. He followed fellow Gtrampers on Instagram and developed friendships with many of them. Eventually, many of the boys connected in person at an organized meetup. Although they are usually separated by many miles, the boys continue give feedback and advice to one another in near real-time via the internet.

DON'T INSTANTLY GO TO "NO"

"No" is the default response for many of us whenever our kids ask
to do something novel or risky. Our hearts are in the right place; we
don't want our boys harmed emotionally or physically. So when
they ask to ride their bikes to school, we're tempted to say no.
(*They might get hit by a car or truck!*) When they express a desire to,
say, melt metal, we say *absolutely not!* (*The melting point of aluminum
is 1,221 degrees F!*) We know that we can avoid the worst possible
outcomes by keeping our child away from the risk at hand.

What we often fail to realize is the potentially far-reaching impact
of those nos. When psychologist and author Michael C. Reichert
spent time with his two-and-a-half-year-old grandson, he noticed
that the boy spent most of his time jumping off the couch.

Many adults would quickly halt such activity, but Reichert
perceived "what we call the drive for mastery and competence,"
he says. The boy was "using his body and discovering what it
can do, and it's enormously interesting and reinforcing to him.
Now, if I project my fears or worries onto him and allow myself to
control the situation, essentially substituting my judgment for his,
he gets the message that he has to operate within my parameters
and that what he wants and who he is aren't important."[7]

Boys, in particular, frequently receive this message from
parents and educators. In our well-intentioned desire to raise good,
caring, civilized men, many of us are quick to kibosh loud, active,
and physically risky behavior. Unfortunately, we may also be
stunting our children's growth.

Whenever possible, observe and ask questions instead. (*Why
do you want to use the circular saw?*) If your son's answers are
reasonable—and he knows how to safely engage in the activity—
say yes.

If you don't know much about the proposed activity, educate
yourself. Watch a couple of videos or talk to knowledgeable
adults. Got a kid who wants to play rugby? Go watch a match and
chat with the coach afterward.

PROTECT HIS INTERESTS

Other people won't always welcome your son's talents. Jeanette knows that Quinn's gymnastic talent includes a healthy dose of energy and a tendency toward movement—two traits that aren't particularly valued in a classroom setting. So while Quinn learns to channel and control his movement, Jeanette advocates for her son.

At the beginning of each school year, Jeanette tells her son's new teachers that "his superpower is his energy." She puts a positive spin on Quinn's propensity toward motion before it can be labeled as a negative and helps his teachers understand that movement is a huge part of who Quinn is and how he understands the world.

Most teachers have appreciated the heads-up and successfully managed Quinn's need for movement while meeting his academic needs. One elementary teacher, though, took away recess as a punishment for minor infractions such as not turning in or completing work or being too wiggly in the classroom. Jeanette spoke up.

"My son needs recess," she says. She used her reporting skills to dig up information and stats to back up her assertion and learned that most students listen and learn better after recess because they're more focused. She found that recess time is particularly important for active children and children with ADHD—ironically, the kids who are most likely to lose their recess privileges. But despite a pile of evidence, loss of recess time remains a common punishment. (According to a survey by the Robert Wood Johnson Foundation, 81 percent of schools use recess as a disciplinary tool.[8])

Armed with this information, Jeanette talked to the school's principal. Ultimately, her son was reassigned to another classroom. The new teacher, Jeanette says, is a much better fit for Quinn.

Is this yet another instance of a helicopter parent interfering in her child's education or expecting special treatment? No. It's a great example of a parent advocating for her son's best interests. Jeanette recognizes that the need to move is innate to Quinn. Her years of parenting him taught her that he can't—and shouldn't—fully suppress that urge because he learns better when he has ample opportunities to move.

Not everyone will recognize or respect your son's talents. Make sure your son knows that you value his interests. Defend him as needed; if grandma or grandpa comments negatively, verbally affirm your support for your son and ask them to withhold their criticism in the future. Be prepared to leave places where your son is under attack. Jeannette once left a family celebration after her sisters yelled at Quinn for doing handstands.

"We'd spent two hours in the car and sat through an extra-long baptismal Mass. We were finally at brunch, in a separate event room," Jeanette explains. "When my sisters yelled at Quinn, he cried. At that point, I just took my kid and left."

Protecting your son's interests can also include giving him time to develop his unique talents, especially once he reaches school age. Remember, many boys' interests are a poor fit for elementary and middle school classrooms; the curriculum typically doesn't allow most boys to spend time nurturing their curiosity—which may be one reason why so many boys disengage from academics. In fact, a 2008 article published in the journal *Cognitive Development* suggests that "some of this drift from academically oriented interests may be the result of a mismatch between the knowledge-rich interests children bring to the classroom and the particular curricula and opportunities for learning that the school provides."[9]

You can ameliorate this situation by allowing your son to devote ample out-of-school time to his passions. My mechanically inclined son Sam didn't get to operate machinery or study engine repair in middle school, so I prioritized his "garage time" in the evenings because I believe that the time he spends customizing and caring for his lawn mower is just as important—if not more important—to his development than the hours he spends in school.

GIVE HIM CONTROL

All boys need guidance, but it's important to allow your son to self-direct the pacing of his development. Some boys are ready to dedicate themselves to an activity at a young age; some are not. At age ten, Quinn decided to devote twenty-two hours a week to gymnastics. At the same age, most of my boys weren't ready (or interested in) spending twenty-two hours a week on *anything*. But by the time my oldest was in high school, it was practically impossible to reign in the hours he spent on his lawn-mowing business.

Your son may well know what he needs better than you do. It's important, however, to watch him for signs of exhaustion, stress, or disinterest. If you find yourself nagging your son to gear up before *every single* baseball practice, it's possible that he's no longer as interested in the sport as he once was. Mentioning your observation to him—*You don't seem as enthusiastic about baseball as you once were*—can help you pinpoint the issue. Sometimes, kids are hesitant to reveal their declining interest because they fear disappointing their parents or because they know you've already spent a lot of money on fees and equipment. Listen to your son carefully. Make sure he knows that you love and support him no matter what.

Alternately, if your son is emotionally energized after games and asking for extra hitting practice, you might want to consider spending more time in the batting cages or backyard. Often, kids we consider "too young" or "immature" for a particular activity are more prepared than we think. Generally speaking, boys come with a pretty accurate internal timetable; they usually know, before we do, whether they're ready to take on the next challenge.

Bean Garner, an unusually motivated eleven-year-old boy when I first interviewed him, recommends that parents "Let your kid try it for a couple of days. If they don't like it or can't handle it, then you can pull them out and wait until they're a little bit older."

That's the approach Jeanette has used with Quinn. "I'm letting him drive," she says. When her son wanted to drop competitive diving to spend more time on gymnastics, she supported him. In fact, she let him quit before the end of the season.

"He was kind of burned out," she says. "It was a reasonable decision." Pushing a child to "finish" an activity when they're already showing signs of mental strain, Jeanette knew, is almost never a good idea.

If you're used to controlling your son's life, it may be difficult for you to step back and allow him some freedom to make choices. However, when it comes to finding and discovering his purpose in the world, your son is the number one expert. Respecting his choices and facilitating the development of his talents will increase his confidence, competence, and motivation—and confident boys who feel respected and valued grow into men who respect and value others.

❧

To build boys:

- *Reflect on what your son loves to do and whether you get in his way. (Be honest!)*
- *Connect your son to others who share his interests.*
- *Give your son space, time, and materials to pursue his passions.*

6

⸎

Give Him Time

Have a little faith in your sons. This journey will be the making of them.

—C. J. Milbrandt

Tyler didn't read fluently until he was eleven years old.

When he entered public school at age eleven, he was reading at a second-grade level. ("Second grade level" may have been a generous assessment of his reading abilities at that time.)

Prior to that time, we homeschooled, and despite my best efforts, Tyler was not interested in the written word. We had reading material in every room of the house (including the bathroom), and I read multiple books to the kids every day. But unlike his older brother, Tyler hadn't yet showed any interest in writing or decoding words. At age four, his oldest brother spontaneously began copying letters from books during quiet time (aka nap time for the little ones). When I handed Tyler a basket full of books to occupy him during quiet time, he built a tower with them.

We had a solid three years of homeschooling experience by the time Tyler turned six, the age at which most American children are expected to read. By that point, I understood a few things:

1. All kids grow and develop at different paces.
2. Kids learn best (and easiest!) if they're interested.
3. There are many ways to learn.

I'd also heard numerous reliable stories about homeschooled children who didn't learn to read 'til later (often, age eleven or twelve) and did just fine in life. At that point, we had no plans to send our children to an institutional school, so I was able to give Tyler the gift of time.

Instead of pressuring him to read, I let him learn at his own pace. We didn't spend hours practicing letter sounds or tracing letters; instead, we followed Tyler's interests and watched documentaries about butterflies. We caught butterflies and categorized them, identifying them with books we checked out from our local library. Tyler played with play dough (sometimes, scratching a few letters of his name into it) and built block towers. We had magnetic letters on the fridge as well as a learning toy that electronically enunciated the names and sounds of letters, but Ty and my other boys used it only occasionally.

I read to the boys daily, and though Tyler rarely appeared to be paying attention—he was usually on the floor, playing with Legos or action figures while I read *Harry Potter*—he was the first to ask why I stopped whenever I paused. He always knew where we were in the story and recapped plot points for us each day before I resumed reading.

As a writer, I realized Tyler was learning a lot about reading and writing. He was learning sentence and story structure. Vocabulary. Plot, pacing, and word choice. The tough stuff, as far as I'm concerned.

So instead of forcing Tyler to focus his energies on learning to read, I supported his continued exploration.

Of course, if Tyler had attended a traditional school then, he would have been expected to turn his attention to the page. His lack of interest wouldn't have mattered; our local kindergarten, like most, expects students to print their first and last names and read emergent-reader texts with purpose and understanding. Tyler's days would have been oriented around those goals, and if he failed to reach those milestones, he may have been referred for extra reading instruction. Likely he would have learned to dislike reading and hate school. He might have labeled himself "stupid" or "dumb."

When he started public school, Tyler was placed in the remedial reading group and realized right away that the other students in his group weren't considered the "smart ones." By age eleven, though, he'd developed a strong sense of self; he knew his reading ability didn't determine his worth.

Within a year, Tyler was reading high school–level texts; his reading skills blossomed quickly, as they often do in students who learn to read at their own pace. A few years later, he graduated high school and earned an academic scholarship. Now a young adult, he still prefers audiobooks, lectures, and hands-on learning over reading, just as he did when he was a small child.

Did Tyler suffer lasting harm because he didn't learn to read 'til "later"? I don't think so. However, I *do* think he may have experienced significant academic, social, and psychological harm if he'd been required to read and write before his brain and body were ready to do so.

Which is exactly what happens to far too many boys. Even though boys' brains mature more slowly than girls', four-, five-, and six-year-old boys are regularly expected to read and write. When they struggle to do so, they assume they're "dumb" or otherwise incapable. (After all, most of their female peers are easily mastering the material!) Academic success—which, in early elementary school, is defined almost exclusively as the ability to read and write—seems out of their grasp, so many boys assume that school "isn't for them."

What would happen, I wonder, if we allowed boys to grow at their own pace?

WHY EARLIER ISN'T BETTER

Doing things first isn't necessarily best. In fact, a slower pace of development may be most beneficial to our children's long-term well-being.

Research has found that chronic stress accelerates physical development. Faster maturation may sound like an advantage, but it's not. Not always, anyway. A study published in 2021 found that children who grow up in low-income families—an experience that's typically linked to increased exposure to all kinds of chronic stress, including food insecurity and environmental instability—get their adult teeth earlier than children who grow up in higher-income, lower-stress families.[1] This study added further evidence to the existing mountain showing that children (and animals) who develop in stressful environments typically mature more quickly than their counterparts.

Faster maturation makes sense if the goal is to get the next generation going because the current one isn't expected to survive much longer. Under those conditions, early puberty and childbearing are adaptive, at least at the collective level.

In humans—a species that can usually expect to live five, six, seven, eight, or more decades—faster maturation can create unnecessary cognitive limitations. According to research by Allyson Mackey, PhD, an assistant professor of psychology at the University of Pennsylvania, adverse experiences (such as abuse, hunger, or loss of a caregiver) make children's brains grow up too quickly.[2] That's a problem because brains lose plasticity—or flexibility—during maturation. A young, not-yet-fully mature brain is more open to experience and learning, whereas a mature, less "plastic" brain is more or less set. Brain circuits have been established and set for maximum efficiency.

Picture a Lego set. Before the bricks are pieced together into a recognizable model (say, the Star Wars Death Star), they could become *anything*. You could build a house, car, or fantastical creature with the plastic components.

It's an imperfect analogy because you can tear apart a model composed of toy bricks at any time and make an entirely new creation. The human brain is flexible but not nearly as easy to reshape. Yet the idea remains: prematurely locking the circuits of the brain in place may limit their potential. It's a bit like clicking a particular brown bit into the corner of a Harry Potter Hogsmeade village model. Once that brick is in place, it will probably remain a plastic cornerstone. A piece that once had nearly unlimited potential—you could have used it to build a tree or car, for instance—has been assigned a permanent job.

Regular exposure to a varied environment and diverse learning materials extends the brain's plasticity.[3] It's almost as if the brain is hesitant to lock anything in place because it's not quite sure what it will encounter next. Will it be required to build a metaphorical Death Star or a racing car?

Research by Mackey and others suggests that it's beneficial to give children the time they need to develop optimally. As Alison Gopnik,

PhD, noted in her 2021 *Wall Street Journal* article, "What Children Lose When Their Brains Develop Too Fast," high-quality preschools and social policies such as child tax credits and parental leave lead to improved child well-being "not because they made children develop faster but because they let them remain children longer."[4]

Despite a general societal push toward early education, there's no evidence suggesting that early attainment of academic skills is particularly beneficial. In fact, an important longitudinal study that followed more than fifteen hundred children with high cognitive ability from 1922 to 1991 found that children who read earlier than their peers experienced early academic success but were less likely to complete advanced degrees. Researchers reported that for males, "normal-aged reading was associated with better long-term adjustment . . . and less alcohol use."[5] Individuals who started school at earlier ages died earlier, on average, than those who started school at later ages.[6]

Interestingly, there's also no solid evidence to support early academic intervention. A 2021 study found that both younger and older children benefited from reading interventions or interventions designed to facilitate geometrical and spatial thinking. But younger children showed no greater gains than older children. The researchers concluded that, "Educational interventions are frequently designed to occur during early childhood, based on the idea that earlier intervention will have greater long-term benefits . . . [but there] is no clear evidence for an overall younger age benefit."[7]

In fact, evidence suggests that prematurely pushing children to reach academic milestones may hinder their overall development. As noted in *Nature News*, "rote practice is likely to drive faster maturation of the brain systems involved, which would be beneficial for the task practiced (for example, reading and writing), but it could compromise the ability to learn novel tasks. By contrast, rich and varied experiences that capture children's attention and enhance their motivation . . . could decelerate the rate of brain maturation."[8]

Remember: slow brain maturation seems to be optimal for human development. Rushing our boys to adulthood can be disastrous for boys—and, ultimately, for the rest of us.

BOYS DEVELOP MORE SLOWLY

Multiple research studies (and thousands of years of anecdotal experience) have demonstrated that boys mature physically and emotionally more slowly than girls. Six-month-old girls have significantly better fine motor skills than similarly aged boys, on average.[9] By age sixteen months, females have an average vocabulary of ninety-five words, compared to boys' twenty-five words.[10] Boys develop bowel and bladder control later, on average, than females, and boys are nearly three times as likely as girls to wet the bed at night after age eight.[11]

Girls' skeletons reach adult bone maturity nearly two years earlier than boys.'[12] The parts of the brain that process language mature, on average, six years later in boys than in girls. The prefrontal cortex, the part of the brain that handles emotional control and executive function, matures, on average, around age twenty-one in females and twenty-five in boys.[13]

To be sure, some boys develop more quickly than some girls. One of my sons, for instance, was potty trained by eighteen months of age, a full year-and-a-half before most girls are toilet trained. He was the exception, however. Expecting my other boys to control their bladders by age eighteen months would have been an exercise in frustration—as proven by the fact that another one of my sons struggled with bedwetting after age ten.

Each of my boys developed according to his own unique schedule. I parented them more or less the same, under similar conditions. One child's brain and body simply took longer to develop the connections necessary to retain urine during sleep. (In hindsight, this same child reached nearly all his physical milestones later than his brothers and many of his peers, indicating a body that operated according to a prolonged timetable.)

Let's take a closer look at some common developmental milestones.

Walking

Most humans take their first independent steps sometime between nine and twelve months of age—though it's perfectly normal for a child to walk many months earlier or later than that nine-to-twelve-month window. My third son, the one who was potty trained by eighteen months, learned to walk "early." Another son didn't walk until a few months after his first birthday.

The age at which a child learns to walk has little bearing on the rest of his life. Although at least one study has found that children who walk at earlier ages tend to display superior fine motor skills and balance in preschool,[14] most children are on equal footing (pardon the pun!) by the time they're in elementary school. Swiss researchers who followed a cohort of more than two hundred children from birth to age eighteen noted that, "by the time they reach school age, children who start walking later than others are just as well-coordinated and intelligent as those who were up on their feet early." The researchers found no correlation between the age at which a child walked and later intelligence or motor skills.

Because some health conditions can affect a child's ability to walk, it's a good idea to seek a medical evaluation for a child who's not walking by eighteen to twenty months of age. If no medical problems are detected, it's likely your child is simply slower than others to develop—and that's okay!

Talking

Available evidence suggests that testosterone influences speech and language development. Researchers have found that babies with low levels of circulating testosterone can better discriminate different spoken sounds than infants with higher levels of testosterone, and babies with high concentrations of the so-called male hormone typically babble less at five months of age than babies with lower testosterone levels.[15] Interestingly, researchers have even found changes in language activity in female-to-male trans men who take high doses of testosterone.

Boys account for more than 70 percent of "late talkers," and boys string together words on average three months later than girls. Differences in the rate of language acquisition are even seen in adult men and women learning a foreign language.[16]

Researchers have conducted exhaustive studies of the structure and functioning of male and female brains and concluded that the "speech and language regions may mature at different rates in males and females."[17] Any significant differences between boys' and girls' language abilities in childhood are "likely due to different rates of maturation between the sexes."[18]

You can't expect a four- or five-year-old boy to elegantly explain to you why he hit his friend over the head with a truck. He not only lacks the insight needed to elucidate the emotions fueling his action, but there's a very good chance that he can't quickly produce a coherent sentence.

It can be really difficult for parents and educators of boys to determine if and when boys need extra help with language development. Because boys' oral communication skills typically develop more slowly than girls,' there's no need to freak out if you son isn't talking by age two. However, you don't want to miss any hidden issues either. (One of my sons talked significantly later than his brothers, and we didn't learn 'til later that he hadn't been hearing well for most of his young life.)

According to the American Academy of Pediatrics' Bright Futures guidelines,[19] two-year-old children of all genders and sexes should:

- Use fifty words.
- Combine two words into short phrases or sentences.
- Follow two-step commands.
- Name at least five body parts.
- Speak in words that are 50 percent understandable to strangers.

Between ages two and three, a child's vocabulary should grow to at least two hundred words.[20] If your child seems a bit behind, mention your concern to a healthcare provider. You may need to ask for a physical and audiological assessment, as many healthcare providers are quick to dismiss concerns about boys' language development because they know that male language acquisition typically lags behind females.' But that general truth can hide specific concerns. In my child's case, the initial physician and speech-language pathologist we consulted attributed my two-year-old's nearly absent verbal language to the fact that he was one of four children; they assumed I didn't speak to him as much as I did to his older brothers. A later evaluation revealed accumulated fluid behind his eardrums. My son wasn't talking clearly because he'd never *heard* clear speech. (Insertion of ear tubes, which allowed the fluid in his ears to drain, plus a couple of years of speech therapy resolved his speech issues.)

Potty Training

According to a 2001 study, boys in the United States ditch diapers around thirty-nine months of age (approximately three-and-a-quarter years old); girls do so at thirty-five months.[21] Although the age of potty training has varied throughout history and according to cultural practices, males worldwide generally develop bladder and bowel control later than females.[22]

More than 6 percent of boys ages eight to eleven experience nocturnal enuresis (the medical term for bed-wetting). Approximately six out of one hundred eight- to eleven-year-old boys occasionally wake up with wet sheets—and that's normal. Though bed-wetting is often distressing for boys and their families, nighttime accidents don't necessarily signal a problem. Most children grow out of it as their minds and bodies mature.

It's worth noting, though, that researchers have found a strong association between attention deficit hyperactivity disorder (ADHD) and bed-wetting.[23] It may be a good idea to consider an ADHD evaluation for boys who experience nocturnal enuresis, especially if the boy in question also struggles with inattention or impulsivity or there is a family history of ADHD.

Given the typical timeline of male development, it is normal for some tween boys to wet the bed, and totally normal for a three-year-old boy to need diapers or training pants. Many three-and-a-half-year-old boys are not yet reliably potty trained—a situation that creates great distress for working parents who rely on preschools to provide childcare, as many schools require children to be potty trained because they simply don't have enough staff to attend to toileting issues.

The potty-trained-for-preschool rule is often parents' and boys' first encounter with systemic and institutional guidelines that are out of sync with boys' development.

Reading

The mismatch between male development and societal expectations becomes even more apparent as boys begin school. In the United States, explicit reading instruction begins in kindergarten, and almost everyone expects first graders to read. Parents and educators place a lot of importance on when a child learns to read; 85 percent of the two hundred adults surveyed for the 2017 "Early Readers and Academic Success" study said that the age at which a child learns to read is important.[24]

But as we've noted, male and female language development proceeds at different rates, and the average five- or six-year-old boy is less ready to read than his female classmates. (The researchers who conducted the 2017 study note that "it is interesting that the two respondents who learned to read at age eight and ten or over were both male."[25])

Boys' ability to decode and comprehend words and sentences lags behind girls' throughout school. Internationally, girls have outperformed boys on reading assessments for decades, in countries as diverse as Qatar, Finland, the United States, and Indonesia.[26] The gender reading gap is apparent as early as first grade and persists throughout high school. However, tests of adult reading ability show no gender gap by twenty-five years of age in the United States, according to the Brookings Institution.[27] Probably not at all coincidentally, age twenty-five is about when the male brain finally reaches full maturity.[28]

Some researchers, educators, and others have attempted to pin boys' delayed reading acumen on adults' tendency to interact differently with male and female children, insisting that boys' language development would parallel their sisters' if parents talked to, sang with, and read to boys as frequently as they did with girls.

It's probably true that parents of young boys sing or read to their boys less than parents of young girls, at least on the whole. But that fact does not necessarily contribute to boys' poor performance on reading assessments. (As the saying goes, correlation does not equal causation. In other words, the fact that two things are related does not mean that one caused the other.) It may be, instead, that parents are reading less to their young boys because the boys are less interested in looking at books or listening to stories.[29]

Either way, a 2016 paper noted that "the measurable differences in parental interaction with boys and girls at the age of three can account for only 10% of the gender gap in language at the start of primary school."[30]

Regardless, many current educational systems expect boys and girls to read fluently (and with understanding) no later than age eight. The result? A whole lot of little boys who "now need extra support in the forms of tutoring, additional help from classroom aides, extra small group work, extra homework, and summer school," writes Marie A. Leahy and Nicole M. Fitzpatrick, in their article, "Early Readers and Academic Success."[31] The duo note, "Pushing children to read before they are ready is truly an injustice."

DON'T RUSH BOYS THROUGH CHILDHOOD

The world doesn't allow little boys to remain little for long. At every stage of their development, parents, educators, and society at large urge boys to grow up.

Young males aren't even referred to as "boys" for very long. It's not uncommon for adults to use the term "little man" when addressing a small boy or to tell the male child of a single mom that he's the "man of the house."

Black boys are allowed even less time in childhood than white boys. A 2014 study found that college students shown photos of Black, white, and Latino boys ages ten to seventeen overestimated the age of Black boys by four and a half years.[32] The police officers who responded to the Cleveland park where twelve-year-old Tamir Rice was playing in 2014 said they thought he was about twenty years old.[33] They didn't see a Black boy playing; they "saw" a Black man that they perceived as a threat and fired shots, wounding and ultimately killing Rice.[34] George Zimmerman, the man who shot seventeen-year-old Trayvon Martin, said at his bail hearing that he thought Martin was "a little bit younger I am."[35] Zimmerman was twenty-eight years old at the time.[36]

Male children deserve our protection. To develop optimally, they need safety, nurturing, and *time* to grow.

Giving them this time is not easy. In the United States, parents of young children are expected back at work within weeks of a child's birth. Childcare and preschool rules are oriented around adult convenience and staffing concerns. School curriculum accentuates academics, and the culture at large has little tolerance for little boys behaving like, well, little boys. Add on top of that the well-founded fears of parents of Black and brown boys, which cause some to limit their boys' play (no toy guns or pretend gunplay, no horsing around with friends at the park) because they're trying to keep their sons alive and are terrified about how others might interpret their sons' actions.

Giving boys time means pushing against cultural norms. You may not have the time, energy, or resources to implement each of these suggestions. That's okay. You don't have to undertake them all; you can make a positive difference in boys' lives by creating pockets of opportunities for them to relax and grow. And you can reassure the boys you know that they are okay, just as they are.

Here are a few strategies you can use to give boys the time they need to grow.

Delay Formal Education If You Can

Kindergarten today is a lot like first grade thirty years ago. Preschool, in many places, is not a place of playful exploration, but a place where children learn to stand in line, take turns, sit still during story time, and begin writing and reading. Most boys are not developmentally ready for these things at ages three, four, and five— which may be one reason why boys are exponentially more likely to be suspended or expelled from preschool than girls. (During the 2017–2018 school year, boys accounted for 83 percent of preschool suspensions and 85 percent of preschool expulsions.[37])

Statistically speaking, younger children do worse in school, behaviorally and academically, than slightly older children in the same class.[38] Remember: one study found that kindergarteners with August birthdays—who may be nearly a year younger than other kindergarten students—were 34 percent more likely to be diagnosed with ADHD,[39] and a 2018 study published in *Frontiers in Psychology* found that teachers often have a negative view of young boys' playfulness.[40]

A boy's first days, weeks, and months of school set the tone for his entire educational experience. If he feels safe, welcomed, and valued, he will likely enjoy school. If he does not feel safe, welcome, or valued . . . well, it's going to be a long twelve years. A child whose early school experience is one of frustration, discipline, and humiliation is unlikely to feel enthusiastic about school. (If the word "humiliation" seems strong to you, think about how exquisitely sensitive some young children are to criticism and reprimands. Young boys are particularly vulnerable to shame.)

I strongly encourage you to consider waiting to enroll your son in formal education, especially if he has a summer birthday and would be among the youngest in his class if he starts as soon as he hits the cutoff age. Remember: boys' brains take longer to mature, and an average five-year-old boy is significantly less developmentally ready to sit still, write, and read than the average five-year-old girl. Think of the long game too. Would you rather your son graduate high school (and potentially leave home) at age seventeen or eighteen?

Note: if you believe your son is developmentally, cognitively, and psychologically ready for kindergarten, go ahead and enroll him! You know your son better than I do. Some boys thrive in kindergarten and elementary school.

Also note: you can change your mind at any time. My mother pulled one of my brothers out of kindergarten less than halfway through the year after hearing numerous complaints from the teacher about his behavior. He spent the next year at home (our mother was a stay-at-home mom at the time, raising six kids), and when he entered kindergarten again nearly a year later, he did well. No complaints from the teacher nor from my brother. He simply needed an extra year to mature.

⚭

THE REDSHIRTING DEBATE

To send him or not to send him, that is the question!

Some people believe that almost all boys should wait a year before starting kindergarten; others argue that "redshirting" (the practice of enrolling a child a year after they're first eligible) creates an uneven playing field. Richard V. Reeves, a Brookings scholar and author of *Of Boys and Men: Why the Modern Male Is Struggling, Why It Matters, and What to Do about It*, recommends redshirting all male children; boys, he says, should start school one year later than similarly aged girls.[41]

One researcher—a mom of two boys with summer birthdays—studied fifty-five families and found that teenage boys who waited a year before starting kindergarten showed significantly higher levels of life satisfaction at adolescence than those who started earlier.[42]

⌒∞⌒

Create Space for Relaxed Learning

As best you can, let go of academic expectations and simply allow your boys to explore, grow, and develop.

It's not at all easy to ignore the ever-present drumbeat of societal expectations: *He should be reading by now! He should know how to tie his shoes! He should be able to do his homework independently!* If you regularly spend time with young girls or "girl parents," it may be especially difficult drown the *shoulds* that crowd your head. It is all too easy to compare our boys to their female peers and forget that boys develop according to their own unique timetable.

Do your best to still your doubts and focus on the boy in front of you. Create and facilitate opportunities for learning. Go to interesting places (the library, local landmarks, natural areas, etc.). Read together. Talk, wonder, and discuss. Together, look up things online that interest him. Whenever possible, encourage his interests.

The world places so many expectations on boys. To whatever extent is possible, create space for him to simply *be*.

Stop Struggling—Wait

At age five, Tanisha Henderson's son was *not* getting the hang of writing. He did okay with copy work—tracing and reproducing letters—but had a panic attack when she asked him to write letters independently. Wisely, Tanisha decided not to push him. She waited somewhere between six months to a year before she brought out paper and pencil again and asked her son to write something independently—and this time, "he was ready," she said. "There was no pushback. No 'I can't.' He just grabbed the pencil and wrote."

My oldest son, Nathan, was extremely frustrated with reading at age six. He wanted so badly to read chapter books, but he hated reading aloud. *Hated it*. So I stopped requiring him to do so. We ceased all formal reading instruction and I continued to read aloud to him and his brothers. A few months later, he snuck down the stairs, well after bedtime, to inform his father and me that he'd just finished his first chapter book.

If your son is struggling with a skill—particularly if learning this skill is creating chaos and distress—simply stop. Drop it for the time being. Try again in a few months. What was difficult a few months earlier may be significantly easier with a bit more maturity.

Don't Stress about School Expectations

It really doesn't matter how old your son is when he learns to read or write. You may not have the power to change schools' expectations of young children, but how you handle those expectations is entirely up to you.

It can be *very difficult* to push back against school expectations. Teachers do not always agree with the "let's wait and try later" approach. You may (or may not) be able to switch teachers or schools. But your reaction to what's happening at school has a tremendous amount of power. If you add your voice to the "you must learn to read now" chorus, your son will feel the weight of your expectation and may conclude that there's something very wrong with him if he can't read. If, on the other hand, you express empathy and say things like, "Reading can be difficult, and everyone learns in their own time," your son won't take his "failure" to meet the school's expectation so personally. He'll feel reassured and understood—and a child who is reassured is far more likely to persist at a tough task than one who feels like he's failed already.

Let me reiterate: it is entirely up to you to decide if you want to uphold, reinforce, or resist school expectations. If completing a handwriting worksheet or math homework regularly sends your son into a tizzy, you can stop. You don't have to make him do it. You can, instead, talk to his teacher about what's happening. (*"Alex ends up crying every night he tries to do the worksheet. We've tried taking breaks and coming back to it later, but it always ends in tears. This is creating a lot of stress in our family."*) The teacher may suggest an alternative—or you can. (*"We're going to take a break for a few nights, and when we try again, I'm going to have him work for just ten minutes/ do only three problems/etc."*) The teacher may or may not approve of an alternate approach. However, it is still ultimately your decision.

That's a difficult truth for people pleasers and rule followers (like me) to accept. Most of us grew up in a system that posits educators as experts—and they are! We've also been taught that school success is the key to life success. But it's not. Not really. In the end, it doesn't matter if your child completes every first-grade math worksheet or reads twenty-five books independently by the end of second grade.

If a school expectation is causing serious stress for your son or family, back off for a bit. Persistent stress is far more damaging to boys' overall development than a slight delay in academic gains.

Talk to Boys about the Mismatch between Male Development and Academic Expectations

Young boys who see their female classmates succeeding while they and their buddies are getting in trouble for wiggling and talking often assume that something is wrong with *them*. They don't understand that girls' brains mature at a different pace than theirs. They don't know that today's academic expectations are wildly different than the ones you experienced two or three decades ago.

Explaining the typical developmental pace of males can help young boys hold on to hope. When you explain that reading, for instance, might be hard now because their brains are still developing, boys begin to realize that their current struggles aren't due to a lack of effort or intelligence, but related to the fact that they're still growing.

Teenage boys can benefit from similar reassurances when they see self-assured young women leading nearly every club and extracurricular activity at school while they and their friends are still bumbling through most days.

Encourage Healthy Risk-Taking

Remember: rich and varied experiences capture children's attention, boost motivation, and help maintain brain plasticity. Allowing children to self-select "risky" activities that challenge their current level of functioning is a fantastic way to facilitate their development. Boys will rarely choose activities that are completely beyond their reach, so supporting boys' efforts is one way to support their natural developmental timeline.

In practice, it's difficult for parents and caregivers to say yes to risk. Our risk-adverse society values harm avoidance. And if we say, "no, you can't climb the tree," we decrease the chances of our son breaking an arm by falling out of a tree. But we also squelch their self-motivation and eliminate any chance of them feeling the sense of pride, accomplishment, and mastery they'd feel when they climb the tree. We take away the opportunity to practice in-the-moment problem-solving.

So whenever possible, say yes to reasonable risks. Give scrap wood and a hammer to the boy who wants to build a bike jump. Hold your tongue when your son announces his plan to climb to the top of the monkey bars; instead, smile, nod, and watch as he takes on the challenge. (Of course, it's a good idea to remain nearby, just in case he needs help.)

When we allow and encourage risk taking, boys are much more likely to tackle the challenges that will help them move forward in their development.

Educate Others about Male Development

Most parents and educators don't know that males develop according to a unique timeline. Teachers typically don't learn about male development in school, and although some are aware that current educational standards are out of sync with child development, they are pressured to adhere to the required curriculum and prepare students for the standardized tests that are so often used to judge teachers' and schools' effectiveness.

Share what you're learning about male development with friends and family members. Talk to your son's childcare providers and teachers and let them know that you don't expect your son to do things that may be developmentally beyond his reach. Tell them you support slow-and-steady growth.

If possible, discuss the gap between academic expectations and male development with the educational leaders in your community. Support developmentally appropriate initiatives like efforts to assure recess time for elementary students; oppose efforts to decrease recess, art, or physical education.

When more people understand and respect male development, more boys will be allowed adequate time to grow.

TEEN BOYS NEED TIME TOO

My husband will be the first to tell you that his relative success today is not the result of a series of wise decisions made in his teens and twenties.

Like many young guys (particularly guys with ADHD), he was a thrill seeker as a young man. He did a lot of the things that you hope your son never does. Despite their sturdy family values and solid example, my husband's parents got more than a few middle-of-the-night phone calls from officers of the law.

Today, my husband is a solid citizen. He's a father, grandfather, and all-around good guy who will do whatever he can to help a fellow human (or dog) in need. More than a few of his high school teachers might be surprised by the man he is today.

Many guys take a long time to grow up. You will need to remind yourself of that fact again and again as you watch your boys flounder through adolescence.

All available evidence tells us that teenage boys and young adult males are prone to making seriously sketchy decisions. During adolescence—which, remember, extends into the early twenties—humans are more likely to take risks than at any other time in their development. Because the prefrontal cortex of the brain is not yet fully developed, teens and young adults are more likely than older humans to act on impulse. The reward system of the brain also goes into high gear during adolescence, so teenage guys typically overestimate the potential reward of an activity while underestimating the possible risks. The presence of friends influences boys' calculations as well. In an interview with NPR, Sandra Aamodt, a neuroscientist and coauthor of *Welcome to Your Child's Brain: How the Mind Grows from Conception to College*, stated that, "a 20 year old is 50 percent more likely to do something risky if two friends are watching than if he's alone."[43]

That's why my husband did a lot of the "stupid" things he did in his teens and twenties. And why my boys have gotten speeding tickets, experimented with substances, and earned a couple in-school suspensions.

The fact that teen boys' slow-to-develop brains are encased in physical bodies that can create and destroy life seems a bit like a cosmic joke. Our boys and young men possess the power to irreversibly alter their lives (and others'), but cognitively and emotionally speaking, many of these same humans are functionally children.

Talk about a conundrum! The world sees teenage and young adult males as men and treats them accordingly. In New York and North Carolina, all crimes committed by sixteen- and seventeen-year-olds are handled in adult court,[44] and throughout the United States, young Black males accused of crimes are significantly more likely to be charged, prosecuted, and penalized as adults than young white males.[45] Meanwhile, schools, communities, and families often fail to offer young men appropriate emotional and logistical support as they grow. Teen boys often unwittingly make things worse by refusing external assistance or support—because they've learned that men can't show weakness.

Our teenage boys need love, compassion, support, and protection. They need us to simultaneously give them time to grow while also holding them accountable for serious missteps. And they need us to believe in their potential and trust the process of development without necessarily lowering the bar. That's a tough thing to do, especially in a culture that misunderstands male development.

That's (part of) why parenting a teen boy is so exhausting, and why I'm absolutely convinced that all parents of teen boys need a support group of their own. (Come join us in the Building Boys Facebook group!)

BUT WHAT ABOUT THE BASEMENT DWELLERS?

It's true: more young adult men live at home and are not working or going to school than in recent generations.[46] Approximately 55 percent of guys ages eighteen to twenty-four lived at home in July 2020,[47] and male college attendance and workforce participation are down. Experts point out that this apparent decrease in independence is not due to male laziness or apathy but societal change and economic pressure.[48] (COVID-19 didn't help either!)

Giving teen boys time to mature will not increase the likelihood of your son living in your basement. On the contrary: it may allow him to develop the skills and confidence he needs to pursue independence.

Expect Uneven Development

Human growth and development are not a linear process. A teenage boy who expertly prepares a family meal one day may melt down completely the next when you suggest he make himself a PB&J as an afterschool snack.

Regression—an apparent inability to do something that an individual could do previously—is common during both the toddler and teenage years. Just as a one-year-old will sometimes seem to "forget" that he walked independently a few days ago, so too will a teenager become overwhelmed by a task he's successfully completed numerous times, such as gathering up his materials for school.

There's a reason for this "two steps forward, one step back" behavior, and it has nothing (well, almost nothing) to do with teenage stubbornness. During adolescence, the teenage brain undergoes significant remodeling. Imagine a dense garden full of tangled weeds, vines, plants, and flowers. That's the brain of a young teen, teeming with neural connections. Humans are born with approximately one hundred billion neurons, and throughout life, the brain creates countless connections between these neurons. More isn't necessarily better, though, so the brain also engages in a pruning process, eliminating less frequently used connections and strengthening others—just as a gardener trims back less productive shoots to allow other ones to flourish.

This pruning process intensifies during the early teen years. (Picture the gardener, frantically working to get the garden show-ready. That's your teen's brain, preparing for adulthood.) As Maggie Dent explained in a 2015 article initially published in *Teachers Matter*, "The initial brain pruning that occurs in the first stage of adolescence . . . often creates very unexpected, confusing changes for our teens. Forgetfulness and a decline in organizational skills are clear signs that brain pruning is happening"[49]

Some days, your fourteen-year-old may act like a man. Other days, he'll act like a toddler. Hang in there. Uneven development during adolescence is completely normal.

Don't Force Driving

According to a 2019 *Wall Street Journal* article, only about one-quarter of sixteen-year-olds in the United States had their driver's license in 2017, compared to half of sixteen-year-olds in 1983.[50]

In an era of mass transit and ridesharing, many teens simply don't feel the need to drive. Others don't feel ready for the responsibility. If your son is expressing hesitation regarding driving, don't push him.

Male drivers ages sixteen to nineteen are twice as likely as similarly aged girls to be involved in a deadly motor vehicle accident, according to the US Centers for Disease Control and Prevention.[51] They are also more likely to speed and drive after drinking alcohol, perhaps due to their slower-developing brains.[52]

No one should be pressured into taking driver's education classes or driving.

Encourage Independence

We cannot expect boys to function well as independent men if we continue to control most aspects of their lives while they are living in our homes.

It's scary to think of releasing control to a not-yet-mature teenage boy who can be so easily influenced by the presence of peers and the possibility of reward. But humans learn best via experience and natural consequences, so it's crucial to give teenage boys multiple opportunities to manage their time, responsibilities, relationships, and resources.

Giving him more independence can include giving him full responsibility for getting up and getting ready in the morning—and allowing him to experience consequences if he oversleeps or forgets his Chromebook at home. It may include not nagging him about his homework—which, yes, may result in him not completing it. As difficult as it may be to watch a teenage boy self-sabotage, it is far better for him (and you!) that he experiences the consequences of his choices now, while he still has plenty of time to course correct. (Getting a D or F in a high school math class really does not matter in the grand scheme of life.)

All kids, of course, need different levels of support. Some are itching for independence; others require extra encouragement. You don't need to make any radical changes; instead, seize opportunities. The next time your boy needs clothes, for instance, consider offering him a set dollar amount and let him shop for his own clothing instead of stopping at TJ Maxx for him.

In a 2021 *Washington Post* article, former CIA analyst and mom Christina Hillsberg wrote, "I believe that giving my kids more independence at earlier ages is not optional—it's essential."[53] As she and her husband Ryan Hillsberg, a CIA operative, learned (and detailed in their book, *License to Parent: How My Career as a Spy Helped Me*

Raise Resourceful, Self-Sufficient Kids), giving kids ever-increasing amounts of independence and responsibility is the best way to prepare them for self-sufficiency in adulthood.[54]

Stop Stressing about "the Future"

In an effort to prepare children for the workforce, schools in the United States have devoted a lot of effort in recent years to ensuring that students are "college and career ready." Middle school teachers and guidance counselors talk about career pathways and encourage students to choose classes that will facilitate entry into their chosen careers. First-year high school students are routinely reminded of college admissions requirements. Parents hammer home the importance of education and are often distressed by their sons' apparent utter lack of interest in school. Parental distress morphs into desperation when parents realize that their sons have no realistic plans.

Relax.

Today's boys are growing up in a time of tremendous transition. The economy, climate, and political leadership are in flux. The future is uncertain—and we somehow expect fourteen-year-old boys to have a serious plan for what they'll do in this yet-to-be-determined future?

It is completely normal for teenage boys (and young adult men) to not have solid plans for adulthood. "A 19-year-old struggling with the question 'What do I want to do?' is normal," Jeffrey Jensen Arnett, the author of *Emerging Adulthood: The Winding Road from the Late Teens through the Twenties*, told journalist Sari Harrar, author of a 2021 AARP article entitled "Fighting the Failure to Launch in Young Adults."[55]

It's okay to talk about the future but keep your concerns and anxiety to yourself. Listen more than you talk. Ask open-ended questions (*"How do you picture your adult life?"* or *"What kinds of things do you* not *want to do when you're older?"*) rather than agenda-driven questions like, "Did you start your college applications yet?"

Mark McConville, a clinical psychologist, advises parents and other caring adults to "discover what excites" young men and "support that."[56] That's easier said than done, given that we adults have far more life experience than the boys and young adults in our lives. We may see, very clearly, that a chosen academic major (say, accounting) is not a good fit for an outdoors-loving, can't-stand-to-be-inside-and-sit-still young man, but (1) he may surprise us and (2) it's far more powerful for him to discover his strengths and stressors than it would be for him to shape his life according to others' perceptions of him.

It is normal for teenage boys and young men to experiment with multiple career and educational paths. Detours and missteps are also normal and expected. Your compassionate support and understanding will be far more helpful than criticism and judgment. (Please note: you do not have to enable unhealthy or dangerous decisions.)

Have Faith

A teen boy's behavior at fourteen (or sixteen or nineteen) is not indicative of the man he will become. Do not assume the worst about your boy because he made a bad decision (or a series of bad decisions.) Remember: his brain is still maturing. He is still developing impulse control, still learning to resist peer pressure and accurately weigh the risks and benefits of a potential action. He will make many, many, *many* mistakes on the path to maturity, and his mistakes aren't an indicator of poor parenting or sociopathic tendencies.

More than anything, teenage boys need the adults in their lives to believe in them. We can (and should) hold them to high standards, but when our boys fall short, they need to know that we still love them, care about them, and see their worth.

My husband, the former teenage risk taker, is a good man today because his family loves and accepts him. They never gave up on him, so he never gave up on himself.

With time, our boys can grow into incredible men.

❧

To build boys:

- *Reflect on whether your son is an early developer, a late bloomer, or somewhere in between.*
- *Push back against developmentally inappropriate expectations.*
- *If your son is struggling with a skill, back off. Try again in a few months.*
- *Let your son develop at his own pace.*

7

❦

Challenge Him with Chores and Caregiving

Achieving gender equality requires the engagement of women and men, girls and boys. It is everyone's responsibility.

—Ban Ki-moon

Mere hours after my oldest son left home for college, his brothers dismantled his bed, carried the cedar chest up to the attic, unstacked the bunk beds, and moved one of our former bunk beds into what was quickly becoming Nathan's former bedroom.[1]

Nathan had been in Nashville for the better part of a year already. I'd insisted on keeping his room "his" after he moved out, but when he was home during spring break, he announced his plans to remain in Nashville for the summer. His brothers immediately asked him if they could take over his turf.

He said yes, and they wasted no time in getting to work.

The boys started while I was working in my basement office. When I went upstairs an hour or so later, the job was nearly done.

At this point in our lives, my boys (then tweens and teens), routinely threw a fit whenever I asked them to empty the dishwasher. They tried to pawn chores off onto one another—often, by offering cash. (*"Hey Sam, I'll give you $2 if you empty the dishwasher for me!"*) Their dirty clothes and wet towels littered the bathroom floor, and

131

plates, cups, and food wrappers marked their movements through the house.

They kept up with school, work, and extracurricular obligations, but they didn't contribute much on the home front. Well, aside from making messes. I tolerated these messes because I didn't want to fight about chores, and it was quicker, easier, and less stressful to simply clean up myself. So I'd pick up paper plates and crinkled chip bags as I walked through the living room and deposit them in the garbage. I'd rinse out the dirty cereal bowls left on the kitchen counter and load them into the dishwasher. I'd hang wet towels to dry and put dirty boxer shorts in the laundry hamper.

I didn't realize it at the time, but I was sabotaging myself and shortchanging my sons. Until the Great Bedroom Switcheroo, I did not realize that my sons could independently handle such a complex household task. I didn't expect cooperation and productivity; I expected fighting and arguing. I was sure that my boys would lose interest and make a mess and that, in the end, the task of cleaning, rearranging, and organizing the bedrooms would fall to me.

I was wrong. The Great Bedroom Switcheroo taught me that I'd inadvertently assigned myself too many household responsibilities while entrusting my boys with too few.

That's a mistake made by parents all over the world, and the effects reverberate in households, boardrooms, and communities. In most families, women still shoulder the bulk of household responsibilities. According to a 2019 Gallup poll, 58 percent of surveyed females in married or partnered heterosexual relationships carry primary responsibility for laundry, and 51 percent for both cooking and cleaning.[2] Opposite-gender couples ages eighteen to thirty-four were no more likely than older couples to divide household chores equitably,[3] and a majority of US-based high school seniors of all genders told researchers that the most desirable work/life arrangement for a family involves the male working full time while the female partner cares for the home and children, according to a 2020 article published in *Sociological Science*.[4]

In the United States, teenage boys ages fifteen to nineteen spend, on average, twenty-four minutes on housework per day, while teenage girls devote approximately thirty-eight minutes to cleaning and cooking.[5] And a 2016 survey of more than fifty thousand children in sixteen different countries on four continents found that twelve-year-old girls spend more time than boys do on housework.[6]

We aren't doing ourselves—or our boys—any favors by letting them off the hook at home.

"The point of chores is to make sure that everyone has the life skills they need when they go out into the adult world," says Gemma Hartley, author of *Fed Up: Emotional Labor, Women, and the Way Forward* and a married mom of two sons and a daughter. "That's something we really need to be cognizant about as we're raising our kids."[7]

And yet, in most homes and communities, gender stereotypes still limit boys' involvement in chores and caregiving. Despite personal commitments to gender equity and extensive (and frustrating!) experience with uneven workloads, many adults unconsciously perpetuate the gender-based division of household responsibilities. My boys' dad and I did; for years, he did the "outside work" (lawn mowing, snow shoveling, car maintenance) and I did the "inside work" (vacuuming, dusting, toilet scrubbing, decorating, and homemaking). We "shared" cooking and childcare responsibilities, but because I was an at-home parent for many years, most of that work fell to me. Neither the boys' dad nor I believed that males are inherently better at lawn mowing than females or that childcare is predominantly a woman's responsibility, but we both grew up in a highly gendered society, so he learned to cut lawn and perform oil changes and I did not. He learned that a man's worth is tied directly to his ability to provide for his family; I learned that motherhood is the "greatest thing a woman can do." (What can I say? I grew up Catholic in the 1970s and 1980s.) Confronted with the stress and logistical challenges of raising a family and managing a household, we reverted to what we knew. Neither of us made time to consciously examine the gender stereotypes that shaped our experience and therefore our boys'.

The results were predictable. Our sons learned to cut lawn. Their interest in mopping the floor waned after they grew old enough that my "splash soapy water on the floor and slip and slide in swimsuits and on towels" approach was no longer attractive. As they entered school, they spent more time on their own activities and less helping inside the home. As young adults, each is more competent in the garage than in the house.

There are a few common unconsciously accepted myths that inter-fere with boys' involvement in chores and caregiving:

1. Boys are messy.
2. Males don't "see" mess.
3. Women are natural nurturers. (And males, therefore, are not.)

Let's tackle them one by one.

MYTH 1: BOYS ARE MESSY

Picture the bedroom of a teenage boy.

What did you just envision?

If you imagined a cluttered, stinky room with an unmade bed and food wrappers, water bottles, energy drink cans, and clothes in a jumbled heap on the floor, your vision is likely a relatively accurate representation of the majority of teen boys' bedrooms in the United States. (I have zero stats to back up this assertion. I do, however, have four sons and know a lot of parents of teenage boys.)

But is that reality—a messy room—due to a biological tendency toward sloth or filth? Or do we parents tolerate and excuse boys' environmental disasters because we believe that boys are inherently messier than girls? Or because, on some level, we believe that boys' time is better spent doing other things?

According to Susan McHale, a Penn State professor of human development, "There's no evidence of inherent, biologically based sex differences in cleanliness or messiness."[8] She notes that there are individual differences—some humans seem to have an innate preference for orderliness and others are more tolerant of mess—and that's definitely something I've noted within my own family: Sam, my youngest, is naturally neater than his brothers, despite being raised in the same household with similarly low expecta-tions for cleanliness. As a young boy, he routinely lined up his dump trucks and tractors when he was done playing with them. (Just as his grandpa did with full-sized dump trucks and heavy equipment in the years before Sam was born.) As a tween, he insisted on organizing the tools in the garage and typically maintains a much cleaner and neater workspace than the rest of us.

The *idea* that men and boys are naturally messier, though, is deeply ingrained in our culture. Consider the opening sentence of a 2016 *Vice* article entitled "Men Are Definitely Dirtier Than Women, According to Science": "Intuition tells us that men are, generally, far more vile and dirty than women."[9] Note: not just dirtier, but *vile*— extremely unpleasant; morally bad; wicked; of little value.

The *Vice* article never actually proves its point. Instead, the author cites studies that show that men generally have more bacteria on their hands than women and that the offices of men usually have more bacteria than the offices of women. But more bacteria doesn't necessarily equal "dirtier." Our bodies are colonized with bacteria and much of that bacteria helps maintain health and homeostasis.

The article does, however, prove that society equates messiness with morality—a holdover from the time when "cleanliness is next to godliness" was a common maxim, perhaps? One striking finding of a 2019 study examining gender and housework norms was that men are judged as significantly less moral when they occupy a messy room than women who occupy equally messy rooms.[10] Women who occupy messy rooms are also judged as less moral than women who occupy clean rooms, but men, unexpectedly, are judged more harshly for mess than women—a finding that researchers suggest can be explained by the fact that "mess activates negative stereotypes about men."

Basically, we expect men and boys to be messy and dirty, *and* we think less of them when they are. Which may be one reason why dirt-smudged boys and their cluttered bedrooms are so intolerable to so many moms. On some level, we know that people find it difficult to respect dirty boys, so we want our sons to present freshly scrubbed faces and hands to the world.

There may be another evolutionary reason why many mothers are repulsed by mess. A 2017 research paper published in *Emotion Review* examined sex differences in disgust and found that women set a much lower bar for feeling sickened by stimuli related to potential pathogens or germs.[11] The authors theorize that females' "low bar" for mess, dirt, and smells may be associated with our desire to protect ourselves and our young from infection and disease, as foul smells and disgusting sights often signal the presence of dangerous pathogens. The authors also suggest that males may be more sensitive to disgusting sights and smells than they let on, noting that males may "suppress their disgust in front of the opposite sex."

Another confounding factor: teens' sense of smell may not be as acute as adults', so it's entirely possible that our tween and teen boys really don't know how bad they (and their sports shoes!) smell. A 2017 study compared the odor identification abilities of adults and teens and found that teens were less adept at detecting spice and environmental odors than adults were.[12] (Teens, however, were better at detecting candy scents.)

So although there is no biological reason for males to be messier than females, there is a collective cultural assumption that guys are grubby and grimy. There is also the distinct possibility that moms are more inclined than boys to be repulsed by chaotic bedrooms and backpacks. Gender doesn't *cause* mess, but it certainly influences our perception and response to it.

MYTH 2: MALES DON'T SEE MESS

Women have long complained that their male partners and sons simply walk past discarded socks, dirty cereal bowls, and empty food boxes, effectively leaving the clutter for "someone else" to clean up. Wives and moms profess amazement (and frustration) at guys' ability to ignore glaringly obvious messes and out-of-place objects.

The idea that men "don't see" messes, though, has been debunked. Researchers at Emory University and the University of Melbourne showed 622 men and women photos of a messy or neat room and asked them to rate the cleanliness of the room. Males and females ranked the rooms similarly, suggesting that men are just as capable as women at noticing mess.[13]

The study, however, did not assess the mess-detecting capabilities of young boys or girls. Children and teenagers are developmentally self-centered; their immediate needs typically take precedence over the needs of others. It is entirely possible that our sons (and daughters) do not notice messes that don't obstruct their actions. A basket of unfolded laundry simply isn't likely to attract the notice of a tween who's focused on heading out the door to meet friends.

The challenge, of course, is helping our children recognize—and respond to—household needs. And historically, females were the only ones who were taught to cook, clean, and respond to domestic disorder. That's changed in recent decades, but gender stereotypes and expectations continue to affect individual activities. In many households, males get out of housework by claiming (perhaps accurately) that they're not as good at [*enter household chore here*] as their spouse, parent, sibling, or roommate. And because it frequently takes longer to explain or show someone how to properly do the chore than it would take to do the $&%# thing, moms and wives often just do whatever needs to be done.

Although doing things yourself may seem the most expedient choice in the present, singlehandedly (or primarily) running the household deprives children of essential learning opportunities. With practice, children of all genders can learn to maintain a home and manage mess.

MYTH 3: WOMEN ARE NATURAL NURTURERS (AND MALES ARE NOT)

It's a lot easier for males to opt out of childcare duties than women.

That's a biological fact. The researchers who conducted the 2017 "disgust" study[14] noted that female mammals (including humans) are "characterized by greater minimum obligatory parental investment than males." Female mammals' bodies protect, gestate, and nourish the next generation.

The close physiologic relationship between mother and child almost certainly underlies the cultural belief that females are naturally more nurturing than males. However, males are capable of nurturing behavior. Boys and men can comfort, feed, encourage, and protect others. Historically, though, they haven't been encouraged to do so.

Gary Barker, a developmental psychologist and the founder and CEO of Promundo, an international organization devoted to healthy masculinity and gender equality, has noted that women and girls are taught that they are natural caretakers, whereas men and boys are not. He told American University Radio that most men and boys want to be more involved in caregiving and housework but worry about how other males will perceive them.[15]

In many places, males and females look suspiciously upon males who choose caregiving roles. According to a 2019 study conducted by the Better Life Lab at New America, twice as many men as women say that society doesn't trust them to give care.[16] Some patients refuse care from male nurses. Some parents are uncomfortable leaving their children in the care of a male daycare provider, citing concerns about possible sexual impropriety. Is it any wonder that males steer away from caregiving?

WHY BOYS NEED CHORES AND
CAREGIVING RESPONSIBILITIES

The biggest predictor of young adults' success in their mid-twenties is their involvement in household tasks at the age of three or four, according to longitudinal research conducted by Marty Rossman, a professor of family education.[17] Kids who learn how to perform household tasks and regularly contribute labor to the family grow into adults who can competently manage an independent life. Boys who do not learn how to do laundry turn into clueless men who ask their female dorm mates how to wash a load of clothes.

Caregiving—playing with or supervising siblings or cousins, assisting an elderly relative, or babysitting other children—can teach boys empathy, compassion, and patience while also building boys' well-being. As noted in a 2019 *Psychology Today* blog post, human "brains are wired to give. Acts of giving to others release neurochemicals that are far more powerful and rewarding than receiving gifts."[18]

Linsey Knerl, a freelance writer and homeschooling mom of six, often asks her ten-year-old son to read to or play an educational card game with a younger brother. It's a win-win-win-win arrangement for the family: Linsey can work, the younger brother is supervised and engaged, both boys develop academic and communication skills, and the older brother feels a sense of pride and empowerment.

"I think that for future strong, kind, honest, amazing men, that's one of the best things you can give boys," says Knerl.

Evidence also suggests that caring for others may decrease suicide risk. A study published by Colorado State University professor of psychology Silvia Sara Canetto in 2021 found that male suicide rates are lower in countries where men do family care work.[19] Although male suicide risk is often correlated with unemployment, Canetto's study found that higher unemployment rates were not associated with increased suicide risk in countries where men perform more caregiving. The study, which examined male employment, caregiving, and suicide in twenty countries including the United States, Japan, Austria, Belgium, and Canada, underscores the "stronger benefits of giving support over receiving it—in terms of longevity as well as quality of life."

Because industrialized societies have traditionally valued males as employees and providers, male self-worth has historically been linked to their ability to earn an income. Men are less likely than women to cite "family" as a reason for living—perhaps because males who are focused on work are often less likely than women (who've been socialized to focus on family) to have close, intimate relationships with family members. Engaging in caregiving shows males the value of such relationships and allows them to "diversify their sources of meaning and power," in the words of Dr. Canetto.[20]

When your son complains about having to help grandma or watch a younger sibling, it might not *seem* like he is developing an appreciation for his relatives or diversifying his "sources of meaning and power." You might worry about burdening your son with caregiving responsibilities or fear that asking (or requiring) him to help will somehow backfire, leading him to conclude that family equals a lack of freedom and drudgery. In reality, he's learning that caregiving is hard work—which may (emphasis on *may*) lead to increased (if unspoken) appreciation for the care you provide. Boys who care for others also begin to see the subtle rewards involved in caregiving work, such as the sense of joy he feels when he makes his younger sister laugh.

Chores and family responsibilities teach interdependence. Boys who are expected to contribute to the family learn vital communication skills. And when all members of a household contribute to the upkeep and maintenance of the family, long-standing, limiting stereotypes crumble. Caregiving experience can expand boys' employment opportunities as well. A 2021 report by New America, a think tank and civic action organization, notes that "jobs in childcare, elder care, and education are some of the most future-proof jobs as they . . . require human touch and interaction."[21] To date, males remain underrepresented in both nursing and education—two essential fields facing critical employee shortages.

GETTING HIM TO DO CHORES

Busting through the mental clutter and societal beliefs that limit boys' involvement in home and family is the easy part. Getting your son to pitch in is the real challenge.

There are no surefire ways to ensure that your son does his chores promptly and without complaining. In fact, I encourage you to adjust your expectations. Assume that your son will whine. Assume he'll procrastinate and do a less-than-stellar job. Assume that you will have to remind him of his responsibilities. And please—please!—assume that you'll have to constantly renegotiate household expectations, because I guarantee that no chore system will work indefinitely. Your son's needs, desires, and capability will grow in the coming years, and your family's needs will change as well.

With that in mind, these seven tips can help.

Tap into His Desire to Contribute

The earlier your son becomes involved in the work of the household, the better. Young children are eager to imitate their parents. They *want* to sweep, mop, and wash the car. They're just not very good at it yet, so our tendency as busy, often overscheduled adults is to shoo them away and tell them to go watch a video (or play on a tablet) so we can get the job done in the fifteen minutes we've allotted, rather than the forty-five to sixty minutes it would take if we let our kids "help."

In the long run, though, we're really not saving any time. Toddlers and preschoolers who are shooed away—when they are developmentally primed to learn from adults—turn into tweens and teens who have the manual dexterity to help but no desire to do so. The "extra time" it takes to do a chore with your child is an investment in his overall growth and development. He'll learn the skills he'll need to one day manage a household, and the two of you will share conversation and closeness. You'll hone his intellectual, verbal, and motor abilities while knocking a task off the to-do list, and your son will feel valued because you're including him in your life and activity.

Older boys also want to contribute, so don't worry that you've missed some sort of critical window of development if your son hasn't been cleaning alongside you ever since he learned to walk. However, if you have a tween or teen who hasn't previously been expected to do household chores, don't expect him to cheerily adapt to a new household routine.

Try tapping into your son's desire to do grown-up things. A four-teen-year-old may be far more eager to learn how to use the hedge trimmer (and take on hedge-trimming responsibilities) than he is to dust the bookshelves. Certainly, he needs to learn how to dust, too, but if you're just getting started with regular responsibilities, there's no harm in starting with tasks that appeal to your son.

In fact, giving kids chores that are bit beyond their current level of capability is usually a better choice than assigning them tasks they can do easily. As noted in a 2015 *Parents* magazine article, "8 Ways to Motivate Kids to Do Chores," "taking away difficult tasks makes chores even more boring."[22] The article suggests gradually ramping up the difficulty of kids' chores. Instead of having your son wash the dishes again, challenge him to plan and prepare a meal for the family.

Felix Bedolla, a dad of a daughter and son, gives his children additional responsibilities annually.

"We add one more chore each year and remind them that learning to take responsibility for their living environment will help them when they live on their own," Felix says.

Make It Fun

It's easy to have fun with chores if you have little boys—as long as you set aside your rigid ideas about how they must be done. My guys had a ball slipping and sliding on soapy water on our kitchen floor, and though the method was nontraditional, the floor was decently clean by the time they were done "playing." (At the end, I gave everybody a used bath towel and asked them to help sop up the remaining wetness, then I threw the towels in the wash. Kitchen floor cleaned, laundry started, kids occupied and amused. Win-win-win!)

Putting on music is another way to amp up the fun (and train your son's ear and develop his vestibular system, which is critical for balance and reading, according to Joan Koenig, author of *The Musical Child*.)[23] Encourage your son to play his favorites or take turns creating playlists. (Challenge each other to name the artist.)

Music can even serve as a pleasant timer. See how much you can get done in one or two songs.

"We do a lot of quick interventions such as a 20-minute Tidy Up, where we crank up the music and everyone just tidies until the 20 minutes is up," says Sandra Prins Harrop, a mom of two. "You would be amazed what four people can accomplish in 20 minutes— and with the music on, we have fun doing it."

The Center for Parenting Education, a nonprofit organization, suggests using humor "to lighten the mood and engage cooperation" and says that "a note from the family pet about being hungry might remind a child that the dog is depending on [him] for dinner." (Note: this approach is unlikely to work with a teenager, unless you get really creative and sarcastic with the note. Teen boys speak sarcasm.)

You can also turn chore assignment into a game. A May 2021 viral "Chore Challenge" video posted by @globalmunchkins, a family of eight, featured some innovative ideas, including a game that involved bouncing a ping-pong ball into a muffin tin, each of which contained a piece of paper labeled with a chore; a conveyor belt game with chores listed on a long sheet of paper that's placed on a table in front of a blindfolded "contestant" who randomly slams his hand down and is responsible for whichever chore his hand landed on; and a version of spin-the-bottle, with chores listed on pieces of paper concealed by plastic cups placed in a circle around the bottle. Key to success is including some desirable options: @globalmunchkins' choices included "no chores," and "bag of Takis + garbage duty," along with "mop," "dishes," and "backyard cleanup." Use your imagination and encourage your kids to contribute some fun choices as well.

Avoid using chores as punishment. Though assigning extra labor to a child who misses his curfew or mistreats a classmate may seem like a good way to simultaneously impose a consequence and get some tasks checked off the family to-do list, you may inadvertently create another problem.

"When you use punitive measures like, 'you're going to have to clean the gutters,' you may cause a major negative association," says Gemma Hartley, author of *Fed Up*. "If cleaning gutters was a punishment in your childhood, that job is going to be loathsome to you as an adult."

Avoid the Pink/Blue Divide

Deliberately expose children of all genders to all chores—even (or especially) if you and your parenting partner tend to gravitate to traditional divisions of labor. My boys' dad and I did not do so, and as result our boys spent a lot more time working alongside their dad, doing traditionally "masculine" things such as lawn mowing, vehicle maintenance, and yard care and much less time cooking and cleaning—and it shows. As teens and young adults, they're all adept at car maintenance but lousy in the kitchen.

Hartley and her husband are doing a much better job of avoiding unwitting propagation of gender stereotypes.

"A lot of people who have boys and girls tend to subconsciously focus on teaching domestic stuff to girls," Hartley says. "I make sure we're not dividing jobs up into 'pink' and 'blue.'"

A subtle shift in language also helps Hartley convey the idea that household chores are a shared responsibility. She no longer asks her kids to "help mom," which, she realized, implies that the chores are really mom's responsibility.

"I think that language is really dangerous, because even if everyone is doing their share, if they're thinking of it as 'helping mom,' that attitude will come up later when they partner as adults," Hartley says. Boys will grow into men who think, "I'm helping my wife. I get a gold star because this is really her responsibility."

In the Hartley home, chores are simply "part of how you learn to be responsible for yourself," she says.

Play to His Strengths

Although you want to make sure that all family members learn how to do crucial chores, it's okay to consider individual preferences and talents.

"I'm keen on playing to everyone's strengths, just like in the work world," says Amanda Barnes, a married mom of two boys. "I'm good with routine and regular chores, so I tend to do those—things like grocery shopping and daily cooking. My husband is better at handling bigger chores and mental loads, so he manages things like ordering Christmas gifts and regular supplies, changing air and water filters, organizing finances and filing taxes, and programming and maintaining our Roomba."

My youngest currently has few regular "inside" chores (aside from cleaning up his own messes and doing his laundry), but he manages lawn and yard care for our household—because he has his own lawn care business and can do the work far more quickly and efficiently than any other member of our family. Allowing him to utilize his unique skill set also makes it easier for my busy teen to contribute to family, as he can do the work on his own schedule.

Invite His Input

Kids are much more likely to do something *they've* chosen to do. Tweens and teens, especially, almost reflexively resist directives issued by someone else, so respect their desire for autonomy. As noted by Christine Carter and Christina Vercelletto, "bossiness is not motivating to kids. Letting them give input is essential in preserving their sense of self-reliance and self-assurance."[24]

Family meetings and planning sessions are a great way to solicit boys' input while also helping children understand the "big picture" of home and family maintenance. Unless your kids are intentionally exposed to things like gutter cleaning and sorting through outgrown clothes, they may remain entirely unaware of those necessary chores. Laying out what needs to happen in a week or month helps all members of the family understand the communal workload. It's also an opportunity to create plans of action.

"I really involved my kids in deciding how we were going to do chores," says Hartley, the *Fed Up* author. "We were having huge morning issues with things like dawdling and not getting stuff done on time, so I started with my oldest son—the one who was having the most trouble—and we talked through what he needs in his routine." Hartley repeated this intervention with each of her children and allowed each to customize their own morning routine. Then, "we printed out charts so they could see what their day looks like and what things they need to be doing."

The Hartley family also deliberately rotates chores. "One month, someone has the dishes. The next month, they may have laundry," Hartley says. "That way they all develop the skills they need, and everyone knows that the garbage and laundry, for instance, are things that need to be done, instead of oh, my sister always did that, so it's not on my radar."

Although it can be helpful to have regularly scheduled family meetings, you can also have impromptu family discussions. "Seize opportunity when it arises," Hartley advises. "Pop some popcorn and talk about how things are going." Be prepared to *listen* rather than lecture or dictate. Your son's needs and desires are legitimate too, and he'll be far more likely to willingly contribute to the family if you make space for his ideas.

Resist the Urge to Micromanage

Nitpicking is the quickest way to kill your son's motivation and ambition. You can tell your son *what* to do—and establish some boundaries and expectations, such as, "This chore needs to be completed to our agreed-upon standards before you play video games"—but you'll see the most success if you give him some leeway regarding *when* and *how* to do the job.

Pro tip: your son likely won't do things your way or according to your preferred timeline, and that's okay. Dishes don't have to be washed immediately after a meal. Laundry doesn't need to be folded as soon as it's removed from the dryer. You don't have to use cleaning spray to effectively clean a bathroom mirror; wiping it down with a clean towel after a steamy shower can work just as well.

Give your son some autonomy and allow him to experiment with routines and rhythms that fit his needs. (Of course, it's fair to insist that his routines respect the rest of the family as well—vacuuming at midnight is probably not a good idea.) Also adjust your expectations to your son's developmental level.

"You can't expect your children to come up to your standards and simply accept them," Hartley says, while noting that "it's hard to let go, to let things get done in a way that doesn't always please you. My children's idea of *what is clean* and my idea of *what is clean* are different."

She's worked with her kids to establish reasonable expectations. Each child must make their own bed in the morning, but how well it's made is up to the child. "Done is better than perfect," Hartley reminds herself. "When kids are getting things done, they feel in control of their lives, and they feel they've accomplished something. Me going in behind them to 'fix' their bed is going to rob them of that. And if you nitpick every single day, kids start to think, 'whatever I do is not good enough. Why am I even trying?'"

Often, boys need to experience the natural consequences of their action (or inaction) before they try another (potentially more effective) approach. At age thirteen, Brooke Borden's youngest son "took forever" to wash the dinner dishes.

"He complained of backaches and knee pain," says Brooke, a Texas-based mom, "so we switched and had his older brother go back to dishes for a while. But it was clear that our older son had already mastered that task. We realized we had to give it back to the youngest so he could learn it. Now he can finally get the dishes done in a few minutes after dinner—counters cleaned and everything."

Give boys space to make mistakes and self-adjust.

Don't Accept Subpar Work

Sounds a little contrary to the advice above, eh? But there's a significant difference between allowing your son to skim the surface of his responsibilities and giving him some autonomy. Autonomy is healthy; skipping through chores while claiming incompetence is not.

In a 2018 *New York Times* article,[25] author Steve Almond wrote, "One of the most despicable tricks of the patriarchy is to peddle the myth that men can't do more around the house because they weren't raised doing so. Trace that logic out a bit, and you arrive at a kind of weaponized incompetence: Your husband isn't good at certain tasks, so he shouldn't have to do them."

Don't want to raise a boy who becomes a man who convinces his partner to iron his shirts for him because they're "better at it"? Make sure your son knows how to iron his own shirts, and rebuff all attempts at weaponized incompetence.

That's what Kristen Mae did when her fifteen-year-old son did a less-than-stellar job of folding the family laundry.

"Most of [the laundry] was folded, but sloppily, with the shirts bunched in such a way that you couldn't really tell what you were looking at," Mae wrote in a 2021 essay[26] for *Scary Mommy*. "The basket still had a pile of clothes in it—a mix of various people's underwear, socks, and workout clothes. . . . A pair of my shorts was mixed in with my son's clothes, and my daughter's skirts and joggers were in the pile that I was pretty sure was meant to be mine."

Mae reminded her son he couldn't go online until the chore was complete. The boy insisted he *was* finished. Mae pointed out the unfolded clothes; her son claimed he didn't know how to fold underwear or socks.

Mae called him out—"I told my son there was a name for what he was doing . . . weaponized incompetence"—and said she wouldn't tolerate it.

"I told him if he didn't understand how to accomplish any part of a task I'd given him, part of the job was to *figure out how* to accomplish it. It's totally unacceptable," she wrote, "to just *opt out.*"

Obviously, this discussion would have gone differently if her son was four rather than fifteen. Four-year-olds cannot neatly fold t-shirts or underwear; their hands are simply too small and clumsy. A fifteen-year-old, though, has near adult-level coordination, and most fifteen-year-olds are perfectly capable of seeking the information needed to complete a task. (Kids today regularly check YouTube to learn how to do all kinds of things!)

Know your son's abilities and hold him to reasonable standards. Expect him to complete chores that are well within (or a bit beyond) his capabilities. Even, perhaps, when doing so means stretching the limits of your tolerance.

Inspired by the competence my sons demonstrated during the Great Bedroom Switcheroo, I let a pile of wet towels remain on the bathroom floor the next time the toilet overflowed.

My then-sixteen-year-old had simply tossed the towels into the mess and headed off to dinner with his girlfriend. When he returned, I told him he had to put the towels in the washing machine and start it. In snarky teenager fashion, he told me that's exactly what he was *going* to do—but now that I'd told him to, he wasn't going to do it.

I let the towels lie and remained silent because I knew that we had no clean towels in the house and that my sixteen-year-old son liked to shower before school. I went about my evening—and by the end of the night, the towels were in the washing machine. By morning, they were dry.

It's not easy to step back long enough to let our sons take responsibility, and for some, it's difficult to allow our sons to experience the consequences of their inaction. But that's exactly what our sons need us to do. After all, how can we expect our children to confidently handle toilet explosions as adults if we swoop in and clean the mess every single time?

❧

AGE-APPROPRIATE CHORES

Ages 1–3:

- Pick up toys
- Dust
- Put dirty clothes in hamper
- Help make beds and do dishes
- Put away silverware
- Wipe up spills

Ages 4–5:

- Set and clear the table
- Put away groceries
- Help with cooking (crack eggs, cut with blunt knife, mix and stir)
- Feed pets
- Sweep
- Help wash car

Ages 6–9:

- Vacuum
- Wash mirrors
- Clean toilets
- Weed garden
- Rake leaves
- Take out trash
- Fold and put away laundry
- Mop floors
- Pack school lunches

Ages 10–13:

- Help with vehicle and home maintenance
- Mow lawn

- Clean out fridge
- Iron
- Cook simple meals

Ages 14 and older:

- Independently manage laundry
- Cook and clean up meals
- Babysit

⚭

INVOLVING BOYS IN CAREGIVING

When my second son was about four years old, he asked for a baby care center for Christmas. He'd noticed the molded plastic set in a toy catalog. It featured a nursery area (complete with a changing station, crib, and mobile) and baby bath area, as well as a vinyl doll with all the necessary accessories, including clothes, bottles, diapers, washcloths, and pretend baby shampoo and powder.

The baby care center was pictured in the "girl" section of the catalog; it wasn't among the trucks or building sets, and it included a lot of pink and other pastel colors. My son clearly didn't care and neither did I. He wanted the toy and I wanted to wrap up my holiday shopping. I clicked "buy."

My son was thrilled when he opened his gift on Christmas morning, and he and his brothers spent many happy hours—over many years!—playing with the center.

This story shouldn't be exceptional, but two-plus decades into the twenty-first century, some people still insist boys shouldn't play with dolls. "I got my almost three-year-old a baby doll today [because] every time we've gone to Walmart, he asks for a baby. . . . But his Dad, oh my god his Dad threw a fit," one mom wrote recently in a Facebook group for parents of boys. "He said, 'Boys shouldn't play with girl toys! I can't believe you spent money on a baby doll.'" Sadly, such posts are not rare. They pop up regularly, a reminder that many boys don't yet have the freedom to play with whatever they'd like.

Step one to involving boys in caregiving: bust outdated gender stereotypes. Here's how.

Broaden Your Son's Perspective

Make sure your son sees caring men. Allow him to spend as much time as possible with uncles, grandfathers, older cousins, and men in your community who care for others. When possible, seek out male caregivers and teachers for your son. (Need someone to keep your kids busy while you work or get a few things done around the house? Consider hiring a teenage boy.) Read books that include and highlight male caregiving; *Daddies Do It Different*, by Alan Lawrence Sitomer,[27] is a picture book that celebrates dads' unique approach to parenting, and *A Father's Love*, by Hannah Holt,[28] showcases the many ways animal fathers care for their offspring.

Talk about portrayals of male caregivers in TV shows and movies, both the good (Phil in *Modern Family*, Pa on *Little House on the Prairie*, Dre Johnson on *Black-ish*) and the not-so-good (Homer on *The Simpsons*, Darth Vader in *Star Wars*, the bumbling dads in commercials).

Prioritize Care

You want to raise a son who cares for others, but does he know that? According to an article posted by the Making Caring Common Project, most parents say that raising caring children is a top priority, but children aren't getting that message. A 2014 study by the Harvard Graduate School of Education found that middle and high school students value achievement over caring, largely because they think their parents do.[29] Only 20 percent of the ten thousand kids surveyed chose "caring for others" as their top priority.

If you're like most modern parents, you probably spend a lot more time talking to your son about his school grades and extracurricular achievements than you do talking about his interactions with others. No wonder our kids—and boys in particular, steeped as they are in historical norms linking male achievement and worth—grow up thinking we value achievement over caring.

We must explicitly and deliberately counter this message. "It's very important that children hear from their parents and caretakers that caring about others is a top priority and that it is just as important as their own happiness,"[30] the Making Caring Common article says.

It's helpful for children to *see* this message in action. Linsey Knerl, the homeschooling mom of six, spent two years caring for her elderly grandmother. She often brought her children along when she visited her grandmother, and her boys learned to scan great-grandma's house and help with necessary chores, including unwashed dishes or laundry. The kids often saw their mother set aside what she was doing to attend to her grandmother's needs.

"I'd get phone calls that she'd fallen or she couldn't get the TV on, and I'd run into town to help her. The boys would have to finish making dinner or put their siblings to bed," Knerl said. "There was a shift of responsibility, and they learned to care for others."

Spend Time in Mixed-Age Groups

Children who spend most of their time with similarly aged children—who are similarly driven to achieve independence—don't have nearly as many opportunities to practice care as children who routinely spend time with older and younger people. Linsey says that spending time with her grandmother helped her boys see the limitations and challenges often associated with old age. "They developed empathy watching her lose function and independence," Linsey says, "and it really changed their outlook on how we treat people." Time with her grandmother also presented her boys with multiple opportunities to provide care.

When they were about fifteen years old, each of Linsey's sons volunteered as a camp counselor at the same camp they (and their siblings) attended beginning at age eight. The experience helped them understand the developmental needs of different age groups and allowed them to appreciate the work that goes into caregiving. "They'd come home and say something like, 'Wow, I was with eight-year-old all day. They really have a lot of needs!' or "Twelve-year-olds—what an interesting time,'" Linsey says. "Through caregiving, they're learning how to relate to everybody."

You may need to purposefully seek out mixed-age opportunities for your son, as schools and clubs often segregate kids by age. Support friendships with older and younger children and encourage your son to share his skills and talents as a volunteer. Your basketball-loving son may be able to help run basketball practices for a younger team. My young lawn entrepreneur mows his grandparents' lawn as needed and works with many elderly clients in town.

Present Caring Careers as an Option

At present, there are no national initiatives to encourage boys to pursue caregiving careers. No counterpoint to the now decades-long push to facilitate girls' involvement in STEM careers. Google "girls and STEM" and more than 181 billion results appear, including stemlikeagirl.org,[31] a NASA initiative (Girls in STEM 2021), and an American Association of University Women (AAUW) report, "The STEM Gap."[32] Search for "boys and caregiving" and you'll get fewer than four million results—and one of the top ones is a 2017 research article entitled, "Is Caregiver Gender Important for Boys and Girls?"[33] (According to the excerpt presented, "there is currently no clear empirical evidence that boys and girls can benefit from the presence of male professional caregivers.") Search for "boys and nursing," and approximately half of the suggested articles are about breastfeeding male children.

The United States and other countries have invested millions of dollars to ensure that girls are aware of and prepared for lucrative careers in science, technology, math, and engineering,[34] fields that have been historically male dominated. There has been no complementary investment in boys' futures, despite statistics that show persistent male underrepresentation in healthcare, early education, and domestic roles and strong demand for teachers, healthcare, and childcare workers.[35]

You'll have to make sure your son is aware of career opportunities in nursing, education, childcare, and eldercare. Introduce him to men who work in caregiving and encourage his school to include men in caring careers in career day presentations. Tell him about the American Association of Men in Nursing; the organization's FutureRN PowerPoint presentation (available on the website[36]) succinctly outlines the career potential of nursing, as well as multiple paths to a nursing career. When your son is looking for moneymaking opportunities, suggest babysitting and tutoring in addition to traditional options such as newspaper delivery, lawn mowing, and snow shoveling.

FAMILY: THE FIRST AND FINAL FRONTIER

Work/life balance is a key concern for humans of all genders. Yes, our government and workplaces can (and should) eliminate gender-based discrimination and implement family friendly policies. But real, sustained change also requires individual action. In our homes and families, it's up to us to quash limiting gender stereotypes. It's on us to teach our children—*all* of them—to cook, clean, and care.

To build boys:

- *Reflect about whether you think males are less competent at household chores and caregiving than females.*
- *Discuss and divvy up household responsibilities.*
- *Teach your son to cook, clean, and care for others.*
- *Make sure your son spends time with people of all ages.*

8

⌘

Keep Him Close

The need for connection and community is primal, as fundamental as the need for air, water, and food.

—Dean Ornish

John B. Watson did not believe in keeping his sons close.

In fact, Watson, a behavioral psychologist who was once the president of the American Psychological Association, counseled parents to avoid closeness with their children. His 1928 book, *Psychological Care of Infant and Child,* advised parents to "never hug and kiss" their children and included a chapter entitled, "The Danger of Too Much Mother Love," which called mother love "a dangerous instrument which may inflict a never-healing wound, a wound which may make infancy unhappy, adolescence a nightmare, an instrument which may wreck your adult son or daughter's vocational future and their chances for marital happiness."[1]

Watson was so concerned about the negative impact of parental affection that he thought it might be best if children were housed separately from their parents, cared for by no-nonsense nurses who would meet the kids' physical needs without fuss or affection. He wrote, "It is a serious question in my mind whether there should be individual homes for children—or even whether children should know their own parents."

Watson's book was a best seller.

No wonder Kate Stone Lombardi felt a bit ashamed to admit her close relationship with her son. Watson was long dead by the time Lombardi became a mother, but his ideas persisted. Lombardi wasn't explicitly instructed to avoid showering affection upon her two children (a son and a daughter) but neither was she advised to keep her kids close. Especially not her son. Boys, society told her, needed space and independence.

Lombardi distinctly recalls a moment in the 1990s when she noticed a slightly older woman looking at her intently when Lombardi mentioned an insightful comment her son made after she told him about a challenging work situation. Sensing potential judgment, Lombardi said, "I hope you don't think it's odd, but we're really close." She added, "Not in a weird way."

"I'm just surprised," the other woman responded, "because my adult son calls me, and we also talk about work." She too added, "It's not anything weird."

Lombardi, a journalist, noticed the defensiveness with which they both talked about their relationships with their sons and decided to explore it in a 2012 book, *The Momma's Boy Myth: Why Keeping Our Sons Close Makes Them Stronger.* Her book is a counterpoint to the culturally persistent idea that "if you're close to your son, you're going to raise this wimpy, dependent guy who will never have an adult relationship," she told me.

That idea reaches directly back to Dr. Watson, who called the "inability to break nest habits" (his term for a continued need for affection) "probably our most prolific source of divorce and marital disagreements." He and his wife, Rosalie Rayner Watson, were determined to raise self-sufficient, independent humans, so they did not "coddle" (their word) or show much physical or emotional affection to their two sons. Rosalie was "unanimously in favor of breaking the mother attachment as early as possible," and the boys were not allowed to cuddle.[2]

Sadly, their sons William and James Watson both attempted suicide as adults. William completed his attempt.[3] James later wrote, "I honestly believe the principles for which Dad stood . . . eroded both Bill's and my ability to deal effectively with human emotion . . . and it tended to undermine self-esteem in later life, ultimately contributing to Bill's death and my crisis."[4]

Kate Stone Lombardi continues to enjoy a close relationship with her son, who is now in his thirties and happily married.

WHY IT'S CRUCIAL TO KEEP BOYS CLOSE (AND SO DIFFICULT TO DO SO)

"Holding boys in relationship where they are known and loved is the best way to build good men,"[5] according to Michael C. Reichert, PhD, founding director of the Center for the Study of Boys' and Girls' Lives.

Because the stress-regulating circuits of the brain mature more slowly in males than in females, researchers believe that "developing males . . . are more vulnerable over a longer period of time to stressors in the social environment."[6] Premature physical or emotional separation from their caregivers may be more damaging for boys, on average, than females, which may explain why boys who grow up without actively involved fathers tend to do worse in school (and in life) than girls who have uninvolved fathers. (Research from 2011 found that teen girls' behavior is largely independent of their relationship with their fathers.[7])

"There's so much literature out there about how boys are developmentally more sensitive, about how important close bonds are," Lombardi says. "When boys are prematurely separated from those attachments, they have so many more behavioral problems" than boys who retained close attachments.

Teenage boys and girls who feel connected to and supported by their mothers and fathers generally have better self-esteem than teenagers who feel disconnected from their parents. Adolescents who do not perceive parental support are more likely to experience depression than those who enjoy a close, supportive relationship.[8] Parental nurturing is important for all children, but boys are less likely to maintain close connections to their parents because social norms have long suggested that "too much" nurturing will inhibit boys' development.

"Myths and stereotypes prey on parents, teachers and coaches and cause us to forget that boys are indeed relational," Dr. Reichert said during an *On Boys* podcast episode. "We all harbor the myth that boys are the Lone Ranger in training, and that if we keep them close, we're likely to undermine their achievement of masculine stereotypes."[9]

That's the belief at the heart of the mama's boy myth. Though many cultures believe that it's essential for boys to spend time with men so that the boys can "learn to become men," it's *not* true that spending time with mothers, aunts, grandmothers, or other adult females is damaging to a boy. Yet the idea that parents (particularly mothers) should push their boys away (for the boys' own good) has so infiltrated society that many people accept it as essential truth.

"The mama's boy myth will cause you to question whether you really have what it takes to raise a boy to be a good man," Dr. Reichert says. "It can cause you to consciously—or unconsciously—move away from your son. Some mothers even believe they need to build a metaphoric bridge and then get out of their son's way so he can join the fraternity of manhood."

For decades, society has counseled parents to keep their daughters close and their sons at arm's length, which may be one reason parents hug their female children more often than their sons. Studies have found that boys—particularly boys ages twelve and older—are the group most likely to "never" be hugged or cuddled.[10]

Tween and teenage boys may shy away from physical affection because they too are surrounded by societal messaging that suggests boys should be strong and independent. According to Michael Thompson, PhD, coauthor of *Raising Cain: Protecting the Emotional Life of Boys*, young boys will usually ask for a hug when they want (or need) one.[11] But most boys carefully monitor their parents' responses. Boys who sense parental discomfort with hugging or other physical affection eventually stop asking for or initiating contact. Instead, they may fulfill their human need for physical touch via aggression. Given that context, it's not particularly surprising that a 2002 study of forty-nine cultures found that cultures that exhibited minimal physical affection toward young children had significantly higher rates of adult violence, whereas cultures that showed significant amounts of physical affection toward children had virtually no adult violence.[12]

Adolescents' developmental tendency to pull away from their parents is often interpreted as a sign that they don't want (or need) continued parental attention. And frankly, it's easier to *not* engage with a teenage boy who prefers to spend time alone in his room. But it's a mistake to assume that our teen boys don't need us. In fact, boys may assume that our lack of engagement—which often derives from a well-intentioned desire to give our boys space—means that there's something terribly wrong with them.

"If mom starts with withdraw during that turbulent time, to a boy, it's almost like, man, my own mother doesn't even want to be near me," Lombardi explains.

CLOSENESS AND CONNECTION
CONFER LIFELONG BENEFITS

Pushing a boy out of the nest too early and insisting he go it alone with minimal support does not lead to strength, resilience, and grit. Boys who do not have a strong relationship with a parent or other adult are adrift—and these boys not infrequently grow into men who harm themselves and others. In contrast, boys and men who have strong relationships with their mothers are mentally healthier and more empathetic; they're almost more likely to enjoy close relationships with women.[13]

Animal science seems to support the continued importance of the mother/son bond throughout the lifespan. Chimpanzees are our closest nonhuman biological relatives, and *National Geographic* reports that "Generations of primatologists have documented strong relationships between [chimpanzee] mothers and their adult sons."[14] Researchers Rachna Reddy and Aaron Sandel wanted to know if such close relationships were the norm for chimpanzees or if the strong bonds noted by other researchers were simply heartwarming aberrations. So, Reddy and Sandel spent three years observing twenty-nine adolescent and young adult males within the Ngogo chimpanzee community of Uganda's Kibale National Park. Though the male chimps' daily lives were largely separate from their mothers, the duo noticed that when mothers' and sons' "paths crossed, the sons sought out their moms and groomed them for long periods, likely repeating behaviors from their childhoods."[15]

The chimp moms "play a crucial role" during their sons' adolescence and young adulthood "by defending their sons during conflicts with older males, as well as offering comfort through touch." (Which brings to mind the conflict and confusion many human moms experience when they find themselves in the middle of clashes between their sons and their boys' fathers.)

Reddy and Sandel also found that about one-third of adult male chimps are "essentially best friends with their mothers."[16]

In both the chimp world and the human world, it seems, strong bonds between mothers and sons confer lifelong benefits. Continued closeness with our offspring can reverberate through the generations as well.

"We know from attachment theory that I'm likely to reproduce the kind of attachment I experienced with my own children," Dr. Reichert says. "So if we parents can offer a secure environment for our sons and keep them close to us, it's more likely that they'll be able to resist the hypermasculine cultural norms that are trying to tear them away." Boys who receive consistent physical and emotional connection grow into men who can connect with others.

EXTREMIST GROUPS PREY ON BOYS WHO DON'T HAVE CLOSE CONNECTIONS

White supremacy groups. Gangs. The Taliban.

Extremist groups have long preyed on—and been fueled by—boys and men who are hungry for acceptance and camaraderie.

Russell Schultz, a former member of the Proud Boys, a neofascist, exclusively male organization that's been identified as a hate group by the Southern Poverty Law Center,[17] told CNN that guys "join the group . . . because it gives them a sense of belonging. . . . They're men who've never had wingmen before. . . . The Proud Boys are the vehicle that attracts those people and accepts them in."

If you don't keep your boys close, someone else may swoop in.

HOW TO KEEP BOYS CLOSE (WITHOUT HINDERING THEM)

It is never too late to develop or deepen your relationship with your son. These seven tips can help you keep your boy close.

1. Carve out time for connection.
2. Use your natural gifts and talents to connect.
3. Listen to and validate their thoughts and feelings.
4. Create a "Dad plan" (or a "Mom plan").
5. Offer daily warmth.
6. Be available.
7. Repair as needed.

Carve out Time for Connection

Emma Brown, author of *To Raise a Boy: Classrooms, Locker Rooms, Bedrooms, and the Hidden Struggles of American Boyhood,* says one of the most powerful things parents can do for their sons is to "intentionally create space for high-quality connection."[18]

That's not easy to do given our busy lives. We're occupied with work and home, and between school and extracurricular activities, boys don't have a lot of free time, either. But if you don't deliberately create time for connection, your relationship will likely devolve. You'll issue orders and directives, he'll respond with as few words as possible, and that'll be the extent of your relationship. You won't know what he's thinking or dealing with in his personal life because boys are reluctant to share their internal truth with people who don't show genuine interest in them.

So make it a point to spend time with your son. Amanda Bartrom, an Indiana-based mom, carves out time before her twelve-year-old son's weekly boxing sessions. "We always leave fifteen minutes before we need to," she says. "He thinks it's so I can find a decent parking space. But the main reason is because for those fifteen to twenty minutes, he actually talks to me."

Brown, the book author, was struck by the close relationship between a father-son duo she interviewed. The father, she learned, regularly walked the dog around the block with his son.[19]

Such simple rituals can maintain connections. Arriving early to boxing practice or walking the dog together don't require eye-to-eye contact or conversational effort. But the regularity of these sessions creates opportunities for parent and sons to share. Some days, you might walk in silence or simply listen to music in the car. That's okay. Quiet time together is powerful.

Spontaneous moments of connection can be a lot of fun too— and may be particularly helpful during times of stress. Invite your son to get ice cream (or another favorite treat) with you. Or, if you can, take a couple of hours off work, excuse your son from school, and do something together (visit a park, take in a baseball game, work on the car, play Legos . . .). Australia's Maggie Dent frequently shares the story of a father who was frustrated because his teenage son barely communicated with the family. After hearing Maggie speak, the dad invited his son to get "chips" (French fries) with him. On their walk home, "the boy opened up to his dad about what was really happening at school. A couple of older boys had targeted him and were bullying him and physically harassing him. They had a good conversation about what they could do to resolve the issues."[20] What a great return on investment for the price of some chips!

Use Your Natural Gifts and Talents to Connect

Charlie Capen, a father of two boys and vice president of GISH (Greatest International Scavenger Hunt), takes his role as father so seriously that he initially tried to play "Good Dad"—part Ward Cleaver, part Mike Brady. But parenting à la Cleaver and Brady felt stilted and awkward. Capen eventually realized why: he was suppressing his natural instincts.

"Every time I tried to be what I thought was a 'good dad,' I removed my creativity and my ability from parenting," he says. "I left out whole parts of myself." Once Capen embraced his creativity, silliness, and sense of adventure, "more power and ability arose," he says.[21] He and his sons connect more easily (and have more fun) when Capen is comfortably being himself.

That's a lesson mom Caren Chesler learned after purchasing (and attempting to construct) a model car with her nine-year-old son. As the only female member of their family, Chesler sometimes felt left out.

"My husband already has a lot of common ground with our son, pitching and hitting baseballs, tossing a football and just plain reveling in the sameness of their gender," Chesler wrote in an essay.[22]

She had fond memories of making models in the 1970s with her father, and her son loves Lamborghinis, so the mother-son duo bought a kit and embarked upon some memory making.

It didn't go well. The kit was complicated, the directions unhelpful. The tiny plastic parts broke, and her son quickly lost interest, hitting small rocks against the shed with his hockey stick while Chesler grilled dinner. After dinner, mom and son watched the movie *City Slickers* in the living room.

"That was fun!" her son said as the closing credits rolled—and Chesler realized she'd made a mistake in trying to force bonding via model building. She remembered a cardinal sports rule: play your position. A soccer midfielder plays both offense and defense, but generally leaves goal tending to the goalie. A midfielder needs excellent ball-handling skills and endurance; a goalie, great reflexes and agility. With the right players at each position, teams can excel.

"When I bought the model car, I wasn't playing my position, not because I'm a girl and girls don't do model cars but because it's not what I enjoy nor is it the skill set I bring to the table," Chesler says. "Cooking a delicious lavish meal, enjoying a good movie, sharing my sense of humor, these are the positions I like to play."[23]

Each of us has natural gifts and talents. Use yours to connect with your son. Whatever you enjoy, consider sharing it. Your boy may not share your interest; in fact, it's best to assume that he won't. (That way, you can be pleasantly surprised if he does, but not *too* disappointed if he declares your beloved hobby the most boring thing ever.) Inviting him into your life and your interests shows him another side of you, creating more possibilities for connection. And when you share your interests with your son, he may feel safer sharing his with you.

Listen to and Validate Their Thoughts and Feeling

All humans want to be seen and heard. We want our thoughts and feelings to matter. There's no quicker way to sever connection than to dismiss what someone else is saying.

Unfortunately, adults all too often dismiss children's concerns with comments like, "Oh, it's not so bad!" or "Don't let it bother you." This well-meaning advice—intended to help children put life's disappointments into perspective—signals a lack of interest in the child's experience. Essentially, these words tell a child that his perception of an experience is wrong. That message does not engender trust or respect. Quite the opposite: kids whose thoughts and feelings aren't validated soon learn to keep their thoughts and feelings to themselves.

Kate Hurley, an adolescent psychotherapist, says that one of the "best things" parents can do to connect with their kids is to give them "the undivided attention of listening, empathizing, and compassion."[24]

Whatever your child shares with you is *important to him*, no matter how small or insignificant it may seem from your adult perspective. So when a boy shares a problem or frustration with you, "first validate their emotions," Hurley says, by saying something like "That sounds really hard" or "That stinks." Then ask, "Is this a problem you think you can solve or is this a problem we need to endure? Are you looking for an answer or do you want help riding out the storm by talking you through it, guiding you through it, or just listening to you through it?"[25] (You'll have to adapt your language a bit if you're talking to a four-year-old or a six-year-old.)

There's no need to squash boys' hopes and dreams, either, no matter how unrealistic they seem to you. After mom Kristin Shaw realized that her reality-based responses to her tween son's stated desire to become a professional gamer were creating distance and distrust between them, she decided to try another approach. Following the advice of a friend, she started saying, "Wouldn't that be great?" when her son dreams aloud. The difference was remarkable.

Her son started daydreaming more—and taking creative action.

"He built a roller coaster for his stuffed animals in our living room. . . . He and my husband created a game with wood and power tools," Shaw wrote in a 2020 essay. "It's as if he started to bloom again, nurtured by rain and rich soil and someone to bathe him in sunlight instead of putting a blanket over him."[26]

Create a "Dad Plan" (or a "Mom Plan")

Don't worry—moms can make a plan, too.

A "Dad plan," as described by Maggie Dent (who coined the term while pondering ways to help fathers connect with their sons) is simply a plan you develop in conjunction with your son.[27] First set the stage: Talk to your son and say express your desire to connect. You can say something like, "I haven't been around much lately and I'm sorry. I want to be a good dad [or mom] to you." Or "I noticed we're not as close as we used to be, and I think I might be part of the reason." Then ask your son how you can be a better parent. Don't be surprised if he doesn't answer you immediately; most boys won't because they're not used to being asked for their opinion! Tell him he can think about it. Invite him to write down a few ideas and share them with you when he's ready. (If face-to-face conversations are tough for him, tell him he can leave a note on your desk or send you a text message.) Encourage him to go into detail—"go fishing with me," for instance, rather than "spend more time with me."

When you have your son's ideas, make a list of three things he'd like you to do. Commit to doing those three things during the next month. Also schedule a parent/son outing (perhaps a trip to get some chips? Or a picnic in a nearby park?) for month's end and encourage your son to review your progress.

Boys like being offered opportunities to express their thoughts and opinions, and most boys will be moved by the fact that you're committed to improving your relationship. Even resistant boys may eventually buy in after they see you putting in the effort.

Get creative if you'd like. Charlie Capen, the dad who learned to lean into his natural gifts, created a hilarious "parenting performance review" video featuring his then-barely-verbal son Finn assessing his performance as a dad, office style.[28] You could share the video with your son and then encourage him to offer you a performance review.

Offer Daily Warmth

Boys of all ages need physical and verbal affection. It's relatively easy to love little ones who clamor for your affection. It gets a bit harder as boys grow. The older they get, the less likely they are to ask for affection (thanks, gender pressure!), so it's vitally important that parents (and other caring adults) demonstrate tenderness and care every day. Something as simple as a fist bump and a smile shows your son that you see him, care about him, and—perhaps most importantly—like him.

A *Greater Good Magazine* article aimed at helping parents show love to teenagers says, "Offering . . . teens daily warmth that isn't conditional on their behavior can strengthen [your] relationship, especially in the face of conflict. That might mean offering a compliment or a hug or expressing empathy with whatever they're going through."[29]

Please note: boys most need warmth and affection when you probably feel least like giving it. When my son ignores my request, hurts someone else, or gets in serious trouble (via his own foolish decisions), I don't necessarily feel like hugging him. More often, I feel angry. And if he's yelled at me in anger? I feel angry, hurt, *and* resentful. My natural inclination in those moments is to ignore and shut out the person—in this case, my son—who's hurt me, so he can't hurt me anymore. And while that's an okay response in the moment, it's not healthy for me to withhold affection and support from my son. I can instead take time to soothe myself, establish and maintain personal boundaries (example: walk out of the room if cursing or physical threats occur), *and* connect with my son. I can offer him a silent hug or simply say, "I still love you."

Tween and teen boys will not always obviously appreciate (or even acknowledge) your gestures of affection. Remember: they've also been influenced by the mama's boy myth, and most are desperately trying to fit in with their peers. Boys' responses to parental affection generally have more to do with whatever is going on in their lives than in your relationship with them. Keep offering warmth, even if your efforts aren't noticably appreciated. Years from now, your son may thank you for your persistence.

Be Available

According to Danial J. Siegel and Tina Payne Bryson, authors of *The Power of Showing Up: How Parental Presence Shapes Who Our Kids Become and How Their Brains Get Wired*, parental presence helps kids feel safe, seen, soothed, and secure.

You've certainly been present in your son's life. By now, you've probably spent thousands of hours bathing and feeding him. You've bandaged his wounds, taught him to use the toilet, tucked him into bed, and wiped his tears. But there's a difference between physical presence and emotional presence, and our children require both. Being present, Siegel told the *Washington Post*, means being "receptive to moments to connect with your child, able to stay with them in the moment when they are feeling distressed and uncomfortable."[30]

You convey your willingness to connect by being available and responding when needed. It's easy to miss (or misread) boys' invitations to connect. A toddler who tackles you is looking for attention and interaction. A preschooler who proudly shows you the rocks and sticks he collected wants conversation and validation. And the tween who taps your shoulder or playfully punches your arm as he walks past is trying to connect. Acknowledging these bids for attention—by wrestling with the toddler, admiring the preschooler's rocks, and play punching or smiling at the teen—signifies your emotional availability. He's looking for consistent, steady responses, and when you respond more or less consistently in everyday interactions, he's more likely to approach you with the tough stuff.

Many parents (myself included) find it difficult to "be available" to tweens and teens who would rather be left alone or with their friends. Yet evidence suggests that backing away from our boys at this critical stage of development is exactly the wrong thing to do. Research has repeatedly shown powerful, positive links between parental presence and adolescent outcomes.[31] I adopted the "potted plant" technique outlined by clinical psychologist Lisa Damour, who wrote, "The quality parenting of a teenager may sometimes take the form of blending into the background like a potted plant."[32] For me, that frequently meant scrolling on my phone in the living room while my boys played video games. Or folding laundry in the dining room after supper. Often, the boys didn't interact with me at all during these moments. But the mere fact that I was present in a public part of the house signaled my availability, and sometimes we'd end up in conversation. Or watching silly YouTube videos together.

As your boys get older, being available may require you to bump back your bedtime. When puberty hits adolescents, their circadian rhythms shift, which is why most teens struggle to sleep any earlier than 11:00 p.m. (and struggle to get up in the morning!). Teenagers often come alive after 9:00 p.m., so you may find it beneficial to engage in "potted plant" activities until at least 10:00 p.m. or so.

Repair as Needed

You will hurt your son. In moments of anger and frustration, you will say or do something you'll later regret. Parents are human, too, and humans make mistakes.

Your mistakes are not a death knell for your relationship. In fact, how your handle your mistakes can be a powerful teaching tool.

"The key," says Tina Payne Bryson, coauthor of *The Power of Showing Up*, "is repair." When you realize you've messed up (and after you've calmed down), go to your child and make things right. Apologize if needed. As tempting as it may be, do not ignore what happened. It's better to own your mistakes and model responsibility and repair. When parents do so, "not only are we not damaging the relationship" but "building a deeper connection and intimacy" with our children, Bryson says.

"It's a real sign of strength to be able to say . . . 'What I did two minutes ago, I don't think that was a great way to go,'" says Siegel, Bryson's coauthor. "Instead of being weak, it teaches them how strong you are."[33]

I lost my temper on more than a few occasions and said words I regretted nearly as soon as they were out of my mouth. I've made plenty of parenting mistakes, but my relationships with my boys remains strong. My young adult sons are making their way in the world. Like Kate Stone Lombardi and her son, my boys and I continue to reap the benefits of a close relationship.

To build boys:

- *Reflect on when you last hugged your son.*
- *Schedule time to do something fun with your boy.*
- *Ask your son what he'd like to do with you.*
- *Apologize to your son when you lose your temper or overreact.*

9

⌒∞⌒

Connect Him to
the Real World

Nothing ever becomes real 'til it is experienced.

—John Keats

When Nathan was four years old, he wanted to sell dandelions. Dandelions. The sunny yellow blossoms that dot lawns and decorate sidewalk cracks. The endemic, easily accessible, freely available weeds that practically every preschooler has plucked and proudly presented to his parents.

When my son told me his plan, I almost said no. I mean, part of our jobs as parents is to acclimate our children to the real world, right? I was *this close* to explaining to him that people pay to get rid of dandelions; no one purchases them. But I saw the hope on my son's face and held my tongue.

I don't remember exactly how I responded. Maybe I shrugged. Smiled? Managed to mutter a couple vaguely supportive words while trying to temper his high hopes? Whatever I said, it wasn't *no*, and I'm so glad because that dandelion sale changed our lives.

I know that sounds dramatic but let me tell you what happened. Little Nathan scrawled a sign to advertise his wares: *Dandelion Sale 1 for 1¢. 6 for 5¢.* (The 6 was backward.) He set up a table in our front yard—which happened to be on one of two major streets in our small town—arranged his dandelions in vases, and waited.

People bought his dandelions! Someone even called our local newspaper editor—in a small town, a dandelion sale counts as news—and she showed up, interviewed my son, and took his photo. Nathan's photo ended up in the paper the following week, launching his reputation as an entrepreneur.

A few days after the sale, my son received a handwritten card in the mail. It contained a $5 bill. The sender said my son reminded her of her now-grown boys. She didn't stop the day of the sale because she didn't have any cash on hand but applauded his initiative.

Before he had even reached the kindergarten cutoff age, Nathan's emerging entrepreneurial instincts had not only been acknowledged but celebrated and encouraged. And though I didn't fully realize it at the time, the dandelion sale was his first big step beyond the confines of our family into the community.

Encouraged by his success, Nathan asked if he could sell vegetables at our local farmer's market. We didn't say yes immediately—he was four!—but when he was six, we relented. My best friend's mother, a former kindergarten teacher, regularly sold plants at the market and agreed to supervise Nathan during market hours. That summer, he spent nearly every Wednesday morning at the market, honing his math skills as he weighed produce, calculated prices, and made change. He developed customer service savvy and became quite adept at conversing with people of all ages. At home, he worked in the garden and prepared produce for market. He also tracked his income and expenses.

Most importantly, Nathan was living, working, and learning in the "real world," a term we adults use to refer to life outside school and the internet. Although he hadn't yet hit puberty, he was an engaged member of the community. He contributed to others' well-being via his presence and veggie sales, and he developed relationships with people who eagerly shared their interests and expertise with him.

Historically, boys' work was essential to the survival of their families and communities. Today, most boys spend their childhood and adolescence segregated from the larger community, supposedly developing the skills they'll one day need to become productive citizens. The first eighteen or so years of their lives are spent *preparing* to act, rather than actively engaging in service.

That's a mistake. Boys are hardwired to contribute. They *want* to do work that makes a difference. When we deny them those opportunities, we all lose. HundrED.org, a nonprofit working to improve K–12 education, notes that "Motivational issues occur when young people see little attachment between school and their outside lives," which is nice way of saying that kids (especially boys) tune out and stop trying when they realize that what they're being asked to do in school has absolutely no bearing on the real world.[1]

Michael Gurian, author of *The Minds of Boys, Saving Our Sons,* and *Raising Boys by Design,* has also noticed a link between boys' mental health and a lack of real-world activity.

"The more real life they have—including the tasks, relationships, and bonds they establish in *real life*—the less depressed they're like to be," Gurian says.[2]

Our communities also lose when our boys withdraw to their rooms. When they are not encouraged to share their gifts and talents, we miss important insights and ideas. Our boys can be—and want to be!—change makers, but we must first connect them to the real world.

BOYS WANT TO CONNECT AND CONTRIBUTE

Helpful and *kind* are two of the four adjectives that boys ages eight to fifteen most commonly use to describe themselves, according to *The State of America's Boys: An Urgent Case for a More Connected Boyhood,* a 2020 report from the Global Boyhood Initiative.[3] (The other two adjectives are *smart* and *outgoing*.) Not coincidentally, the three adjectives they use to describe a "good man" include *helpful, nice,* and *caring*.

If you have (or regularly interact with) an eight- to fifteen-year-old boy, you know that *helpful* and *kind* aren't always the first two words you'd choose to describe him. But the fact that boys consistently choose "helpful" as both a descriptor of themselves and of "good men" means that boys put tremendous value on being of service to others.

That claim may sound strange to you if you've just spent your morning trying to get your son to put his own cereal bowl into the dishwasher. Boys, particularly preteens and teens, can seem incredibly self-centered and selfish. Unlike little boys, who scamper to grab a broom or wrench so they can work alongside you, older boys often make themselves scarce when there's work to be done. But don't let them fool you: boys of all ages crave purposeful action.

"Boys want to feel as though they are needed to do some kind of important work," says Dr. Adam Cox, a psychologist and author of *Cracking the Boy Code: How to Understand and Talk with Boys*.[4]

By approximately age seven, most boys are aware of world problems and eager to get to work, says Rick Ackerly, a retired educator, father, and grandfather to five boys (and four girls).[5] "Kids come into the world pre-motivated," says Ackerly, author of *The Genius in Every Child: Encouraging Character, Curiosity, and Creativity in Children*.[6] "Each has their genius, almost like a little engine inside them, that's telling them to *do this, do that*. Often, when boys are getting in trouble in class, it's because they're chomping at the bit, just sitting there and having to absorb information when they really want to *do* stuff."

The work of boys and young men was once essential to the health, safety, and well-being of their communities. Throughout the world, boys and young men hunted, labored, and fought alongside their elders. A formal system of apprenticeship developed in what is now Europe during the late Middle Ages, with young boys (usually ages ten to fifteen) serving as sources of cheap labor for master craftsmen who, in return, taught the boys their trade.

The system, of course, was not perfect. Apprentices were sometimes (often?) abused. In the early days of the United States, enslaved Black boys were forced to labor. Poor boys who worked to support their families often did so in unsafe conditions. (Think kiddy coal miners and textile workers.) Even into the twentieth century, many boys infrequently attended school because their skills and muscles were required to keep families safe, warm, and fed. My father, born in 1936, was the first of his siblings to graduate from high school because he grew up in a time and place where boys' labor on the farm was necessary to sustain the family.

Child labor laws were eventually passed to protect children from exploitation and unsafe working conditions; these laws are also intended to ensure that work doesn't jeopardize children's educational opportunities.[7]

But when school became the focus of children's lives, children became separated from the daily lives of their communities. Kids today no longer regularly interact with people of varying ages, and adults no longer rely on them to complete essential work. Instead, children spend most of their hours—most of the first two decades of their lives, in fact—completing tasks designed to prepare them to *eventually* contribute to their communities. (In 1934, psychologist and educational reformer John Dewey said that "The purpose of education has always been . . . to give the young the things they need in order to develop in an orderly, sequential way into members of society."[8] In 1957, the Association for Supervision and Curriculum Development stated that "The main purpose of the American school is to provide for the fullest development of each learner for living morally, creatively, and productively in a democratic society,"[9] and today, nearly every K–12 school in the United States is laser-focused on college and career readiness.[10])

Kids, however, still want to be part of the wider world. Given access to both a toy and "real" version of a tool (say, a hammer, lawn mower, or broom), almost all children gravitate toward the real thing. That's because "their real interests lie in the real world," says preschool teacher Tom Hobson.[11] His colleague, John Yiannoudis, founder of the Dorothy Snot preschool and kindergarten, notes that "What children really need is to discover the world," and he encourages parents and educators to put meaningful activity at the center of children's lives.[12]

Boys who do not have the opportunity to engage in meaningful activity often act out, disconnect, or shut down.

BUT THERE'S PLENTY FOR HIM TO DO!

The apparent disconnect between boys' innate desire to contribute and their lack of enthusiasm for chores or work boils down to two words: *important work*. (Emphasis on *important*.)

Remember: boys want to feel as though they are needed to do some kind of important work, according to Dr. Adam Cox. They want to do work that is important to them, to the welfare of others, or to the world.

Instead of focusing on getting your son to do things that are important to you, help him do things that matter to him. Encourage him to use his skills and talents to tackle a problem that's relevant to his interests.

⟨∞⟩

UNUSED ABILITIES LEACH
MOTIVATION AND LIMIT GROWTH

In most modern societies today, it is possible for a child to reach adulthood without ever having done something upon which someone else depends.

That might be good preparation for today's highly individualistic American culture, but it's not necessarily healthy. The journal *Nature Human Behaviour* notes that "human beings are a social species that relies on cooperation to survive and thrive."[13] We are intended to be interdependent, to rely upon one another's labor, skill, and support. We often do our best when others are counting on us. That's as true for our children as it is for us adults.

So many boys, Ackerly says, "are suffocating in their unused abilities." Without opportunities to test their skills, ideas, and initiatives in the real world, they stagnate.

Jacob Navarro stopped trying in high school. Actually, his efforts (and grades) began declining after elementary school. The former A and B student got his first C in middle school, and by the time he got to high school, he decided simply passing classes was good enough.

"The main reason my friends and family wanted me to get good grades was so I could go to college," Jacob says. "But I really did not want to go to college."

School offered nothing of interest to Jacob—no opportunities to stretch or test his skills in the real world. So he spent most of his freshman year (and planned to spend the rest of high school) waiting for his compulsory education to end so he'd finally be free to explore.

That's a waste of time and talent—both Jacob's and his teachers'. It's also potentially dangerous. We now know that boys who are disengaged from their schools and communities are at increased risk for social exclusion, risky health behaviors (including substance use), unemployment, criminal activity, and suicide.[14] Those who are disconnected from the community at large are more likely to join gangs or extremist organizations.[15] And nearly every mass shooter to date has been a young man who felt like a loser and needed to prove himself.[16] Boys who do not have a role or who do not feel valued by their communities sometimes seek to make a mark in devastating ways.

Thankfully, only a tiny minority of disenfranchised boys commit horrific acts of violence. Far more commonly, such boys languish in plain sight. A 2015 report that examined the experiences of children in Western Australia found that 25 percent of fifteen-year-olds said that school has not prepared them for life; 10 percent said school is a "waste of time."[17] The report didn't break down results by gender, but I'm willing to bet that many (if not most) of those who didn't see value in school and declared it a waste of time were boys.

Though they may not say so directly, boys want to be an integral part of their communities. They don't want busywork and they don't want to take on superfluous tasks. When boys know their efforts don't really matter, they're not likely to exert much effort. In fact, they may not try at all. Or they may direct their energies in less-than-useful directions.

Often, we unwittingly make things worse.

"The way that we deal with misbehaving boys the world over is to ratchet down on their freedoms. We take away freedom and privileges," says Dr. Cox, who recommends what he calls a counter-intuitive approach.[18]

"I think that we should instead try to get them to ally themselves with us by giving them an important job," he says.

Research supports Dr. Cox's idea. Work by Dr. Daniel Offer, a psychiatrist who specialized in adolescence, and Dr. Kimberly A. Schonert-Reichl, an applied developmental psychologist, has found that children are far more competent than most adults think—and that "the more opportunities for decision-making that children are given, the better they are able to exercise informed choices."[19]

In contrast, when we restrict kids' opportunities, we set in motion a "self-fulfilling cycle. . . . Kids learn helplessness, understand their decisions can be easily over-ruled by adults, become reluctant to even make decisions, and finally lash out in frustration."[20]

When boys know that others are counting on them, though—that their effort is important to their family or community in some way—they will stretch, persevere, and often manage to accomplish things that even they thought might have been beyond their reach.

BARRIERS TO BOYS' INVOLVEMENT IN THE REAL WORLD

The modern world is created for the convenience and comfort of adults, not children. Since the lives of children and adults diverged in the early twentieth century, children now spend most of their time in institutional settings with similarly aged peers, and adults spend their time in the community, effectively running society. This age-related division of labor has been codified into systems and structures that make it difficult for children to engage in the real world. Compulsory education, child labor laws, municipal curfews, and local ordinances that require children under certain ages to be supervised at all times limit children's opportunities in the community.

Though created to protect children from harm, such broad guidelines may also inhibit growth and development, as most ordinances and laws don't consider the capabilities and circumstances of individual children.

"Many young people who want to make a go of their lives . . . are blocked at many turns and so give up," noted Professor Tanya Byron, a clinical psychologist and founding chancellor of England's Edge Hill University. "Blocked by an education system that narrows the definition of achievement . . . blocked by a society that discriminates against youth and so reduces the participation of upcoming generations in the development of the social and cultural landscape."[21]

Harmful stereotypes and prejudice also limit boys' involvement. Teenagers are commonly viewed as apathetic, self-indulgent, and uninterested in civic activities.[22] Boys of all ages are considered unpredictable, impulsive, and potentially destructive. Older boys are perceived as dangerous; Black boys and teenagers are often assumed to be troublemakers or criminals.[23] Due in part to stereotypes that portray teenage boys as irresponsible and sex crazed, some community organizations, churches, camps, schools, and parents are reluctant to allow boys to work with children.[24] Adult misunderstanding of autism, attention deficit hyperactivity disorder (ADHD), and other behavioral and learning challenges further complicate matters for many boys.

Ephebiphobia—extreme fear of teenagers—plays a role as well. Though most people are not pathologically fearful of adolescents, a general distrust of teens permeates society. Young people (especially boys) often encounter adults who seem to go out of their way to avoid them (say, by crossing the street). Shopkeepers and citizens carefully monitor boys' actions, assuming the children intend to steal, damage, or otherwise create chaos.

These factors collectively restrict boys' contributions, yet society is quick to blame boys for their supposed lack of drive and desire.

"We label children as troublemakers or failures," Professor Byron says, "because, as a society, we often fail to see their potential."

REAL-WORLD EXPERIENCES HELP BOYS BLOSSOM

Urie Bronfenbrenner, a child psychologist who served as professor emeritus of human development and psychology at Cornell University, believed that child involvement in the community could decrease antisocial behavior. In a 2005 paper, Bronfenbrenner "proposed a two-part solution to problems of alienation and anti-social behavior:

- Involve adults directly in the life space of children, rather than warehousing students in stockade schools or letting peer groups dominate youth development.
- Involve youth in finding solutions to problems, rather than having them grow up disengaged from the community, without ever making contributions to others."[25]

In other words, allowing boys to solve real-world problems alongside adults may decrease the number of disengaged, apathetic, antisocial boys. That, in turn, could decrease crime and juvenile delinquency, freeing up dollars that could be invested in programs to sustain youth engagement.

Real-world experiences also have been shown to increase learning. One (unsurprising) study found that four- to nine-year-old children who participated in a hands-on zoo camp dramatically increased their ability to classify animals and connect bits of information. "Children didn't just learn piecemeal facts," the lead researcher said. "They learned how different birds such as ostriches and ducks are related to each other even when they look very different or live in different habitats. . . . This kind of knowledge organization helps children retrieve what they have learned from memory. It helps them reason . . . and helps them integrate new information."[26]

A child who has seen and experienced the behavior of a penguin, for instance, is much better equipped to note similarities and differences in the behavior of a robin because real-world, first-hand experiences are multisensory. Someone who has seen, heard, smelled, and maybe even touched a penguin has a visceral—and much deeper—understanding of what a penguin is than someone who only reads or hears about penguins.

Children who use their skills in real-world settings may learn more quickly, as they must adapt their actions as necessary to achieve desired outcomes. Real-world experiences can increase a child's sense of belonging and boost their self-confidence. And according to the Australian Research Alliance for Children and Youth, young people who engage in meaningful activities in their communities experience a better quality of life in the here and now, as well as good physical and mental health in adulthood.[27]

Jacob's life started trending positively when his mother suggested he enroll in the video game design program at the regional occupational center (ROC) in Bakersfield, California. Jacob has always loved games; in fact, he doesn't remember life without video games. ("My youngest memories were going to LAN parties with my dad," he says.) Though Jacob initially resisted the idea, he signed up during his sophomore year—largely to please his mom. As part of the game design cohort, he attended game design classes at the ROC in the morning and returned to his home high school for core class in the afternoon.

A few months into the program, Jacob "started to actually enjoy it," he says. He downloaded the game design tools he learned about in class and started working on projects at home. "I practiced on my own pretty much every day," he says, "even on weekends."

The kid who didn't care about school didn't magically start exerting extra effort in his other classes. But he found a passion, and after a year of video game design class (and working on his own at home), he started applying for game design gigs he found online. At first, he set his fee at $10 an hour because he knew that he was less skilled and experienced than many people. No one hired him. Jacob raised his price to $25 an hour and started getting jobs. Each job he did expanded his skills and experience. He updated his portfolio and raised his rates accordingly. Within a few months, Jacob was earning $40 to $45 an hour (and sometimes working on game design projects instead of homework).

He graduated high school in 2021 and was hired at age nineteen by Amazon Games.

His future plans?

"I want to start my own game studio," says Jacob, who was living at home when I interviewed him and is saving most of his salary to make his dream come true.

Like Jacob, my son Nathan, the dandelion entrepreneur, grew via his real-world experiences. Motivated by his success selling dandelions and veggies—and fueled by the connections and reputation he earned while doing those two jobs—Nathan started a lawn-mowing business at age eleven. Soon after, he added snow removal. He mowed lawns, shoveled snow, and did odd jobs for dozens of clients throughout middle and high school. His love of music and theater led to performances with community theater groups, choirs, and singing-and-dancing troupes, and these experiences, in turn, connected him with formal and informal mentors who helped him hone his skills and pointed him toward additional opportunities.

Nathan ultimately earned a degree in music business. He put himself through college by cutting lawns.

Before graduating high school, both Jacob and Nathan undertook work that was important to others. Their tasks weren't "made up" or artificial; other people relied on their labor. As a result, both boys learned how to suss out and meet others' expectations. They developed negotiation and time management skills. They also realized that they're valuable to other people.

There's no substitute for that kind of experience.

HELPING BOYS CONNECT TO THE REAL WORLD

There are all kinds of ways to help your son forge connections in the real world. There are also a lot of ways to inadvertently irritate your son and inhibit his initiative.

Scratch any ideas of "making" your boy volunteer or get a job. Don't sign him up for Scouts (or any other activity) unless you are sure that said activity is something he wants to do. Forcing boys into work or community service is almost never effective.

"If a parent cares about something more than the child, it absolves the child of responsibility," Ackerly says. A parent who is set on finding their son a mentor, for instance, is likely to soon be the parent of a son who spends zero time looking for someone who can help him develop his skills. In fact, the son might shut down all together.

Restrain your enthusiasm. When your boy expresses an interest in airplanes and flight, don't immediately sign him up for space camp or flight lessons. Instead, watch and observe. Check out a book about planes from the library, perhaps, and leave it lying around. Stock up on paper or cardstock if you see him making paper airplanes, but resist the urge to arrange a meeting between him and the local guy you know who built his own plane. Instead, casually mention that you know someone who built a plane. If your son asks a bunch of questions or expresses an interest in meeting the plane builder or seeing his plane, *then* schedule a get-together.

Facilitate rather than direct. Whenever possible, let your son lead. Every community contains a wealth of opportunities for real-world connections. For example, consider the following.

Jobs

In the United States, children as young as age fourteen can begin formal employment.[28] However, boys don't have to wait until age fourteen to undertake jobs for money. Many people would love to hire a motivated young man to cut their grass, pull weeds, walk the dog, clean the garage, or babysit (or entertain) younger kids.

Think outside the box—and encourage your son to do so as well. Does he have a unique or desirable skill? Perhaps he could teach it to others. I know a mom who once hired a slightly older boy to play catch and practice baseball skills with her young son. The son was passionate about baseball and wanted to improve, but he didn't want to practice with his parents. The arrangement worked well for both boys.

Get creative if necessary. My son Sam occasionally sells snowmobile and dirt bike parts that he doesn't need anymore. (By age fifteen, he figured that he could make more money selling a used snowmobile in parts than as a whole machine.) He finds willing customers in online groups frequented by others who work on snowmobiles and dirt bikes, but because Sam is a minor and legally unable to maintain a PayPal account, I allow him to use mine (with my direct supervision) to send and receive funds.

Teenage boys who don't enjoy or aren't doing well in school may benefit from a job. Your instinct might be to direct your son to focus more attention on his studies but allowing (or encouraging) him to seek employment can pay unexpected dividends. Some research even indicates that economically disadvantaged Black and Hispanic youth who work during high school are less likely to drop out than those who only attend school.[29]

Liesl Garner's son started working in a warehouse when he was fifteen years old. "It gave him the boost he needed," Liesl says. "Working with people who were older than him, who complimented his work ethic, allowed him to thrive in an area outside of school, which, in turn, I think helped his communication skills and confidence."

Buoyed by his success at work, Liesl's son worked harder at school and his grades improved. He's continued his employment after graduation and plans work his way up the corporate ladder.

Personal Passions

A deep interest in anything can lead any- and everywhere. Got a kid who loves to perform? Look for community theater opportunities. Got a son who's fascinated with bugs or concerned about climate change? Together, investigate citizen science opportunities. When Tyler was deep into his butterfly stage, we helped scientists and other butterfly aficionados track the monarch butterfly migration through Journey North (https://journeynorth.org). (You can also monitor and learn about hummingbird, robin, and songbird migrations via Journey North.) Project Noah (www.projectnoah.org) encourages citizen scientists to upload photos of wildlife in their natural habitat; participants can earn patches (similar to Scout badges) for their contributions.

Science fiction and literature fans have lots of opportunities to create connections via their interests as well. Fandom Forward (https://fandomforward.org) helps fans of all ages tackle real-life challenges. The organization, which was formerly known as the Harry Potter Alliance (and showed members how they, like Harry and his friends, can make "a real difference in this world"[30]) has activities and options for *Star Wars*, Pokemon, Avatar fans, and others. The Avatar toolkit, for instance, encourages fans to think about gender roles, experiment with different forms of self-care, and connect with organizations helping refuges.[31]

Not quite sure how to link your son's interest to real-world activities? Ask him and others to brainstorm with you. When Leah Beatty asked a group of fellow "boy parents" to suggest some new ideas for her sixteen-year-old son who loves to grow plants (and was running out of room in the backyard!), they delivered dozens of great recommendations, including helping at community gardens, propagating and selling houseplants, participating in native gardening projects, joining a local garden club, and enrolling in a Master Gardener program.

VIRTUAL CONNECTIONS CAN LEAD
TO REAL-WORLD EXPERIENCES

Online activity is not a waste of time.

My mechanically minded, snowmobile- and dirt-bike-loving kid learned how to fix machines by watching YouTube videos. He connected with other snowmobile and dirt bike enthusiasts in online forums; they swapped stories and shared tips. Relationships forged online evolved into in-person friendships. Bolstered by their shared enthusiasm, the boys plan meetups and compete against (and cheer for) one another at area races. Together, they continue to refine their skills.

Volunteering

Nearly every charitable and nonprofit organization could use some extra help. The Humane Society, for instance, welcomes children as "Critter Cuddlers," "Feline Friends," and animal assistants.[32] Many organizations (including the Humane Society) require would-be volunteers to complete an application and undergo training;

some require parental or caregiver participation as well. You'll also probably have to fill out a liability waiver.

These hoops are worth the effort. Remember, your goal is to help your son connect with others in the community. It may seem time consuming and tedious to research volunteer opportunities and fill out paperwork, but your son will appreciate your efforts. (He can help too! Encourage him to complete as much of the paperwork as he can independently. It's great training for adult life.)

If your son has unique skills, think about which populations and organizations might appreciate his talents. Local nursing homes sometimes showcase vocalists and musicians; their residents enjoy performances by young people. Don't ignore opportunities close to home either. Boys who enjoy cooking can prepare meals for busy parents or people recovering from surgery. (Don't know anyone who needs help? A local church may be able to point you to people in need.)

Fifteen-year-old Andrii Pokrasa, a drone enthusiast, helped the Ukrainian military protect Kyiv from advancing Russian troops in early 2022. When his father realized that Ukrainian fighters were desperate to learn the precise location of troops and tanks closing in on the city, he told local defenders that his son might be able to help. The local fighters "provided us information where approximately the Russian column cold be," Andrii told *Global News*.[33] He used his drone to surveil the area and shared the GPS coordinates of the approaching convoy with the Ukrainian military.

Hopefully, your son will never need to use his skills to defend your home. Andrii's story reminds us, though, that humans of all ages possess skills that are useful to the community at large. You can help link your son to those who may need his service.

Clubs and Organizations

Boy Scouts, 4-H, and interest-specific clubs (robotics team, Legos club . . . the possibilities are nearly infinite) allow kids to interact with, and learn from others. Many youth-focused clubs also include ample leadership development. My oldest son was elected by his peers to serve as reporter of his 4-H club when he was ten years old. This position required him to attend an officer training program and submit written reports of club activities to our local newspaper. Through his involvement in 4-H, he also participated in countywide public speaking contests and theatrical competitions.

Boy Scouts also offers formal and informal leadership opportunities. Walter, the boy from chapter 4 who sold pocketknives to cover the cost of scout camp, was only ten years old when he somewhat reluctantly attended his first overnight scout campout. His confidence soared, though, when he discovered he had skills that some of the older scouts did not. The teenagers charged with making breakfast were burning the pancakes, so Walter—who started making pancakes with his mother when he was five—asked if he could help. When his mom Brittany arrived to pick him up, the boys told her, "Walter saved breakfast! We're glad he's part of our troop!"

Chris Singer honed his project management and leadership skills while working toward Eagle Scout recognition. His Eagle Scout project entailed building a shed for a church, which required him to obtain building permits, solicit donations, and organize and direct helpers of all ages.

Though Chris has since earned a degree in business administration, his mother, Jen, still describes his Eagle Scout experience as "the best management training" because her son learned at a young age how to deal with different personalities and work habits.

Such practical experiences allow boys to earn recognition and respect, which in turn build authentic self-confidence. Boys who help others—and see the positive impact their actions have on other people—are motivated to continue to serve others. Active participation in clubs broadens your son's social circle as well, exposing him to diverse perspectives, personalities, and possibilities. Regular interaction with people who appreciate and share his interests can also be a literal lifesaver for a boy who feels rejected by his classmates.

Career Technical Education and Apprenticeships

Increasingly, schools are recognizing the value of real-world experiences. That's why many states and school districts are developing career technical education (CTE) programs and youth apprenticeships. These programs give students opportunities to explore career paths, develop skills, gain work experience, and earn certifications (and, in some cases, money) while still in high school.

Jacob, the young video game designer, enrolled in one such program. California, his home state, has invested significant resources into building CTE programs. The state offers at least fifteen different CTE pathways, including agriculture and natural resources; arts, media, and entertainment (video game design falls under this pathway); building and construction trades; engineering and architecture; business and finance; and information and communication technologies.[34] These programs are not a "dumping ground" for failing or uninterested students, as some vocational education programs were in years past. They are robust educational offerings that include hands-on experience with industry-standard technology—a terrific opportunity for experiential learners.

Westley, a Colorado high school student, is one such learner. He was a sophomore in high school when he approached his parents about applying for a CareerWise youth apprenticeship, a program modeled after the phenomenally successful Swiss apprenticeship program. Westley's parents were thrilled ("It was the first time he'd shown some sort of initiative," his mother told me)—and a bit cautious, as they have no experience with, well, experiential high school education.

A CareerWise liaison at Westley's school helped them understand the program, which includes paid work experience (for which students earn high school credits) and weekly mentoring with industry professionals. As a youth apprentice, Westley worked as a project estimator for a construction company approximately twelve hours a week throughout his junior year. He'll put in additional hours (and continue developing his skills) while he completes his senior year of high school; after graduation, he'll work full time as an apprentice for another year. Then he can decide if he wants to pursue additional formal education or if he'd prefer to continue employment.

Your local high school can tell you more about CTE and apprenticeship opportunities in your area. Your son may have more hands-on learning opportunities in school than mine ever did, as the proposed 2023 federal budget included a $200 million investment in career-connected high schools, an initiative intended to provide increased work-based educational options.[35]

CONNECTING BOYS TO THE COMMUNITY
MAY DECREASE IMPLICIT BIAS

Because boys (and girls) are usually cooped up in school, positive, meaningful interactions between boys and other members of the community are relatively rare. News stories about boys behaving badly are not. No wonder so many people harbor negative ideas about boys and young men!

When we link our boys to the community, we give others the opportunity to know them as human beings. And when people get to know our sons, they may also see the potential and promise imbued in each of our boys. They may recognize the many ways in which gender stereotypes inhibit young men and hurt our communities and may join us in the work of building boys.

To build boys:

- *Reflect on whether your son currently does anything upon which others rely.*
- *Help your son find ways to use his skills and talents in the community.*
- *Investigate real-world learning opportunities at your son's school.*

10

⌒∞⌒

Accept Him as He Is

To be fully seen by somebody, then, and be loved anyhow—
this is a human offering that can border on miraculous.

—Elizabeth Gilbert

Jeremy found his son's love of Barbie dolls endearing—at first.

The dolls seemed to remind four-year-old Nixon of his mother. Nixon even called his favorite one "mommy doll" because it had long, blond tresses, just like his beloved mom. No wonder Noah was crazy about Elsa, the blond heroine in the hit Disney movie *Frozen*!

Dressing up like Elsa, though? Jeremy felt uncomfortable seeing his son in a frilly princess dress, but his wife told him not to worry. Jeremy held his tongue and tried to ignore his discomfort as his son's dress collection grew. He hoped Nixon would soon grow out of this stage.

Then Nixon flat-out refused to remove his princess gown before heading to a playdate. A "massive fight" ensued, Jeremy said, and he wrestled the dress off his sobbing, screaming son. All for naught, really, because when Jeremy picked his son up from the friend's house later that day, Nixon met him at the door wearing a dress, wig, and makeup, with a Barbie doll in each hand.

"I was so embarrassed," Jeremy says. "I wondered what his friend's parents thought about him, what they thought about me as a parent. And then I thought about the potential of kids making fun of my son. Worst of all, I caught myself thinking, 'why can't he just be normal? Why can't I have a boy who wants to be like me and play sports?'"

A boy who plays sports, Jeremy knew, is much less likely to be bullied in school than one who wears dresses. So a few nights later, after tucking Nixon into bed, Jeremy gathered up the boy's dolls, dresses, and wigs and threw them all away.

"I told myself it would be better for him," Jeremy says, "that he'd be fine within a couple of days."

Nixon wasn't fine. He was angry. He told his dad to "Go away!" and lashed out aggressively.

Jeremy hoped things would settle down while he was out of town on business. He couldn't stop thinking about his son, though, and discussed the situation with a mentor, who looked him straight in the eyes and asked one simple question: 'What are you afraid of?'"

"I'm afraid he might get made fun of," Jeremy replied.

"What else?"

"That people think I'm a bad parent."

"What else?"

"That he might think he's a girl. That he wants to be a girl."

Then his mentor asked, "What if all those fears come true? Would you still love him?"

Of course! Jeremy thought. And then a realization crashed into his consciousness: tossing his son's treasured toys in the trash probably didn't look much like love.

With tears in his eyes, Jeremy responded: "I want my son to know that I love him and accept him as he is and that I will always be there for him, no matter what."

Like many parents, Jeremy found it difficult to accept his son as is. His fierce love for his son included a powerful desire to protect the boy from harm, and he was afraid that accepting Nixon's interest in dolls, dresses, and makeup would increase the boy's vulnerability to bullying. Jeremy was so focused on preventing future pain that he was blind to the harm he was causing in the present. After realizing that his actions were driving a wedge in his relationship with his child, Jeremy decided to make a change. When he returned home, Jeremy apologized to his son and wife. Then father and son headed to the store to buy an Elsa dress.

WHY ACCEPTANCE IS IMPORTANT FOR BOYS

Parental acceptance is key to boys' emotional and physical health.

A 2019 cross-national study found that high levels of parental acceptance predicted increased prosocial behavior by children. Kids who experienced warmth and affection were more likely to help, share with, and demonstrate caring behaviors toward others. In contrast, children of parents who ignored them or acted annoyed by their presence were more likely to display aggressive behavior.[1]

The link between parental acceptance and children's psychological health or dysfunction is so strong that the authors of another 2019 article describe it as "a kind of natural law."[2] Worldwide, children who feel accepted by their parents tend to fare well.[3] Children who do not feel accepted are prone to maladjustment, conduct disorders, poor academic performance, decreased self-esteem, and decreased satisfaction with interpersonal relationships. There's even evidence to show that parental rejection (the opposite, of course, of acceptance) increases a child's risk for substance abuse.[4]

REJECTION HURTS—LITERALLY

The pain of rejection is very real.

Our brains and bodies respond to perceived emotional rejection and physical pain in almost exactly the same way. Both increase inflammation and the flow of stress hormones like cortisol. And both increase activity in the anterior cingulate cortex, the part of the brain involved in emotion, impulse control, and decision making, and the right ventricular prefrontal cortex, which affects empathy.[5]

A psychological theory dating back to the 1960s posits that children who feel emotionally or physically rejected by their parents may "close off emotionally in an effort to protect themselves from the hurt of further rejection." This tendency to restrict emotional reaction and involvement can persist into adulthood and may negatively affect the individual's ability to form and maintain relationships. Some people who experience parental rejection as children become "defensively independent"—they capably manage their personal business without asking for support or validation, but continue to crave approval, warmth, and support. They may not recognize or acknowledge their emotional needs and may be quick to anger when confronted with stressful situations.[6]

If you're thinking right now, "wow, that sounds like a lot of guys," you're right. The stereotypical go-it-alone, I-don't-need-close-friends man may well be the result of actual or perceived parental rejection. Unfortunately, parents in years past were often *advised* to push their sons away. My maternal great-grandmother almost certainly based her parenting, at least in part, on the advice contained in a prayer book she treasured. The book, *Mother Love: A Manual for Christian Mothers*, cautions that, "Among boys, in particular, we . . . find a certain spirit of independence which brooks no restraint, an ambition that tolerates no rivalry, and a coarseness of feeling that borders on brutality. All these qualities are evidences of a hard heart and must be corrected with a firm hand; and, if no improvement is observed, mother and father should even resort to severe corporal punishment."[7] A few pages later, the book states, "It is also necessary to make the child feel humiliation. This may be done by showing preference to its brothers and sisters, by being brief and curt, by disregarding its advances, by isolating it from the others, and by other minor humiliations."

There may well be a straight line between this style of parenting—characterized by deliberate parental rejection—and my maternal grandfather's eventual death from alcoholism. And from him to my mother's inability to recognize or accept emotions and my tendency to contort my actions to fit the needs and desires of those around me.

If we want our boys to grow into healthy, resilient men who know themselves and respect the emotions, needs, and boundaries of others, we must accept and love them unconditionally. We cannot withhold our affection and mete it out only when they please us. We cannot let our ideas of who our boys "should be" get in the way of loving them as they are.

Today's boys desperately need acceptance. Recent public discourse around manhood and masculinity has tended toward the negative; young boys (and some older ones) may believe that the term "toxic masculinity" implies there's something inherently toxic about being male. In response to near-constant criticism of their behavior, interests, and preferred means of expression, many boys subconsciously conclude that they're "wrong."

Dr. Thomas Gordon, a three-time Nobel peace prize nominee and author of *Parent Effectiveness Training*, once wrote that "Whether a child feels that *she as a person* is unaccepted will be determined by how many of her behaviors are unacceptable."[8]

Dr. Gordon used the pronoun *she* in that sentence but mentally change it to *he* and consider most boys' experiences in the modern world. From early on, they are told to *shhhh!*, to *settle down!*, and to *stop!* At parks and playgrounds, boys who chase and tackle one another are asked to "use their words" or "find another game." Boys who pick up sticks and initiate sword fights are often swiftly redirected; some well-meaning adults even snatch the sticks out boys' hands. Boys like Nixon, who love dresses and princesses, are nudged toward "more acceptable" interests or encouraged to pursue their passion in private. Tween and teenage boys who love video games are viewed as "lazy" and "unmotivated"; those who love dance often face bullying and physical aggression.

Boys, Michael Reichert wrote in his book *How to Raise a Boy*, "are vulnerable to feeling inadequate because they are shamed constantly."[9] If you were a young boy, would you feel accepted, as is? Or would you feel like a disappointment or annoyance?

Parental rejection can lead to:

- antisocial behavior
- negative self-image
- problems with emotional regulation
- difficulty with relationships

Parental acceptance leads to:

- healthy self-esteem
- self-competence
- emotional regulation
- healthy interpersonal relationships

⟨∞⟩

WHY ACCEPTING OUR BOYS IS SO DIFFICULT

Whether we admit it to ourselves or not, we all have an idea of who we'd like our boys to be. Some of us want athletic sons; some, compassionate, creative artists. Most of us want respectful boys who do their homework, keep their rooms clean, and generally listen to us and follow our advice and directives.

And that, in most cases, is *not* what we get. Our sons are messy, complex humans, just like we are. They don't always agree with us and often rebel against our advice and example. It can be exceedingly difficult to fully and freely accept a son whose behavior is in direct opposition to our dreams, values, and example.

Many of us believe that it's our duty to correct our sons. After all, it's a parent's job to shape their children's behavior, right?

Yes. We're supposed to socialize our children and teach them the customs of our societies. That's why we introduce small spoons into our babies' chubby hands and why we instruct our preschoolers to say "please" and "thank you."

Shaping our kids' behavior, however, does not require us to constantly criticize or nitpick. We don't need to comment every time our boys do something we'd rather they didn't. We don't need to express disdain or disappointment when their choices don't align with ours. We can calmly reiterate our family rules and values and continue to model the behavior we'd like our sons to emulate. We can also question and expand our definitions of "acceptable" behavior. (We'll get into this later in this chapter, in "Tackling Social Norms—Together.")

Many adults from previous generations believed that accepting children "as is" would decrease motivation and result in adults who lack direction and adequate social skills.[10] You might subconsciously still hold this belief. After all, it seems entirely reasonable that unconditionally accepting a boy who scatters his dirty socks and empty food wrappers all over the floor might lead to a man who leaves his laundry and food wrappers all over the floor.

It can be hard to differentiate between accepting the child and approving (or disapproving) of his behavior. Saying something like,

"You're so lazy! You never pick up after yourself!" is *not* accepting; those harsh words carry a negative value judgment. In contrast, calmly saying, "I see you didn't pick up your room" or "You need to put your socks in the hamper" draws attention to the behavior you hope to change without conveying disapproval that your son might interpret as disappointment in *him*.

I know—it's often difficult to remain calm in the face of boys' or any child's, behavior. Our boys aren't always easy to love. Psychologists who study parental acceptance have noted that "one should not overlook the effect of children's emotional adjustment on the behavior of their parents. . . . Violent behavior would, in turn, feed maternal and paternal criticism and rejection."[11]

It is normal and natural to pull away from a child who is yelling, swearing, threatening, or damaging things. We're human, too, and our instincts compel us to move away from violence. That's productive and healthy. Accepting your boy does not require tolerating abuse. Accepting your son—while respecting yourself—sometimes means protecting yourself physically and emotionally without condemning your son. It means revisiting the moment after the drama has subsided to clarify that you love your son but will not allow yourself (or anyone else) to remain in harm's way.

If you have a son with attention deficit hyperactivity disorder (ADHD), autism, or another physical or emotional challenge, your support and acceptance are absolutely vital to his sense of self-worth, as he's more likely than his peers to experience rejection in the community at large.

Debbie Reber, founder of TiLT Parenting, offers four tips for parents of neurodiverse or physically challenged kids:[12]

1. *Process and accept your child's diagnosis.* "When you're fighting your child's true identity, you can't support him," Reber writes.
2. *Parent from a place of possibility, not fear.* Focus on what your child can do.
3. *Help your child embrace self-discovery.* Encourage your child to explore his gifts and preferences.
4. *Shift your mindset, thoughts, and actions.* Parent the child you have—not the one you thought you'd have.

TACKLING SOCIAL NORMS—TOGETHER

Accepting a boy as is can be challenging for adults who are acutely aware of the physical and psychological dangers a boy faces in the world. Adults who know that dressing or behaving in certain ways exposes boys to ridicule, bullying, and physical aggression may feel a responsibility to warn the child—or to modify his behavior—so the boy can avoid pain.

But despite good intentions, real damage can occur when adults try to contort boys' behavior to meet existing social norms. Boys lose trust in adults who ask them to behave in ways that are contrary to their character. Relationships rupture, as Jeremy discovered. Boys begin to doubt their natural inclinations, which can lead to a lifetime of self-doubt and sever their connection to their intuition. Finally, adult attempts to shape boys' behavior to current norms may hinder boys' ability to flourish in a society that's rapidly changing. The rigid expectations you grew up with are slowly (and, in some places, rapidly) giving way to a more tolerant, flexible understanding and expression of gender.

However, you can't ignore social conventions. The truth is, your son *may* face bullying or criticism if he dresses, acts, or behaves in ways that are out of step with the norm.

Brian Gresko, a Brooklyn-based dad, found himself struggling with his conflicting desires to support his son's self-expression and protect him from harm. When his then seven-year-old son "asked if he could get a dress, just like Mommy," Brian—a man who uses the pronouns *he* and *they* and often wears eye makeup—was a bit surprised by his emotional reaction.

"I imagined him coming home from first grade, pale cheeks blotched with tears, his ego hurt by taunts, and his confidence in me weakened: 'Why didn't you warn me I'd get picked on, Dad?'" Brian wrote in an essay. "To not directly address issues of gender stereotypes with him at this point felt irresponsible."[13]

You can—and should!—discuss possible peer and public reactions to nonconforming behavior with your son in age-appropriate terms. For a seven-year-old, this might sound like, "Some people still think it's weird or strange to see a boy or man in a dress. Some people might laugh or stare or say mean things." You can pause then and give your son a chance to respond; chances are, he's aware of the peer pressure he faces on a daily basis and hearing his thoughts can help you tailor your response.

Brian carefully discussed the issue with his son. "I didn't want him to feel like he was doing something wrong by desiring a dress," he wrote, noting that "this is especially essential for our hypersensitive children, who so often read correction as criticism."

Felix, Brian's son, soon wore a dress to school and was "unfazed" when some older kids made fun of him for "dressing like a girl." The boy simply raised his hand in the universal sign for stop and said, "Let me be."

If your son—like Felix (and Jeremy's son Nixon)—is comfortable and calm confronting prejudice and bias, but you still feel unsettled (as the boys' dads did) . . . well, you've got some inner work to do. Don't beat yourself up, though. It is natural to feel anxious or uneasy when dealing with things beyond our experience. It's normal to feel uncomfortable when your child wants to do something that was unimaginable in your childhood. We are all products of our environment, and most of us have internalized the social and gender norms we learned while growing up. Many of us faced punishment or pain for straying beyond social norms and gained "acceptance" only when we behaved in ways that others deemed appropriate.

Your son doesn't have to live with the same limitations. Together, you can question gender biases and expand social norms. You can help others to do so as well.

Because certain standards have been entrenched for a few generations now, you may need to have some uncomfortable conversations with other adults in your son's life. Jeremy realized he'd have to talk to his parents after he noticed Nixon quietly washing makeup off his face.

"I'd picked him up from a friend's house," Jeremy said. "When I told him we were going to Nanna and Papa's house, he said, 'Hey dad, I'm really thirsty.'"

Without thinking, Jeremy handed back his water bottle. The next time he glanced in his rearview mirror, he saw Nixon using the water to scrub his face.

"What're you doing?" Jeremy asked.

"I don't want Nanna and Papa to see, uh, you know," Nixon said. "I don't want them to make fun of me."

Nixon's grandparents hadn't previously said anything negative to the boy. But Jeremy realized that his son had noticed his grandfather's discomfort. In fact, the last time the family visited, Nixon—usually an affectionate child—didn't hug either of his grandparents.

So shortly after they arrived at Jeremy's parents' home, Jeremy asked to speak with his father privately. He asked his dad, "Does Nixon make you uncomfortable? How do you feel when he comes in wearing makeup?"

His father squirmed and tried to avoid answering the question.

"I've really struggled with it," Jeremy said. "It made me uncomfortable, and I worried. Can you relate to that?"

His father nodded yes, and Jeremy offered reassurance. Then he said, "What's most important right now is that Nixon knows he's safe with you. Is that something you can do?"

The answer, fortunately, was yes. However, additional conversations were needed over time to help Nixon's grandparents understand *how* to demonstrate safety and acceptance. Jeremy had to tell them that giving Nixon toy guns and baseballs as gifts—after the child specifically asked for dolls—not only contributed to clutter in the house (because the boy had no interest in those toys), but also communicated to Nixon disapproval of his interests.

These conversations can be tough. Same-sex marriages have been legal in the United States only since 2015. Social mores have shifted, but many parents, grandparents, aunts, uncles, and others unconsciously use sexist and heteronormative language. (*Heteronormative* is, simply, the assumption that heterosexuality is "normal," expected, and preferred.) Complete strangers, for instance, will ask your son if he has a girlfriend.

Chris Tompkins, author of *Raising LGBTQ Allies: A Parent's Guide to Changing the Messages from the Playground*, remembers feeling deep shame when people asked him that question because by age six, he knew he was gay.

"That question was a reminder that I was 'wrong' or 'bad' or 'different,'" Tompkins says. "I knew I was disappointing their assumption of me."

Use inclusive language whenever you can (and encourage others to do so). Ask, "is there someone special you like?" instead of, "do you have a girlfriend?" Don't inquire which girl your son is taking to prom; ask if he's going with someone. When you discuss sexual and romantic relationships, talk about heterosexual and homosexual relationships. If you don't, your son—who may be gay or know someone who is—may feel judged, unwelcome, and unaccepted as is.

Please note: it is also 100 percent okay for a boy to behave, dress, and act in stereotypically "boy" ways. Due to adults' heightened sensitivity to the potential damage that can result when boys and men are confined to the "man box," some parents feel a bit of panic if their son gravitates toward wrestling and stick-fighting. That was the case for Jay Deitcher, a stay-at-home dad who admits that he "wanted his son to reject masculine stereotypes."[14]

Jay's determination to raise a son unconstrained by stereotypes led him to bury a football-themed outfit his mother-in-law purchased for his infant son in the depths of the boy's closet. But at age two, his son developed a fascination with tractors and construction equipment, and Jay was forced to confront his bias.

"I pride myself on blurring gender lines. I wanted him to, also," he wrote in a 2022 essay.[15] But "I had to make a choice: buy him clothes with pictures of heavy machinery on them and make the kid happy or force him to wear shirts emblazoned with fuzzy animals to appease me."

Jay ultimately honored and respected his son's preference. The boy now happily wears machine-emblazoned clothing and enjoys playing with tractors and trucks—often with his father.

"I realized that I needed to let him discover his own interests," Jay wrote, and "define his own identity, not influenced by my own bias of what I deemed to be too masculine."

❧

GENDER IDENTITY

If your son is questioning his gender identity, love him. Listen to him. Support him. And reach out for additional support and information. Good resources include:

- GenderSpectrum.org
- GenderDiversity.org
- Children's National Gender Development Program (childrensnational.org/departments/gender-development-program)

⸙

UH-OH. . . . I THINK I INADVERTENTLY REJECTED MY SON

Don't fret if, in hindsight, you realize you initially overreacted to your child's interest or behavior. We all react emotionally sometimes, without considering the possible consequences of our words or actions. Simply apologize to your son, as Jeremy did when he recognized his mistake.

It's okay to admit that you're still learning about the world, still learning how to best support your son. Depending on your son's level of maturity and sensitivity, you may even want to share a story of a time when you felt limited by social expectations or unsupported by your parents or other authority figures. In fact, reflecting on your experiences may help you accept your son's desire to authentically express himself.

That's how Ohio mom Judi Ketteler came to accept her son Maxx's preferred spelling of his name. The baby she and her husband officially named "Maxwell" had long been known as "Max." In fourth grade, though, their son announced he wanted to be "Maxx."

"Why would you want to spell it that way?" Judi asked. "It's Max."

A few months later, his teacher emailed Judi to double-check the spelling of his name before sending the school yearbook to print. Judi told the teacher to use "Max." When Maxx told his mom that she misspelled his name online—she'd written Max—Judi laughed.

"Don't laugh," ten-year-old Maxx said quietly.

"That's when I realized this wasn't something he was doing to annoy me," Judi wrote in a 2022 essay.[16] It was also when she remembered that she was eleven when she changed the spelling of her name from "Judy" to "Judi" (after trialing "Judie").

"I . . . remember feeling frustrated that I couldn't get the people closest to me to see me how I wanted to be seen," Judi wrote. She decided to accept Maxx as is. ("It suits him so perfectly," she says four years later. "One little 'x' couldn't possibly contain his wonderful quirkiness.")

HOW TO ACCEPT YOUR SON

Middle school teacher (and father of four sons and a daughter) Braden Bell has noticed that in every school, there's a teacher that all the kids trust. That teacher, he says, genuinely likes the kids. "They even love them in the purest, most unconditional sense of that word," Bell says. "They see the best in kids." These teachers, he notes, "aren't blind" to their students' flaws, but "manage to see the good things . . . see what the kids are trying to do and who they are trying to be."[17]

That is how you accept kids: You see and acknowledge the good in them. You let them know that they matter to you, and you show them, through your words and actions, that you enjoy and appreciate them. When they make a mistake or do something "bad," you remind yourself (and them) that one incident does not define them. You nourish their emerging gifts, while allowing them to be fully human.

Here's how.

Show Interest in His Interests

Dismissing or denigrating a boy's interests feels, to him, like dismissal of him as a human being. Deep interests are intensely personal and often connected to our sense of purpose. When you express curiosity in your son's interests—even if his latest passion is of absolutely no interest to you—he feels seen and welcome.

In practice, this may mean listening to hundreds of hours of conversation about Minecraft, butterflies, cars, or black holes. It could mean driving an hour or more to attend an all-day fishing expo with him and sitting in on sessions about how the phases of the moon influence the behavior of muskellunge, a huge freshwater game fish. (Yes, that extremely specific example is drawn directly from my life, and no, I don't regret a moment of that day.)

When you create time and space for the things your son values, he feels valued as well.

Light Up When He Enters the Room

Listen, I know that boys are not always a bundle of joy. Toddlers and preschoolers are exhausting, and tweens and teens can be downright unpleasant. But no matter how hard or heavy parenting gets, our boys need to know that we love them. *You* know you love your son, always and forever, but does he? Can he tell? Boys pay closer attention to our facial expressions and body language than we sometimes think.

Do you often sigh and look stressed or annoyed when your son walks into the room? Or remain focused on whatever you're doing? You don't need to drop everything when your son enters your space, but a quick smile, wink, wave, or first bump both acknowledges his presence and lets him know you're happy to see him.

Avoid Negative or Judgmental Comments

You will not like or approve of everything your son does. And yes, you have every right (and responsibility) to share your family values with your son. However, refrain from nitpicking and work to erase negative and judgmental comments from your conversations.

You don't need to say, "Those pants look terrible on you" or "This room is a pigsty!" Instead, you can say something like, "I like those other pants better" or "It's been a while since you cleaned your room. Please pick up and throw away the empty bottles, soda cans, and wrappers before dinner."

Steer clear of negative comments about your son's body. Though most popular discourse about eating disorders and body image has focused on females, boys and men aren't immune to societal pressure. They too are bombarded with all sorts of unrealistic body expectations (hulking chest and shoulders, chiseled abs, etc.), which is one reason why almost a third of teenage boys are trying to "bulk up,"[18] with nearly 40 percent of high school boys using or experimenting with protein powder or shakes.[19] The desire to mold their bodies into something that is, frankly, utterly unattainable for most teenage boys can lead to disordered eating and an unhealthy obsession with exercise and nutrition. According to a 2019 study, approximately one out of five young men ages eighteen to twenty-four experiences disordered eating due to a desire to enhance muscles.[20]

You can help your son accept his body by appreciating bodies of assorted sizes and shapes, loving and caring for your *own* body, and drawing his attention to the many things his body can do.

Watch Your Tone of Voice

Try to keep notes of negativity or disapproval out of your voice. Many boys are adept at interpreting vocal cues—and more inclined to trust tone of your voice more than the literal meaning of your words.

Not sure how you're coming across? Ask a close friend who frequently spends time with you and your son. It can be difficult for us to hear implied judgment in our own voices, particularly because many of us unconsciously parrot the vocal patterns our parents and others used to speak to us. Alternately, when you approach your son, consciously adopt the tone of voice you'd use to talk with a coworker. Aim for calm and respectful. (Bonus: if you talk to your son calmly and respectfully, he's more likely to speak that way to others. Not *always* . . . but more likely.)

Look for the Good

It's so easy to hyper-focus on what's wrong. That's the negativity bias, a well-known cognitive bias that causes humans to notice and remember negative experiences more than positive ones.[21] Evolutionarily, the bias is helpful: noticing the negative helps us stay alive long enough to have positive experiences. From a parenting perspective, however, the negativity bias means it's all too easy to gloss over the good parts and believe instead that our boys are destined for failure.

Train yourself to deliberately look for the good in your son, particularly when you're feeling disappointed in his behavior or choices. Do not let occasional behavioral slips cloud your perception of your son; his goodness and gifts are always inside him.

Recognizing the good can help you get through tough moments. And it'll help you communicate unconditional love and acceptance to your son. When you focus on the negative (a failed test, a legal infraction), your frustration, anger, and disappointment is likely to show up in your voice and body language. When you remember the good, your voice and body conveys tenderness (even if it's mixed with anger or exasperation). That tenderness can make all the difference. As Alfie Kohn, author of *Unconditional Parenting*, wrote, "what counts is how things look from the perspective of the children—whether they feel just as loved when they mess up or fall short."[22]

Increase Your Tolerance

Remember, Dr. Thomas Gordon, author of *Parent Effectiveness Training*, said that a child's sense of acceptance is determined by how many of his behaviors are accepted.

"Parents who find unacceptable a great many things that their children do or say will inevitably foster in their children a deep feeling they are unaccepted as persons," he wrote. "Conversely, parents who are accepting of a great many things their children do or say will produce children who are more likely to feel acceptable as persons."[23]

You may need to expand your definition of acceptable behavior for boys *and* increase your tolerance. I planned to have no-toy-guns and no-balls-in-the-house policies—likely because those were my mom's rules when I was growing up. Then I saw my boys' tendencies to turn bread and sticks into "guns" and their near-constant need for physical movement. I realized that upholding those two rules would mean saying no (a lot!) to things that aren't inherently harmful or dangerous. So I loosened my rules. The boys gradually amassed an arsenal of Nerf guns, and for years, we had a small indoor basketball hoop mounted on our dining room door. Increasing my tolerance gave my boys a chance to be themselves at home, and that, I know, helped them feel accepted.

Practice Self-Care

It is much easier to accept your son if you are calm and content. When you are solidly centered, you're less likely to react impulsively, which means you're better able to respond thoughtfully and deliberately.

I cannot stress the importance of foundational self-care enough. To most effectively parent boys, you need regular sleep, rest, nutrition, and movement. You need to decompress and nourish your soul on a regular basis, whether via meditation, art, spiritual practice, or time in nature.

The next time you find yourself obsessing about what's "wrong" with your son (or what you think he needs to do differently), I encourage you to shift your focus to yourself for a minute. Conduct a brief self-exam: Have you been sleeping enough? Resting? Spending time outside? If the answer to any of those questions is no, take some time to address your *own* needs before attempting to change or fix anything about your son.

Deliberate, consistent self-care will help you successfully nurture your boy in a world that misunderstands males. Your example and attention will facilitate his growth and allow him to become the best possible version of himself. With your support, he will blossom into a well-rounded human being who respects himself and others.

Do not doubt your ability to raise a great guy. You care deeply about your son—about boys—and that, as they say, makes all the difference.

"A relationship in which a boy can tell he matters is fundamental to his ability to think for himself and follow an independent course," Michael Reichert wrote. "A young man's self-confidence is not accidental or serendipitous but derives from experiences of being accurately understood, loved, and supported."[24]

Self-confident boys who think for themselves grow into men who travel beyond the paths carved by previous generations. The work you are doing today will lead to a better tomorrow.

Here's to building boys!

⌑

To build boys:

1. *Learn the terrain.*
2. *Emphasize emotional intelligence.*
3. *Discuss and demonstrate healthy relationships.*
4. *Let him struggle.*
5. *Help him find and develop his talents.*
6. *Give him time.*
7. *Challenge him with chores and caregiving.*
8. *Keep him close.*
9. *Connect him to the real world.*
10. *Accept him as he is.*

Acknowledgments

Writing a book is a lot like birthing a baby.

You think you're ready, and then, once the process is in motion, you wonder, *What the #*%$ have I done?* You wonder, *Is it too late to change my mind?* And you start to question why you ever thought you were qualified to undertake such a massive endeavor.

During the transition phase of one of my labors, I uttered a single word aloud: *help*. That one syllable, in that moment, meant *I don't think I can go on*, and in that moment, I needed those around me— my then-husband, my midwife—to get me through.

I reached that point numerous times while working on this book. You would not be holding it in your hands if not for the continual support and encouragement of so many people, especially:

My husband, Mike Tennessen, who believed in me and this project even when I didn't. He cooked for me, picked up my slack, and, most crucially, left me alone when I needed to write.

My writer friends and the American Society of Journalists and Authors (ASJA). Jen Singer gave me the push I needed to shape my ideas into a book proposal. I first pitched my proposal for this book at the 2019 ASJA conference and eventually got my agent, Peter Rubie, via ASJA connections. (Thanks for taking a chance on me, Peter!) Special thanks to *Marijke Vroomen Durning* and

Janine Latus, who checked in often and encouraged me to keep going.

My On Boys cohost, Janet Allison, who helped me build my platform and navigate book writing, parenting, and podcasting. Thanks also to each of our *On Boys guests*.

My Building Boys family. You shared your stories, struggles, and strength with me. Thanks especially to *Liesl Garner, Penny Warnell*, and *Leah Beatty*.

The Rockvale Writers' Colony, a haven that gave me the physical and mental space I needed to start this book.

Sky Hume and Catherine Miller, two ambitious young women who assisted me with research and citations. I could not have done this project without you!

My sons, Nathan, Tyler, Adam, and Sam. The four of you opened my eyes to the many ways in which the world misunderstands males—and then put up with me as I proceeded to share what I learned with the world. Thank you for helping me grow.

Appendix:
Organizations That Support
Boys and Their Families

Building Boys (https://buildingboys.net/). A one-stop shop for parents and teachers of boys. Includes access to Building Boys Bulletin, Jennifer's weekly newsletter; Building Boys Facebook group; and occasional classes and book studies.

MBK Alliance (www.obama.org/mbka/). An extension of the My Brother's Keeper initiative started by President Obama in 2014, the MBK Alliance focuses on building safe and supportive communities for boys and young men of color.

BAM—Becoming a Man (www.youth-guidance.org/bam/). BAM fosters positive development in young men by emphasizing six core values: integrity, accountability, positive anger expression, self-determination, respect for womanhood, and visionary goal settings. A school-based counseling and mentoring program, BAM is currently active in Chicago, Boston, Los Angeles, Seattle, and Kansas City.

Build Up Boys (www.buildupboys.com/). This nonprofit has developed an evidence-based curriculum that uses play, theater, movement, writing, and storytelling exercises to help boys develop social, emotional, and relationship learning skills to combat gender pressure. Programs for parents are under development.

A Call to Men (www.acalltomen.org/). This organization's Live Respect curriculum promotes healthy, respectful manhood and helps build young men of character. They also offer a Call to Boy Moms, a free online community for mother of boys (www.acalltomen.org/introducing-our-new-community-for-boy-moms).

Next Gen Men (www.nextgenmen.ca/). A Canadian nonprofit that offers an online course for parents and educators of boys, as well as an online community for boys in grades seven through nine.

The Boys Initiative (https://boysinitiative.org/). An American nonprofit dedicated to raising awareness about the issues and trends affecting the well-being and success of boys and young men.

Boy Mentoring Advocacy Network (BMAN) (www.bmanadvocacy.org/). This Nigerian nongovernmental organization frequently offers free webinars to help parents and educators understand and effectively guide boys.

Global Initiative for Boys & Men (www.gibm.us/). Collates and supports research to inform policy makers, educators, and parents about issues affecting boys to collectively improve outcomes.

The Boys and Men Project (www.brookings.edu/series/boys-and-men/). A Brookings Institution project that examines the challenges facing many boys and men in the context of progress toward gender equality and potential policies to promote greater male flourishing and agency.

Notes

CHAPTER 1

1. Eliot, Lise. "Neurosexism: The Myth That Men and Women Have Different Brains." *Nature News*, February 27, 2019. www.nature.com/articles/d41586-019-00677-x.

2. Valian, Virginia. "Psychology: More Alike than Different." *Nature News*, February 16, 2011. www.nature.com/articles/470332a.

3. Ounsted, C., D. C. Taylor, eds. *Gender Differences: Their Ontogeny and Significance.* London: Churchill Livingstone, 1972.

4. Nagy, Emese, Hajnalka Kompagne, Hajnalka Orvos, and Attila Pal. "Gender-Related Differences in Neonatal Imitation." Wiley Online Library, March 21, 2007. https://onlinelibrary.wiley.com/doi/10.1002/icd.497.

5. Weinberg, M., E. Z. Tronick, J. F. Cohn, and K. L. Olson. "Gender Differences in Emotional Expressivity and Self-Regulation during Early Infancy." *Developmental Psychology* 35, no. 1 (February 1999): 175–88. https://doi.org/10.1037/0012-1649.35.1.175.

6. Kraemer, Sebastian. "The Fragile Male." *BMJ: British Medical Journal*, December 23, 2000. www.ncbi.nlm.nih.gov/pmc/articles/PMC1119278/.

7. Calkins, Susan D., Susan E. Dedmon, Kathryn L. Gill, Laura E. Lomax, and Laura M. Johnson. "Frustration in Infancy: Implications for Emotion Regulation, Physiological Processes, and Temperament." American Psychological Association, January 18, 2010. https://psycnet.apa.org/record/2002-13294-004.

8. Feldman, Ruth, Romi Magori-Cohen, Giora Galili, Magi Singer, and Yoram Louzoun. "Mother and Infant Coordinate Heart Rhythms through Episodes of Interaction Synchrony." *Infant Behavior and Development*, December 2011. https://pubmed.ncbi.nlm.nih.gov/21767879/.

Rosen, Meghan. "Scienceshot: Human Hearts Beat Together." Science. org, December 5, 2011. www.science.org/content/article/scienceshot-human-hearts-beat-together.

Suga, Ayami, Maki Uraguchi, Akiko Tange, Hiroki Ishikawa, and Hideki Ohira. "Cardiac Interaction between Mother and Infant: Enhancement of Heart Rate Variability." *Nature News*, December 27, 2019. www.nature.com/articles/s41598-019-56204-5.

9. Baron-Cohen, S., M. O'Riordan, V. Stone, R. Jones, and K. Plaisted. "Recognition of Faux Pas by Normally Developing Children and Children with Asperger Syndrome or High-Functioning Autism." *Journal of Autism and Developmental Disorders*, October 1999. https://pubmed.ncbi.nlm.nih.gov/10587887/.

Schore, Allan N. "All Our Sons: The Developmental Neurobiology and Neuroendocrinology of Boys at Risk." Wiley Online Library, January 2, 2017. https://onlinelibrary.wiley.com/doi/epdf/10.1002/imhj.21616.

10. Sax, Leonard. *Why Gender Matters: What Parents and Teachers Need to Know about the Emerging Science of Sex Differences*. New York: Doubleday, 2005.

11. Schore, Allan N. "All Our Sons: The Developmental Neurobiology and Neuroendocrinology of Boys at Risk." Wiley Online Library, January 2, 2017. https://onlinelibrary.wiley.com/doi/epdf/10.1002/imhj.21616.

12. Sciamanna, John. "Preschool Children Have a Higher Expulsion Rates than K-12." CWLA, 2020. www.cwla.org/preschool-children-have-a-higher-expulsion-rates-than-k-12/.

13. Kraemer, Sebastian. "The Fragile Male." *BMJ: British Medical Journal*, December 23, 2000. www.ncbi.nlm.nih.gov/pmc/articles/PMC1119278/.

14. Schore, Allan N. "All Our Sons: The Developmental Neurobiology and Neuroendocrinology of Boys at Risk." Wiley Online Library, January 2, 2017. https://onlinelibrary.wiley.com/doi/epdf/10.1002/imhj.21616.

15. Allison, Janet, and Jennifer L. W. Fink. "ADHD with Ryan Wexelblatt the ADHD Dude." *On Boys* podcast, February 6, 2020. https://on-boys.blubrry.net/adhd-with-ryan-wexelblatt-the-adhd-dude/.

16. Robert Blum in discussion with author, April 14, 2021.

17. ACTM. "Tony Porter (He/Him/His)." A Call to Men, 2022. www.acalltomen.org/about/team/tony-porter/.

Porter, Tony. "Tony Porter's TED Talk: A Call to Men." TED Conferences, December 2010. www.ted.com/speakers/tony_porter.

18. Greene, Mark. "The History of 'The Man Box.'" Medium, October 2, 2021. https://remakingmanhood.medium.com/the-history-of-the-man-box-e6eed6d895c4.

19. Porter, Tony. "Transcript of 'A Call to Men.'" Ted Conferences, December 2010. www.ted.com/talks/tony_porter_a_call_to_men/transcript?language=en#t-638179.

20. Undem, Tresa, and Ann Wang. "The State of Gender Equality for U.S. Adolescents." Plan International, 2018. https://planusa-org-staging.s3.amazonaws.com/public/uploads/2021/04/state-of-gender-equality-summary-2018.pdf.

21. Pearson, Catherine. "How to Raise Boys Who Aren't Afraid to Be Vulnerable." HuffPost, March 4, 2021. www.huffpost.com/entry/how-to-raise-boys-who-arent-afraid-to-be-vulnerable_l_60413b06c5b6429d08320c8f?ncid=tweetlnkushpmg00000067.

Undem, Tresa, and Ann Wang. "The State of Gender Equality for U.S. Adolescents." Plan International, 2018. https://planusa-org-staging.s3.amazonaws.com/public/uploads/2021/04/state-of-gender-equality-summary-2018.pdf.

22. Reynolds, Tania, Chuck Howard, Hallgeir Sjåstad, Luke Zhu, Tyler G. Okimoto, Roy F. Baumeister, Karl Aquino, and JongHan Kim. "Man Up and Take It: Gender Bias in Moral Typecasting." *Organizational Behavior and Human Decision Processes*, November 2020. https://doi.org/10.1016/j.obhdp.2020.05.002.

23. Thompson, Michael, and Dan Kindlon. *Raising Cain: Protecting the Emotional Life of Boys*. New York: Random House, 2000.

24. Robert Blum in discussion with author, April 14, 2021.

25. Blum, Robert Wm, Jo Boyden, Annabel Erulkar, Caroline Kabiru, and Siswanto Wilopo. "Achieving Gender Equality Requires Placing Adolescents at the Center." *Journal of Adolescent Health*, June 1, 2019. https://doi.org/10.1016/j.jadohealth.2019.02.002.

26. Blum, Robert Wm, Jo Boyden, Annabel Erulkar, Caroline Kabiru, and Siswanto Wilopo. "Achieving Gender Equality Requires Placing Adolescents at the Center." *Journal of Adolescent Health*, June 1, 2019. https://doi.org/10.1016/j.jadohealth.2019.02.002.

27. Evans, Erica. "Parents Are More Concerned about Their Boys Becoming Successful Adults than Their Girls." *Deseret News*, September 21, 2020. www.deseret.com/indepth/2020/9/21/21436402/parents-concerned-boys-becoming-successful-adults-gender-differences-afs-2020-byu.

28. Samuels, Christina A. "Pre-K Suspension Data Prompt Focus on Intervention." *Education Week*, March 31, 2014. www.edweek.org/leadership/pre-k-suspension-data-prompt-focus-on-intervention/2014/03?tkn=VLNF2UbEJiDbZ%2Fzwz9ppsCkuEHjCwI1il8As&print=1.

29. Marcus, Jon. "The Pandemic Is Speeding Up the Mass Disappearance of Men from College." *The Hechinger Report*, January 19, 2021. https://hechingerreport.org/the-pandemic-is-speeding-up-the-mass-disappearance-of-men-from-college/.

30. Shaywitz, S. E., B. A. Shaywitz, J. M. Fletcher, and M. D. Escobar. "Prevalence of Reading Disability in Boys and Girls. Results of the Connecticut Longitudinal Study." *JAMA*, August 1990. https://pubmed.ncbi.nlm.nih.gov/2376893/.

31. OECD. "Grade Expectations: How Marks and Education Policies Shape Students' Ambitions." OECD Publishing, December 18, 2012. http://dx.doi.org/10.1787/9789264187528-en.

32. OECD. "Grade Expectations: How Marks and Education Policies Shape Students' Ambitions." OECD Publishing, December 18, 2012. http://dx.doi.org/10.1787/9789264187528-en.

33. Barnett, Lynn A. "The Education of Playful Boys: Class Clowns in the Classroom." *Frontiers in Psychology*, March 1, 2018. www.frontiersin.org/articles/10.3389/fpsyg.2018.00232/full.

34. CDC. "Results from the School Health Policies and Practices Study." Centers for Disease Control and Prevention, August 2017. www.cdc.gov/healthyyouth/data/shpps/pdf/shpps-results_2016.pdf.

35. CDC. "Results from the School Health Policies and Practices Study." Centers for Disease Control and Prevention, August 2017. www.cdc.gov/healthyyouth/data/shpps/pdf/shpps-results_2016.pdf.

36. Layton, Timothy J., Michael L. Barnett, Tanner R. Hicks, and Anupam B. Jena. "Attention Deficit–Hyperactivity Disorder and Month of School Enrollment." *The New England Journal of Medicine*, November 29, 2018. www.nejm.org/doi/full/10.1056/NEJMoa1806828.

37. Kering Foundation and Promundo. "More than 2/3 of Parents in the United States Say Boys Don't Feel Comfortable Sharing When They Feel Scared or Lonely, Reveals New Research." PR Newswire, May 28, 2020. www.wfmz.com/news/pr_newswire/pr_newswire_health/more-than-2-3-of-parents-in-the-united-states-say-boys-dont-feel-comfortable/article_b84091b6-5b56-5cbf-b89c-ac19c672bc17.html.

Barker, Gary, Brian Heilman, and Michael Reichert. "Staying-at-Home with Our Sons: Fostering Healthy Masculinity in Challenging Times." Promundo, June 3, 2020. https://promundoglobal.org/resources/fostering-healthy-masculinity/.

38. Lahey, Jessica. "How a Hot Sauce–Themed YouTube Show Helped Me Get to Know My Sons Better." *Washington Post*, April 6, 2021. www.washingtonpost.com/lifestyle/2021/04/06/kids-addiction-prevention/.

39. Harvard Graduate School of Education. "Making Caring Common Project." The President and Fellows of Harvard College, 2014. https://static1.squarespace.com/static/5b7c56e255b02c683659fe43/t/5bae774424a694b5feb2b05f/1538160453604/report-children-raise.pdf.

Hedegaard, Holly, Sally C. Curtin, and Margaret Warner. "Increase in Suicide Mortality in the United States, 1999–2018." Centers for Disease Control and Prevention, April 8, 2020. www.cdc.gov/nchs/products/databriefs/db362.htm.

40. Dent, Maggie. "Seven Tips for Parenting Teen Boys: 'Nagging Them Is Like Shouting into a Void.'" *Guardian*, October 9, 2020. www.theguardian.com/lifeandstyle/2020/oct/10/seven-tips-for-parenting-teen-boys-nagging-them-is-like-shouting-into-a-void.

41. Habeeb, Lee. "Meet the Man Leading the Charge on America's Boy Crisis." *Newsweek*, July 14, 2020. www.newsweek.com/meet-man-leading-charge-americas-boy-crisis-opinion-1517782.

42. Waters, Lea. "How to Be a Strength-Based Parent." *Greater Good Magazine*, October 2, 2018. https://greatergood.berkeley.edu/article/item/how_to_be_a_strength_based_parent.
Yale University. "Focus on Your Strengths, Focus on Success." Yale University, 2022. https://your.yale.edu/work-yale/learn-and-grow/focus-your-strengths-focus-success.

43. Forman-Alberti, Alissa. "Facets of Peer Relationships and Their Associations with Adolescent Risk-Taking Behavior." American Psychological Association, December 2015. www.apa.org/pi/families/resources/newsletter/2015/12/adolescent-risk-taking.

44. Fink, Jennifer L. W. "Here's How to Motivate Teenage Boys: Encourage Risk-Taking." *Your Teen Magazine*, April 19, 2021. https://yourteenmag.com/health/teenager-mental-health/how-to-motivate-boys.

45. Fink, Jennifer L. W. "How Parenting Teenage Boys Prepared Me for a Pandemic." *Building Boys*, May 24, 2020. https://buildingboys.net/how-parenting-teenage-boys-prepared-me-for-a-pandemic/.

46. Reber, Deborah. "Reframe Your Teen's Bad Behavior with 'Unconditional Parenting.'" *ADDitude*, April 7, 2021. www.additudemag.com/adhd-teens-bad-behavior/.

CHAPTER 2

1. Allison, Janet. "Teacher Tom Talks about Boys, Emotions & Play." *On Boys* podcast, June 8, 2021. www.on-boys-podcast.com/teacher-tom-talks-about-boys-emotions-play/.

2. Allison, Janet. "Teacher Tom Talks about Boys, Emotions & Play." *On Boys* podcast, June 8, 2021. www.on-boys-podcast.com/teacher-tom-talks-about-boys-emotions-play/.

3. Oxford English Dictionary. "Definition of Emotional Intelligence in English." Lexico Dictionaries, 2022. www.lexico.com/en/definition/emotional_intelligence.

4. Bradberry, Travis. "Emotional Intelligence—EQ." *Forbes Magazine*, January 9, 2014. www.forbes.com/sites/travisbradberry/2014/01/09/emotional-intelligence/?sh=482f14501ac0.

5. Kadane, Lisa. "EQ vs IQ: Why Emotional Intelligence Will Take Your Kid Further in Life." *Today's Parent*, August 4, 2020. www.todaysparent.com/kids/kids-health/eq-vs-iq-why-emotional-intelligence-will-take-kids-farther-in-life/.

6. Collaborative for Academic, Social, and Emotional Learning. "What Does the Research Say?" CASEL, February 1, 2022. https://casel.org/fundamentals-of-sel/what-does-the-research-say/.

7. NIMH. "Suicide." National Institute of Mental Health, 2019. www.nimh.nih.gov/health/statistics/suicide.

8. Farr, Kathryn. "Adolescent Rampage School Shootings: Responses to Failing Masculinity Performances by Already-Troubled Boys." *Gender Issues*, October 19, 2017. https://link.springer.com/article/10.1007/s12147-017-9203-z.

9. Reichert, Michael C., and Joseph Derrick Nelson. "The State of America's Boys: An Urgent Case for a More Connected Boyhood." Promundo-US, 2020. https://promundoglobal.org/wp-content/uploads/2020/10/State-of-American-Boys-Report-r3-4.pdf.

10. Reiner, Andrew. "For Father's Day, Let's Redefine Masculinity So Dads Can Give Boys What They Need." NBC, June 20, 2021. www.nbcnews.com/think/opinion/father-s-day-let-s-redefine-masculinity-so-dads-can-ncna1271343.

11. Tapia, Amancay. "World's 20 'Most Admired' Men of 2021—Warren Buffett, Joe Biden Join List." *Newsweek*, December 26, 2021. www.newsweek.com/world-most-admired-men-2021-warren-buffett-joe-biden-join-list-1661028.

12. Dowd, Maureen. "'All Men Are Guilty,' Says Mega-Mogul Barry Diller." *New York Times*, March 24, 2018. www.nytimes.com/2018/03/24/style/barry-diller-iac.html.

13. Ruiz, Rebecca. "How to Raise Boys So They're Comfortable with Their Emotions." Mashable, June 1, 2020. https://mashable.com/article/how-to-raise-strong-sons.

14. Rabinowitz, Fredric, Matt Englar-Carlson, Ryon McDermott, Christopher Liang, and Matthew Kridel. "APA Guidelines for Psychological Practice with Boys and Men." American Psychological Association, August 2018. www.apa.org/about/policy/boys-men-practice-guidelines.pdf.

15. Fink, Jennifer L. W. "129 Grief with Tom Golden." *On Boys* podcast, September 20, 2018. www.on-boys-podcast.com/129-grief-with-tom-golden/.

16. Weir, Kirsten. "The Exercise Effect." American Psychological Association, December 2011. www.apa.org/monitor/2011/12/exercise.

17. Collier, Lorna. "Why We Cry." American Psychological Association, February 2014. www.apa.org/monitor/2014/02/cry.

Newhouse, Leo. "Is Crying Good for You?" Harvard Health Publishing, March 1, 2021. www.health.harvard.edu/blog/is-crying-good-for-you-2021030122020.

Rosman, Katherine. "Read It and Weep, Crybabies." *Wall Street Journal*, May 4, 2011. www.wsj.com/articles/SB1000142405274870392280457630090 3183512350.

18. Mayo Clinic Staff. "Exercise and Stress: Get Moving to Manage Stress." Mayo Foundation for Medical Education and Research, August 18, 2020. www.mayoclinic.org/healthy-lifestyle/stress-management/in-depth/exercise-and-stress/art-20044469#:~:text=Exercise%20increases%20 your%20overall%20health,%2Dgood%20neurotransmitters%2C%20 called%20endorphins.

19. Mascaro, Jennifer S., Kelly E. Rentscher, Patrick D. Hackett, Matthias R. Mehl, and James K. Rilling. "Child Gender Influences Paternal Behavior, Language, and Brain Function." *Behavioral Neuroscience*, June 2017. www. ncbi.nlm.nih.gov/pmc/articles/PMC5481199/#!po=55.0000.

20. Mascaro, Jennifer S., Kelly E. Rentscher, Patrick D. Hackett, Matthias R. Mehl, and James K. Rilling. "Child Gender Influences Paternal Behavior, Language, and Brain Function." *Behavioral Neuroscience*, June 2017. www. ncbi.nlm.nih.gov/pmc/articles/PMC5481199/#!po=55.0000.

21. Mascaro, Jennifer S., Kelly E. Rentscher, Patrick D. Hackett, Matthias R. Mehl, and James K. Rilling. "Child Gender Influences Paternal Behavior, Language, and Brain Function." *Behavioral Neuroscience*. U.S. National Library of Medicine, June 2017. https://www.ncbi.nlm.nih.gov/pmc/ articles/PMC5481199/#!po=55.0000.

22. Pellis, Sergio M., and Vivien C. Pellis. "What Is Play Fighting and What Is It Good for?" *Learning and Behavior*, April 3, 2017. https://link. springer.com/article/10.3758/s13420-017-0264-3.

23. Dodd, Helen F., and Kathryn J. Lester. "Adventurous Play as a Mechanism for Reducing Risk for Childhood Anxiety: A Conceptual Model." *Clinical Child and Family Psychology Review*, January 19, 2021. https://link. springer.com/epdf/10.1007/s10567-020-00338-w?sharing_token=ujN5H-8F59TZTeus9FarJWfe4RwlQNchNByi7wbcMAY4vd7kjnLjh6XnWNaSU4e q6e8JyD9h2vpm7dNXcVqwcVhUUuHlMMoXho9Cg8DTOLNYKCq-sz6v DsB9i0s2EIbifD6br6SiG6Un7hqx-o83YP_SOe9iPk9ubWLZVvDUJ3A0%3D.

24. Dodd, Helen F., and Kathryn J. Lester. "Adventurous Play as a Mechanism for Reducing Risk for Childhood Anxiety: A Conceptual Model." *Clinical Child and Family Psychology Review*, January 19, 2021. https://link. springer.com/epdf/10.1007/s10567-020-00338-w?sharing_token=ujN5H-8F59TZTeus9FarJWfe4RwlQNchNByi7wbcMAY4vd7kjnLjh6XnWNaSU4e q6e8JyD9h2vpm7dNXcVqwcVhUUuHlMMoXho9Cg8DTOLNYKCq-sz6v DsB9i0s2EIbifD6br6SiG6Un7hqx-o83YP_SOe9iPk9ubWLZVvDUJ3A0%3D.

25. Dent, Maggie. "Fidgeting & Farts: Boys in Isolation." *Maggie Dent* (blog), May 2, 2020. www.maggiedent.com/blog/fidgeting-farts-boys-in-isolation/.

26. Salo, Virginia C., Sara J. Schunck, and Kathryn L. Humphreys. "Depressive Symptoms in Parents Are Associated with Reduced Empathy to-

ward Their Young Children." *PLoS ONE*, March 23, 2020. https://journals. plos.org/plosone/article?id=10.1371%2Fjournal.pone.0230636#sec005.

27. Graczyk, P. A., M. C. Lovejoy, E. O'Hare, and G. Neuman. "Maternal Depression and Parenting Behavior: A Meta-Analytic Review." *Clinical Psychology Review*, August 2000. https://pubmed.ncbi.nlm.nih.gov/10860167/.

Humphreys, Kathryn L., Sara J. Schunck, and Virginia C. Salo. "Depressive Symptoms in Parents Are Associated with Reduced Empathy toward Their Young Children." *PLoS ONE*, March 23, 2020. https://journals.plos.org/plosone/article?id=10.1371%2Fjournal.pone.0230636#sec005.

National Research Council (US) and Institute of Medicine. "Associations between Depression in Parents and Parenting, Child Health, and Child Psychological Functioning." *Depression in Parents, Parenting, and Children: Opportunities to Improve Identification, Treatment, and Prevention.* National Academies Press, January 1, 2009. www.ncbi.nlm.nih.gov/books/NBK215128/.

28. Myers, Sarah, and Sarah E. Johns. "Male Infants and Birth Complications Are Associated with Increased Incidence of Postnatal Depression." *Social Science & Medicine*, 2019.

29. Weinberg, M. Katherine, and E. Z. Tronick. "Gender Differences and Their Relation to Maternal Depression." *Stress, Coping, and Depression*, 2000.

30. Pearson, Catherine. "How to Raise Boys Who Aren't Afraid to Be Vulnerable." HuffPost, March 5, 2021. www.huffpost.com/entry/how-to-raise-boys-who-arent-afraid-to-be-vulnerable_l_60413b06c5b6429d08320c8f?nci=tweetlnkushpmg00000067.

31. Fink, Jennifer L. W. "Encouraging Emotional Intelligence in Boys." *Building Boys*, October 4, 2016. https://buildingboys.net/encouraging-emotional-intelligence-in-boys/.

32. Willcox, Gloria. "The Feeling Wheel." *Transactional Analysis*, December 28, 2017. www.tandfonline.com/doi/abs/10.1177/036215378201200411.

33. Thomas, Ian. "Helping Boys Develop Emotional Intelligence." *Building Boys*, October 18, 2016. https://buildingboys.net/helping-boys-develop-emotional-intelligence/.

34. Koenig, Joan. Essay. In *The Musical Child: Using the Power of Music to Raise Children Who Are Happy, Healthy, and Whole*, 95. Boston: Mariner Books, 2021.

35. Palmiter, David, Mary Alvord, Rosalind Dorlen, Lillian Comas-Diaz, Suniya S. Luthar, Salvatore R. Maddi, Katherine H. O'Neill, Karen W. Saakvitne, and Richard Glenn Tedeschi. "Building Your Resilience." American Psychological Association, February 1, 2020. www.apa.org/topics/resilience.

36. Sher, Leo. "Resilience as a Focus of Suicide Research and Prevention." *Acta Psychiatrica Scandinavica*, May 31, 2019. https://onlinelibrary.wiley.com/doi/10.1111/acps.13059.

37. Katey McPherson via email with author, January 3, 2021.

38. Damour, Lisa. "Helping Teens Make Room for Uncomfortable Emotions." *New York Times*, April 20, 2020. www.nytimes.com/2020/04/21/well/family/coronavirus-teenagers-uncomfortable-emotions.html.

39. Orenstein, Peggy. "The Miseducation of the American Boy." *The Atlantic*, December 21, 2019. www.theatlantic.com/magazine/archive/2020/01/the-miseducation-of-the-american-boy/603046/?utm_source=facebook&utm_campaign=the-atlantic-fb-test-1255-1-&utm_content=edit-promo&utm_medium=social&fbclid=IwAR2pp9eObz2tDKbq MC043q1M5OIdO3JQKY2zKldia422LrJTRm5z8hqy910.

40. Carissoli, Claudia, and Daniela Villani. "Can Videogames Be Used to Promote Emotional Intelligence in Teenagers? Results from EmotivaMente, a School Program." *Games for Health Journal*, November 26, 2019. www.liebertpub.com/doi/10.1089/g4h.2018.0148.

Carissoli, Claudia, Daniela Villani, Stefano Triberti, Antonella Marchetti, Gabriella Gilli, and Guiseppe Riva. "Free Access Videogames for Emotion Regulation: A Systematic Review." *Games for Health Journal*, April 1, 2018. www.liebertpub.com/doi/10.1089/g4h.2017.0108.

Ducharme, Peter, Jason Kahn, Carrie Vaudreuil, Michaela Gusman, Deborah Waber, Abigail Ross, Alexander Rotenberg, Ashley Rober, Kara Kimball, Alyssa L. Peechatka, and Joseph Gonzalez-Heydrich. "A 'Proof of Concept' Randomized Controlled Trial of a Video Game Requiring Emotional Regulation to Augment Anger Control Training." *Frontiers*, January 1, 2021. www.frontiersin.org/articles/10.3389/fpsyt.2021.591906/full.

Gaetan, Sophie, Vincent Bréjard, and Agnès Bonnet. "Video Games in Adolescence and Emotional Functioning: Emotion Regulation, Emotion Intensity, Emotion Expression, and Alexithymia." *Computers in Human Behavior*, 2016.

CHAPTER 3

1. Basile, Kathleen C., Sarah DeGue, Kathryn Jones, Kimberley Freire, Jenny Dills, Sharon G. Smith, and Jerris L. Raiford. "STOP SV: A Technical Package to Prevent Sexual Violence." National Center for Injury Prevention and Control, 2016. www.cdc.gov/violenceprevention/pdf/sv-prevention-technical-package.pdf.

2. "The 1 in 6 Statistic." 1in6.org, July 19, 2018. https://1in6.org/get-information/the-1-in-6-statistic/.

"Child Sexual Abuse Facts." YWCA, September 2017. www.ywca.org/wp-content/uploads/WWV-CSA-Fact-Sheet-Final.pdf.

"Prevalence of Child Sexual Abuse." Darkness to Light, September 17, 2021. www.d2l.org/child-sexual-abuse/prevalence/.

3. "11 Facts about Teen Dating Violence." DoSomething.org, 2014. www.dosomething.org/us/facts/11-facts-about-teen-dating-violence.

"Quick Guide: Teen Dating Violence." NCADV: National Coalition against Domestic Violence, February 8, 2017. https://ncadv.org/blog/posts/quick-guide-teen-dating-violence.

4. "Teen Dating Violence and Gender." Youth.gov, 2011. https://youth.gov/youth-topics/teen-dating-violence/gender.

5. Brown, Emma. "How Do We Prepare Boys for Healthy Relationships?" LitHub, March 7, 2021. https://lithub.com/how-do-we-prepare-boys-for-healthy-relationships/.

6. Brown, Emma. *To Raise a Boy: Classrooms, Locker Rooms, Bedrooms, and the Hidden Struggles of American Boyhood.* New York: Simon & Schuster, 2022.

7. HCMC Admin. "Healthy vs Unhealthy Relationships." Between US Health, February 10, 2020. https://betweenushealth.com/2020/02/10/healthy-vs-unhealthy-relationships/.

8. "National Domestic Violence Hotline." *The Hotline*, April 11, 2022. www.thehotline.org/.

9. Fink, Jennifer L. W. "How to Teach Consent to Boys—Without Shaming Them." *Your Teen Magazine*, September 3, 2021. https://yourteenmag.com/family-life/communication/how-to-teach-consent-to-boys-without-shaming-them/.

10. Feinberg, Mark E., Anna R. Solmeyer, and Susan M. McHale. "The Third Rail of Family Systems: Sibling Relationships, Mental and Behavioral Health, and Preventive Intervention in Childhood and Adolescence." *Clinical Child and Family Psychology Review* (March 2012).

11. Weir, Kirsten. "Improving Sibling Relationships." American Psychological Association, March 1, 2022. www.apa.org/monitor/2022/03/feature-sibling-relationships.

12. Feinberg, Mark E., Anna R. Solmeyer, and Susan M. McHale. "The Third Rail of Family Systems: Sibling Relationships, Mental and Behavioral Health, and Preventive Intervention in Childhood and Adolescence." *Clinical Child and Family Psychology Review*, March 2012. www.ncbi.nlm.nih.gov/pmc/articles/PMC3288255/#R25.

13. Feinberg, Mark E., Anna R. Solmeyer, and Susan M. McHale. "The Third Rail of Family Systems: Sibling Relationships, Mental and Behavioral Health, and Preventive Intervention in Childhood and Adolescence." *Clinical Child and Family Psychology Review*, March 2012. www.ncbi.nlm.nih.gov/pmc/articles/PMC3288255/#R25.

14. Psychology Today Staff. "Navigating Sibling Relationships." *Psychology Today*. Accessed June 10, 2022. www.psychologytoday.com/us/basics/family-dynamics/sibling-relationships.

15. Feinberg, Mark E., Anna R. Solmeyer, and Susan M. McHale. "The Third Rail of Family Systems: Sibling Relationships, Mental and Behavioral

Health, and Preventive Intervention in Childhood and Adolescence." *Clinical Child and Family Psychology Review*, March 2012. www.ncbi.nlm.nih.gov/pmc/articles/PMC3288255/#R25.

16. Feinberg, Mark E., Anna R. Solmeyer, and Susan M. McHale. "The Third Rail of Family Systems: Sibling Relationships, Mental and Behavioral Health, and Preventive Intervention in Childhood and Adolescence." *Clinical Child and Family Psychology Review*, March 2012. www.ncbi.nlm.nih.gov/pmc/articles/PMC3288255/#R25.

17. Psychology Today Staff. "Navigating Sibling Relationships." *Psychology Today*. Accessed June 10, 2022. www.psychologytoday.com/us/basics/family-dynamics/sibling-relationships.

18. Delahooke, Mona. *Brain-Body Parenting: How to Stop Managing Behavior and Start Raising Joyful, Resilient Kids*. New York: HarperCollins, 2022.

19. Weir, Kirsten. "Improving Sibling Relationships." *Monitor on Psychology*, March 1, 2022. www.apa.org/monitor/2022/03/feature-sibling-relationships.

20. Evaldsson, Ann-Carita. "Staging Insults and Mobilizing Categorizations in a Multiethnic Peer Group." *Discourse & Society*, November 2005. https://doi.org/10.1177/0957926505056663.

21. Randazza, Janelle. "The Power of Pillow Fights: 5 Reasons Why You Should Be Roughhousing with Your Children." Bay State Parent, March 2, 2021. www.baystateparent.com/story/lifestyle/2021/03/01/parenting-tips-roughhousing-helps-kids-learn-important-life-lessons/6877275002/.

22. Tatter, Grace. "Consent at Every Age." Harvard Graduate School of Education, December 19, 2018. www.gse.harvard.edu/news/uk/18/12/consent-every-age?fbclid=IwAR3Ro2utr-3fcqJF0fFhVMUnJno9X-W19EGKMq2XlEIFFkjNHLBabW_eSSsE.

23. Jacobson, Malia. "Parenting an Only Child: Are Siblings a Must for Childhood Happiness?" ParentMap, January 31, 2012. www.parentmap.com/article/parenting-an-only-child.

24. Denworth, Lydia. "How Monkeys Taught Me to Appreciate Teen Sleepovers." *New York Times*, February 4, 2020. www.nytimes.com/2020/02/04/well/family/teenagers-friendships-sleepovers-video-games-parenting.html/.

25. Denworth, Lydia. "The Outsize Influence of Your Middle-School Friends." *The Atlantic*, January 29, 2020. www.theatlantic.com/family/archive/2020/01/friendship-crucial-adolescent-brain/605638/.

26. Park, Alice. "Why Autism Affects Boys More Than Girls." *Time*, February 8, 2017. https://time.com/4663196/autism-spectrum-disorder-gender/.

Skogli, Erik Winther Winther, Martin H. Teicher, Per Normann Andersen, Kjell Tore Hovik, and Merete Øie. "ADHD in Girls and Boys—Gender Differences in Co-Existing Symptoms and Executive Function Measures."

BMC Psychiatry, November 9, 2013. www.ncbi.nlm.nih.gov/pmc/articles/PMC3827008/.

27. Jo Langford in discussion with author, April 12, 2021.

28. Denworth, Lydia. "The Outsize Influence of Your Middle-School Friends." *The Atlantic*, January 29, 2020. www.theatlantic.com/family/archive/2020/01/friendship-crucial-adolescent-brain/605638/.

29. Blackmon, Freddy. "Young Men Are Lonelier Than Ever before Says Recent Study." Guy Counseling, June 20, 2020. https://guycounseling.com/young-men-are-lonely-study/.

30. YouGov. "Results for YouGov Realtime (Friendship)." YouGov, July 2019. https://d25d2506sfb94s.cloudfront.net/cumulus_uploads/document/m97e4vdjnu/Results%20for%20YouGov%20RealTime%20(Friendship)%20164%205.7.2019.xlsx%20%20[Group].pdf.

31. Reichert, Michael C. *How to Raise a Boy: The Power of Connection to Build Good Men*. New York: TarcherPerigree, 2020.

32. Denworth, Lydia. "How Monkeys Taught Me to Appreciate Teen Sleepovers." *New York Times*, February 4, 2020. www.nytimes.com/2020/02/04/well/family/teenagers-friendships-sleepovers-video-games-parenting.html/.

33. Denworth, Lydia. "How Monkeys Taught Me to Appreciate Teen Sleepovers." *New York Times*, February 4, 2020. www.nytimes.com/2020/02/04/well/family/teenagers-friendships-sleepovers-video-games-parenting.html/.

34. Cole, AmyKay, and Kathryn A. Kerns. "Perceptions of Sibling Qualities and Activities of Early Adolescents." *Journal of Early Adolescence*, May 2001. https://doi.org/10.1177/0272431601021002004.

35. Camarena, Phame M., Pamela A. Sarigiani, and Anne C. Petersen. "Gender-Specific Pathways to Intimacy in Early Adolescence." *Journal of Youth and Adolescence*, February 1990. https://link.springer.com/article/10.1007/BF01539442.

36. Denworth, Lydia. "How Monkeys Taught Me to Appreciate Teen Sleepovers." *New York Times*, February 4, 2020. www.nytimes.com/2020/02/04/well/family/teenagers-friendships-sleepovers-video-games-parenting.html/.

37. Denworth, Lydia. "How Monkeys Taught Me to Appreciate Teen Sleepovers." *New York Times*, February 4, 2020. www.nytimes.com/2020/02/04/well/family/teenagers-friendships-sleepovers-video-games-parenting.html/.

38. Bauers, Sandy. "Philadelphia's Black Teen Boys Lose So Many Friends to Gun Violence. Studying How They Grieve Might Help." *Philadelphia Inquirer*, January 2, 2020. www.inquirer.com/health/gun-violence-black-teen-boys-grief-philadelphia-penn-research-20200102.html.

39. Bauers, Sandy. "Philadelphia's Black Teen Boys Lose So Many Friends to Gun Violence. Studying How They Grieve Might Help." *Phila-*

delphia Inquirer, January 2, 2020. www.inquirer.com/health/gun-violence-black-teen-boys-grief-philadelphia-penn-research-20200102.html.

40. Atkins, Sue. "How to Help Kids with Friendship after Lock Down." Sue Atkins—The Parenting Coach, April 28, 2020. https://sueatkinsparentingcoach.com/2020/04/kids-make-friends/.

41. ADHD Dude. "High School Guys Social Skills Lesson (Perspective Taking)—ADHD Dude—Ryan Wexelblatt." YouTube, July 12, 2020. www.youtube.com/watch?v=Z6oZF1Qeev4.

42. ADHD Dude. "High School Guys Social Skills Lesson (Perspective Taking)—ADHD Dude—Ryan Wexelblatt." YouTube, July 12, 2020. www.youtube.com/watch?v=Z6oZF1Qeev4.

43. Erasmus, Estelle. "What Should I Do about My Tween's Toxic Friend?" *Good Housekeeping*, May 10, 2021. www.goodhousekeeping.com/life/parenting/a36356220/tween-toxic-friend/.

44. Erasmus, Estelle. "What Should I Do about My Tween's Toxic Friend?" *Good Housekeeping*, May 10, 2021. www.goodhousekeeping.com/life/parenting/a36356220/tween-toxic-friend/.

45. Hurley, Katie. "Mean Boys Are a Thing, Too. Here's How to Help Your Son Manage Toxic Relationships." *Washington Post*, November 8, 2018. www.washingtonpost.com/lifestyle/2018/11/08/mean-behavior-isnt-just-girls-heres-how-help-your-son-manage-toxic-relationships/.

46. A Mighty Girl staff. "The Hidden Benefits of Girl-Boy Friendships and How to Foster Them between Children." A Mighty Girl, March 8, 2022. www.amightygirl.com/blog?p=23152&fbclid=IwAR3icNVExx-ciPyhtpTa_Yxr-JajFeqV-GCTy4OrLw5wHVSYfTxJdz7SVqo.

Miller, Claire Cain. "How to Raise a Feminist Son." *New York Times*, June 2, 2017. www.nytimes.com/2017/06/02/upshot/how-to-raise-a-feminist-son.html.

47. Donna, Ilana. "How to Deal with Mean Kids on the Playground." Patch Media, May 3, 2019. https://patch.com/new-york/rivertowns/how-deal-mean-kids-playground.

48. Myler, Carmen. "Please Teach Your Sons about 'the Line in the Sand.'" *Maggie Dent* (blog), May 28, 2019. www.maggiedent.com/blog/please-teach-your-sons-about-the-line-in-the-sand/.

49. Weissbourd, Richard, Trisha Ross Anderson, Alison Cashin, and Joe McIntyre. "How Adults Can Promote Young People's Healthy Relationships and Prevent Misogyny and Sexual Harassment." Making Caring Common Project, May 2017. https://static1.squarespace.com/static/5b7c56e255b02c683659fe43/t/5bd51a0324a69425bd079b59/1540692500558/mcc_the_talk_final.pdf.

50. Blumberg, Dean, and Lena van der List. "Dealing with Your Child's First Crush." Kids Considered, October 25, 2021. https://health.ucdavis.edu/blog/kids-considered/dealing-with-your-childs-first-crush/2021/10.

51. Hinduja, Sameer, and Justin W. Patchin. "Digital Dating Abuse among a National Sample of U.S. Youth." *Journal of Interpersonal Violence*, December 2021. https://doi.org/10.1177/0886260519897344.

52. Hinduja, Sameer, and Justin W. Patchin. "Digital Dating Abuse among a National Sample of U.S. Youth." *Journal of Interpersonal Violence*, December 2021. https://doi.org/10.1177/0886260519897344.

Pittman, Robin. "How to Talk with Kids about Healthy Relationships." Alice Aycock Poe Center for Health Education, January 16, 2018. www.poehealth.org/how-to-talk-with-kids-about-healthy-relationships/.

53. Bell, David L., Joshua G. Rosenberger, and Mary A. Ott. "Masculinity in Adolescent Males' Early Romantic and Sexual Heterosexual Relationships." *American Journal of Men's Health*, May 2015. https://doi.org/10.1177/1557988314535623.

54. Weissbourd, Richard, Trisha Ross Anderson, Alison Cashin, and Joe McIntyre. "How Adults Can Promote Young People's Healthy Relationships and Prevent Misogyny and Sexual Harassment." Making Caring Common Project, May 2017. https://static1.squarespace.com/static/5b7c56e255b02c683659fe43/t/5bd51a0324a69425bd079b59/1540692500558/mcc_the_talk_final.pdf.

55. Weissbourd, Richard, Trisha Ross Anderson, Alison Cashin, and Joe McIntyre. "How Adults Can Promote Young People's Healthy Relationships and Prevent Misogyny and Sexual Harassment." Making Caring Common Project, May 2017. https://static1.squarespace.com/static/5b7c56e255b02c683659fe43/t/5bd51a0324a69425bd079b59/1540692500558/mcc_the_talk_final.pdf.

56. Weissbourd, Richard, Trisha Ross Anderson, Alison Cashin, and Joe McIntyre. "How Adults Can Promote Young People's Healthy Relationships and Prevent Misogyny and Sexual Harassment." Making Caring Common Project, May 2017. https://static1.squarespace.com/static/5b7c56e255b02c683659fe43/t/5bd51a0324a69425bd079b59/1540692500558/mcc_the_talk_final.pdf.

57. Weissbourd, Richard, Trisha Ross Anderson, Alison Cashin, and Joe McIntyre. "How Adults Can Promote Young People's Healthy Relationships and Prevent Misogyny and Sexual Harassment." Making Caring Common Project, May 2017. https://static1.squarespace.com/static/5b7c56e255b02c683659fe43/t/5bd51a0324a69425bd079b59/1540692500558/mcc_the_talk_final.pdf.

58. French, Bryana H., Jasmine D. Tilghman, and Dominique A. Malebranche. "Sexual Coercion Context and Psychosocial Correlates among Diverse Males." *Psychology of Men and Masculinity*, 2015. https://psycnet.apa.org/record/2014-09544-001.

59. Black, Michael Ian. *A Better Man: A (Mostly Serious) Letter to My Son.* Chapel Hill, NC: Algonquin Books, 2020.

60. Fink, Jennifer L. W. "Talking to Boys about Sexually Aggressive Girls." *Building Boys*, March 31, 2014. https://buildingboys.net/talking-boys-sexually-aggressive-girls/.

Black, Michael Ian. *A Better Man: A (Mostly Serious) Letter to My Son.* Chapel Hill, NC: Algonquin Books, 2020.

61. Fink, Jennifer L. W. "Talking to Boys about Sexually Aggressive Girls." *Building Boys*, March 31, 2014. https://buildingboys.net/talking-boys-sexually-aggressive-girls/.

62. McKee, Alan. "Yes, Your Child Will Be Exposed to Online Porn but Don't Panic—Here's What to Do Instead." The Conversation, November 16, 2020. https://theconversation.com/yes-your-child-will-be-exposed-to-online-porn-but-dont-panic-heres-what-to-do-instead-149900#:~:text=According%20to%20some%20sources%2C%20 the,on%20porn%20and%20their%20kids.

"Age Verification for Online Pornography." Parliament of Australia, March 4, 2020. www.aph.gov.au/Parliamentary_Business/Committees/House/Social_Policy_and_Legal_Affairs/Onlineageverification/Report/section?id=committees%2Freportrep%2F024436%2F72615.

63. Fink, Jennifer L. W. "How to Teach Consent to Boys—without Shaming Them." *Your Teen Magazine*, September 3, 2021. https://yourteenmag.com/family-life/communication/how-to-teach-consent-to-boys-without-shaming-them/.

64. Weissbourd, Richard, Trisha Ross Anderson, Alison Cashin, and Joe McIntyre. "How Adults Can Promote Young People's Healthy Relationships and Prevent Misogyny and Sexual Harassment." Making Caring Common Project, May 2017. https://static1.squarespace.com/static/5b7c56e255b02c683659fe43/t/5bd51a0324a69425bd079b59/1540692500558/mcc_the_talk_final.pdf.

65. @Adigoesswimming. Twitter, May 20, 2018. https://twitter.com/adigoesswimming/status/998227660437417985?lang=en.

66. Smiler, Andrew M. *Dating and Sex: A Guide for the 21st Century Teen Boy.* Washington, DC: American Psychological Association, 2016.

CHAPTER 4

1. Holbrook, Sharon. "Capable Kids Q&A: Differently Wired." *Sharon Holbrook, Writer* (blog), June 15, 2021. https://sharonholbrook.com/2021/06/15/capable-kids-qa-differently-wired/.

2. Cornwall, Gail. "Giving Kids No Autonomy at All Has Become a Parenting Norm—And the Pandemic Is Worsening the Trend." Salon.com, January 17, 2021. www.salon.com/2021/01/17/giving-kids-no-autonomy-

at-all-has-become-a-parenting-norm—and-the-pandemic-is-worsening-the-trend/.

3. Francis, Meagan. "Helicopter Parenting and Bulldozer Parenting Are Bad for Everyone—Including Parents." NBCNews.com, October 13, 2019. www.nbcnews.com/think/opinion/helicopter-parenting-bulldozer-parenting-are-bad-everyone-including-parents-ncna1065266?fbclid=IwAR0 h7OPJjRDj38mlggfy9rRQZTLgbf5peVOJK_FlK5WnxS6ufdrvqETAqCU.

4. Duckworth, A. L., C. Peterson, M. D. Matthews, and D. R. Kelly. "Grit: Perseverance and Passion for Long-Term Goals." *Journal of Personality and Social Psychology* 92 (2007): 1087–1101. doi: 10.1037/0022-3514.92.6.1087.

5. Kannangara, Chathurika S. "From Languishing Dyslexia to Thriving Dyslexia: Developing a New Conceptual Approach to Working with People with Dyslexia." *Frontiers in Psychology*, December 24, 2015. www.frontiersin.org/articles/10.3389/fpsyg.2015.01976/full.

6. Dweck, Carol. "Carol Dweck Revisits the 'Growth Mindset.'" In *Mindset: The New Psychology of Success*. New York: Ballantine Books, 2015.

7. Sigmundsson, Hermundur, Stéfan Guðnason, and Sigurrós Jóhannsdóttir. "Passion, Grit and Mindset: Exploring Gender Differences." *New Ideas in Psychology* 63 (2021).

8. Zenger, Jack, and Joseph Folkman. "How Age and Gender Affect Self-Improvement." *Harvard Business Review*, September 11, 2020. https://hbr.org/2016/01/how-age-and-gender-affect-self-improvement.

9. Zenger, Jack, and Joseph Folkman. "How Age and Gender Affect Self-Improvement." *Harvard Business Review*, September 11, 2020. https://hbr.org/2016/01/how-age-and-gender-affect-self-improvement.

10. Kannangara, Chathurika. "Success in Failure." Tedx Talks, University of Bolton, April 18, 2016. www.youtube.com/watch?v=IG2_O5LRkDY.

11. Achor, Shawn, and Michelle Gielan. "Resilience Is about How You Recharge, Not How You Endure." *Harvard Business Review*, June 24, 2016. https://hbr.org/2016/06/resilience-is-about-how-you-recharge-not-how-you-endure?utm_source=twitter&utm_medium=social&utm_campaign=hbr.

12. Achor, Shawn, and Michelle Gielan. "Resilience Is about How You Recharge, Not How You Endure." *Harvard Business Review*, June 24, 2016. https://hbr.org/2016/06/resilience-is-about-how-you-recharge-not-how-you-endure?utm_source=twitter&utm_medium=social&utm_campaign=hbr.

13. Kris, Deborah Farmer. "Listen and Connect: How Parents Can Support Teens' Mental Health Right Now." KQED, December 14, 2020. www.kqed.org/mindshift/57108/listen-and-connect-how-parents-can-support-teens-mental-health-right-now.

CHAPTER 5

1. Allison, Janet, and Fink, Jennifer L. W. "My Boy Can with Sassy Harvey." *On Boys* podcast, August 20, 2020. www.on-boys-podcast.com/my-boy-can-and-my-boy-can-dance-with-sassy-harvey/.

2. Hedegaard, Holly, Sally C. Curtin, and Margaret Warner. "Suicide Mortality in the United States, 1999–2019." National Center for Health Statistics, February 2021. www.cdc.gov/nchs/data/databriefs/db398-H.pdf.

3. National Science Foundation. "ADVANCE at a Glance." NSF, 2021. www.nsf.gov/crssprgm/advance/.

4. Blocka, Katharina, Alyssa Croft, Lucy De Souza, and Toni Schmader. "Do People Care If Men Don't Care about Caring? The Asymmetry in Support for Changing Gender Roles." *Journal of Experimental Social Psychology* 83, (2019): 112–31.

5. Allison, Janet, and Fink, Jennifer L. W. "How to Raise a Boy with Michael Reichert." *On Boys* podcast, May 9, 2019. www.on-boys-podcast.com/how-to-raise-a-boy-with-michael-c-reichert/.

6. DeLoache, Judy S., Gabrielle Simcock, and Suzanne Macari. "Planes, Trains, Automobiles—And Tea Sets: Extremely Intense Interests in Very Young Children." *Developmental Psychology*, November 2007. https://pubmed.ncbi.nlm.nih.gov/18020834/.

7. Fink, Jennifer L. W. "Here's How to Motivate Teenage Boys: Encourage Risk-Taking." *Your Teen.* www.yourteenmag.com/health/teenager-mental-health/how-to-motivate-boys.

8. Fenton Communications. "The State of Play." Robert Wood Johnson Foundation, February 1, 2010. www.rwjf.org/en/library/research/2010/02/the-state-of-play.html.

9. Alexandera, Joyce M., Kathy E. Johnson, Mary E. Leibham, and Ken Kelley. "The Development of Conceptual Interests in Young Children." *Cognitive Development* 23 (2008): 224–34.

CHAPTER 6

1. McDermott, Cassidy L., Katherine Hilton, Anne T. Park, Ursula A. Tooley, Austin L. Boroshok, Muralidhar Mupparapu, JoAnna M. Scott, Erin E. Bumann, and Allyson P. Mackey. "Early Life Stress Is Associated with Earlier Emergence of Permanent Molars." *PNAS*, June 15, 2021. www.pnas.org/content/118/24/e2105304118/tab-article-info.

2. Tooley, Ursula A., Danielle S. Bassett, and Allyson P. Mackey. "Environmental Influences on the Pace of Brain Development." *Nature Reviews*, June 2021. https://static1.squarespace.com/static/53fa2990e4b009642c5e689b/t/61ba605e9cb0f225c5e47df0/1639604321220/s41583-021-00457-5.pdf.

3. Tooley, Ursula A., Danielle S. Bassett, and Allyson P. Mackey. "Environmental Influences on the Pace of Brain Development." *Nature Reviews*, June 2021. https://static1.squarespace.com/static/53fa2990e4b009642c5e689b/t/61ba605e9cb0f225c5e47df0/1639604321220/s41583-021-00457-5.pdf.

4. Gopnik, Alison. "What Children Lose When Their Brains Develop Too Fast." *Wall Street Journal*, December 9, 2021. www.wsj.com/articles/what-children-lose-when-their-brains-develop-too-fast-11639071752?mod=Searchresults_pos1&page=1.

5. Kern, Margaret L., and Howard S. Friedman. "Early Educational Milestones as Predictors of Lifelong Academic Achievement, Midlife Adjustment, and Longevity." *Journal of Applied Developmental Psychology*, 2008. www.ncbi.nlm.nih.gov/pmc/articles/PMC2713445/.

6. Kern, Margaret L., and Howard S. Friedman. "Early Educational Milestones as Predictors of Lifelong Academic Achievement, Midlife Adjustment, and Longevity." Journal of Applied Developmental Psychology, 2008. www.ncbi.nlm.nih.gov/pmc/articles/PMC2713445/.

7. Park, Anne T., and Allyson P. Mackey. "Do Younger Children Benefit More from Cognitive and Academic Interventions? How Training Studies Can Provide Insights into Developmental Changes in Plasticity." *Mind, Brain, and Education*, 2021. https://static1.squarespace.com/static/53fa2990e4b009642c5e689b/t/61d8b028ce20da752b7a74f1/1641590825146/Mind+Brain+and+Education+-+2021+-+Park+-+Do+Younger+Children+Benefit+More+From+Cognitive+and+Academic+Interventions++How.pdf.

8. Tooley, Ursula A., Danielle S. Bassett, and Allyson P. Mackey. "Environmental Influences on the Pace of Brain Development." *Nature News*, April 28, 2021. www.nature.com/articles/s41583-021-00457-5.

9. Dinkel, Danae, and Kailey Snyder. "Exploring Gender Differences in Infant Motor Development Related to Parent's Promotion of Play." *Infant Behavior and Development*, May 2020. www.sciencedirect.com/science/article/pii/S0163638319301742?via%3Dihub.

10. Adani, Shir, and Maja Cepanec. "Sex Differences in Early Communication Development: Behavioral and Neurobiological Indicators of More Vulnerable Communication System Development in Boys." *Croatian Medical Journal*, April 30, 2019. www.ncbi.nlm.nih.gov/pmc/articles/PMC6509633/#:~:text=During%20the%20first%20years%20of,words%20(21%2C22).

11. Kiddoo, Darcie A. "Nocturnal Enuresis." *CMAJ*, May 15, 2012. www.ncbi.nlm.nih.gov/pmc/articles/PMC3348193/#:~:text=Gender%20also%20plays%20a%20role,boys%20and%202.51%25%20among%20girls.&text=Boys%20have%20also%20been%20found%20to%20have%20more%20severe%20bedwetting%20than%20girls.

12. Cole, Tim J., Emily K. Rousham, Nicola L. Hawley, Noel Cameron, Shane Norris, and John M. Pettifor. "Ethnic and Sex Differences in Skeletal

Maturation among the Birth to Twenty Cohort in South Africa." *Archives of Disease in Childhood*, 2015. https://adc.bmj.com/content/100/2/138.
Grgic, Olja, Enisa Shevroja, and Brunilda Dhamo. "Skeletal Maturation in Relation to Ethnic Background in Children of School Age: The Generation R Study." *Bone* 132 (2020).
13. Cox, Tony. "Brain Maturity Extends Well beyond Teen Years." NPR, October 10, 2011. www.npr.org/templates/story/story.php?storyId=141164708.
14. Messerli-Bürgy, Nadine, Tanja H. Kakebeeke, Andrea H. Meyer, Amar Arhab, Annina E. Zysset, Kerstin Stülb, Claudia S. Leeger-Aschmann, Einat A. Schmutz, Susi Kriemler, Jardena J. Puder, Simone Munsch, and Oskar G. Jenni. "Walking Onset: A Poor Predictor for Motor and Cognitive Skills in Healthy Preschool Children." *BMC Pediatrics*, August 27, 2021. https://bmcpediatr.biomedcentral.com/track/pdf/10.1186/s12887-021-02828-4.pdf.
15. Quast, A., V. Hesse, J. Hain, P. Wermke, and K. Wermke. "Baby Babbling at Five Months Linked to Sex Hormone Levels in Early Infancy." *Infant Behavior and Development* 44 (August 2016): 1–10. doi: 10.1016/j.infbeh.2016.04.002.
16. Adani, Shir, and Maja Cepanec. "Sex Differences in Early Communication Development: Behavioral and Neurobiological Indicators of More Vulnerable Communication System Development in Boys." *Croatian Medical Journal*, April 30, 2019. www.ncbi.nlm.nih.gov/pmc/articles/PMC6509633/#:~:text=During%20the%20first%20years%20of,words%20(21%2C22).
17. Etchell, Andrew, Aditi Adhikari, Lauren S. Weinberg, Ai Leen Choo, Emily O. Garnett, Ho Ming Chow, and Soo-Eun Chang. "A Systematic Literature Review of Sex Differences in Childhood Language and Brain Development." *Neuropsychologia*, June 2018. www.ncbi.nlm.nih.gov/pmc/articles/PMC5988993/.
18. Etchell, Andrew, Aditi Adhikari, Lauren S. Weinberg, Ai Leen Choo, Emily O. Garnett, Ho Ming Chow, and Soo-Eun Chang. "A Systematic Literature Review of Sex Differences in Childhood Language and Brain Development." *Neuropsychologia*, June 2018. www.ncbi.nlm.nih.gov/pmc/articles/PMC5988993/.
19. Duncan, Paula M., Joseph F. Hagan, and Judith S. Shaw. "Guidelines for Health Supervision of Infants, Children, and Adolescents." Bright Futures, 2017. https://brightfutures.aap.org/Bright%20Futures%20Documents/BF4_POCKETGUIDE.pdf.
20. Sandeen, Cathy. "200 by Two." CSHA, March 4, 2020. www.csha.org/200-by-two/.
21. Davis, Susan. "Potty Training: Seven Surprising Facts." WebMD, September 5, 2015. www.webmd.com/parenting/features/potty-training-seven-surprising-facts#1.

Schum, Timothy R., Thomas M. Kolb, Timothy L. McAuliffe, Mark D. Simms, Richard L. Underhill, and Marla Lewis. "Sequential Acquisition of Toilet-Training Skills: A Descriptive Study of Gender and Age Differences in Normal Children." *Pediatrics*, March 2002. https://pubmed.ncbi.nlm.nih.gov/11875176/.

22. Schum, Timothy R., Thomas M. Kolb, Timothy L. McAuliffe, Mark D. Simms, Richard L. Underhill, and Marla Lewis. "Sequential Acquisition of Toilet-Training Skills: A Descriptive Study of Gender and Age Differences in Normal Children." *Pediatrics*. https://pubmed.ncbi.nlm.nih.gov/11875176/.

Wald, Ellen R., Carlo Di Lorenzo, Lynne Cipriani, Kathleen Kolborn, Rosa Burgers, and Arnold Wald. "Bowel Habits and Toilet Training in a Diverse Population of Children." *Journal of Pediatric Gastroenterology and Nutrition*, March 2009. https://pubmed.ncbi.nlm.nih.gov/19274784/.

23. Shreeram, Srirangam, Jian-Ping He, Amanda Kalaydjian, Shannon Brothers, and Kathleen Ries Merikangas. "Prevalence of Enuresis and Its Association with Attention-Deficit/Hyperactivity Disorder among U.S. Children: Results From a Nationally Representative Study." *Journal of the American Academy of Child and Adolescent Psychiatry*, January 2009. www.ncbi.nlm.nih.gov/pmc/articles/PMC2794242/?report=reader.

24. Leahy, Marie A., and Nicole M. Fitzpatrick. "Early Readers and Academic Success." *Journal of Educational and Developmental Psychology*, 2017. https://pdfs.semanticscholar.org/5012/35bbd71340c2b89a496345267a8004a05d22.pdf.

25. Leahy, Marie A., and Nicole M. Fitzpatrick. "Early Readers and Academic Success." *Journal of Educational and Developmental Psychology*, 2017. https://pdfs.semanticscholar.org/5012/35bbd71340c2b89a496345267a8004a05d22.pdf.

26. Organisation for Economic Co-operation and Development. "Girls' and Boys' Performance in PISA." OECD, 2022. www.oecd-ilibrary.org/sites/f56f8c26-en/index.html?itemId=/content/component/f56f8c26-en.

27. Loveless, Tom. "The Gender Gap in Reading." The Brookings Institution, March 26, 2015. www.brookings.edu/research/the-gender-gap-in-reading/.

28. Organisation for Economic Co-operation and Development. "Girls' and Boys' Performance in PISA." OECD, 2022. www.oecd-ilibrary.org/sites/f56f8c26-en/index.html?itemId=/content/component/f56f8c26-en.

29. Fink, Jennifer L. W. "Why Treating Boys Like Girls Won't Close the Gender Gap in Education." *Building Boys*, July 26, 2016. https://building-boys.net/why-treating-boys-like-girls-wont-close-the-gender-gap-in-education/.

30. Moss, Gemma, and Liz Washbrook. "Understanding the Gender Gap in Literacy and Language Development." Bristol Working Papers in Education, University of Bristol, July 18, 2016. www.bristol.ac.uk/media-library/

sites/education/documents/bristol-working-papers-in-education/Understanding%20the%20Gender%20Gap%20working%20paper.pdf.

31. Leahy, Marie A., and Nicole M. Fitzpatrick. "Early Readers and Academic Success." In *Journal of Educational and Developmental Psychology 7*, no. 2 (2017): 87–95.

32. Goff, Phillip Atiba, Matthew Christian Jackson, Natalie Ann DiTomasso, Brooke Allison Lewis Di Leone, and Carmen Marie Culotta. "The Essence of Innocence: Consequences of Dehumanizing Black Children." *Journal of Personality and Social Psychology*, 2014. www.apa.org/pubs/journals/releases/psp-a0035663.pdf.

33. Lopez, German. "Police Thought 12-Year-Old Tamir Rice Was 20 When They Shot Him. This Isn't Uncommon." Vox, November 26, 2014. www.vox.com/2014/11/26/7297265/tamir-rice-age-police.

34. Lopez, German. "Police Thought 12-Year-Old Tamir Rice Was 20 When They Shot Him. This Isn't Uncommon." Vox, November 26, 2014. www.vox.com/2014/11/26/7297265/tamir-rice-age-police.

Williams, Vanessa. "Innocence Erased: How Society Keeps Black Boys from Being Boys." *Washington Post*, September 21, 2018. www.washingtonpost.com/nation/2018/09/21/innocence-denied-black-boys-who-face-harsher-scrutiny-consequences-than-their-white-peers/?requestid=c8f5c444-c9d1-4d62-aa1a-62945562a215&pml=1.

35. Liston, Barbara, and Chris Francescani. "Killer of Trayvon Martin Gets Bail, Apologises to Family." Reuters, April 20, 2012. www.reuters.com/article/uk-usa-florida-shooting/killer-of-trayvon-martin-gets-bail-apologises-to-family-idUKBRE83J0K620120420.

36. CNN. "Trayvon Martin Shooting Fast Facts." CNN, February 14, 2022. www.cnn.com/2013/06/05/us/trayvon-martin-shooting-fast-facts/index.html.

37. Office of Civil Rights. "An Overview of Exclusionary Discipline Practices in Public Schools for the 2017–18 School Year." U.S. Department of Education, June 2021. www2.ed.gov/about/offices/list/ocr/docs/crdc-exclusionary-school-discipline.pdf.

38. Kern, Margaret L., and Howard S. Friedman. "Early Educational Milestones as Predictors of Lifelong Academic Achievement, Midlife Adjustment, and Longevity." *Journal of Applied Developmental Psychology*, 2008. www.ncbi.nlm.nih.gov/pmc/articles/PMC2713445/.

39. Layton, Timothy J., Michael L. Barnett, Tanner R. Hicks, and Anupam B. Jena. "Attention Deficit–Hyperactivity Disorder and Month of School Enrollment." *New England Journal of Medicine*, February 14, 2019. www.nejm.org/doi/full/10.1056/nejmoa1806828.

40. Barnett, Lynn A. "The Education of Playful Boys: Class Clowns in the Classroom." *Frontiers in Psychology*, March 1, 2018. www.frontiersin.org/articles/10.3389/fpsyg.2018.00232/full.

41. Reeves, Richard V. Of Boys and Men: Why the Modern Male Is Struggling, Why It Matters, and What to Do about It. Washington, DC: Brookings Institution Press, 2022.

42. Jones, Suzanne Stateler. "Academic Red-Shirting: Perceived Life Satisfaction of Adolescent Males."(PhD diss., Texas A&M, 2012). www.proquest.com/docview/1022333185?pq-origsite=gscholar&fromopenview=true.

43. Cox, Tony. "Brain Maturity Extends Well beyond Teen Years." NPR, October 10, 2011. www.npr.org/templates/story/story.php?storyId=141164708.

44. Scialabba, Nicole. "Should Juveniles Be Charged as Adults in the Criminal Justice System?" American Bar Association, October 3, 2016. www.americanbar.org/groups/litigation/committees/childrens-rights/articles/2016/should-juveniles-be-charged-as-adults/.

45. National Juvenile Justice Network. "Campaign for Youth Justice." National Juvenile Justice Network, May 2020. www.njjn.org/uploads/digital-library/CFYJ%20-%20TRANSFER%20CLOSE%20PPT%20FINAL%20(2).pdf.

46. Fernandes-Alcantara, Adrienne L. "Youth and the Labor Force: Background and Trends." Congressional Research Service, August 20, 2018. https://sgp.fas.org/crs/misc/R42519.pdf.

Harrar, Sari. "Fighting the Failure to Launch in Young Adults." AARP, December 20, 2021. www.aarp.org/home-family/friends-family/info-2021/failure-to-launch.html.

47. Fry, Richard, Jeffrey S. Passel, and D'Vera Cohn. "A Majority of Young Adults in the U.S. Live with Their Parents for the First Time since the Great Depression." Pew Research Center, September 4, 2020. www.pewresearch.org/fact-tank/2020/09/04/a-majority-of-young-adults-in-the-u-s-live-with-their-parents-for-the-first-time-since-the-great-depression/.

48. Hill, Nancy E., and Alexis Redding. "The Real Reason Young Adults Seem Slow to 'Grow Up.'" The Atlantic, April 28, 2021. www.theatlantic.com/family/archive/2021/04/real-reason-young-adults-seem-slow-grow/618733/.

49. Dent, Maggie. "Teaching with the Teen Brain in Mind." Maggie Dent (blog), 2015. www.maggiedent.com/wp-content/uploads/7%20Teaching%20with%20the%20teen%20brain%20in%20mind.pdf.

50. Roberts, Adrienne. "Driving? The Kids Are So over It." Wall Street Journal, April 20, 2019. www.wsj.com/articles/driving-the-kids-are-so-over-it-11555732810.

51. CDC. "Teen Drivers: Get the Facts." Centers for Disease Control and Prevention, October 12, 2021. www.cdc.gov/transportationsafety/teen_drivers/teendrivers_factsheet.html.

52. CDC. "Teen Drivers: Get the Facts." Centers for Disease Control and Prevention, October 12, 2021. www.cdc.gov/transportationsafety/teen_drivers/teendrivers_factsheet.html.

53. Hillsberg, Christina. "Take It from This Spy Mom: Our Kids Are Capable of More." *Washington Post*, June 7, 2021. www.washingtonpost.com/lifestyle/2021/06/08/kids-capable-spy-mom/.

54. Hillsberg, Christina, and Ryan Hillsberg. *License to Parent: How My Career as a Spy Helped Me Raise Resourceful, Self-Sufficient Kids*. New York: G. P. Putnam's Sons, 2021.

55. Harrar, Sari. "Fighting the Failure to Launch in Young Adults." AARP, December 20, 2021. www.aarp.org/home-family/friends-family/info-2021/failure-to-launch.html.

56. Harrar, Sari. "Fighting the Failure to Launch in Young Adults." AARP, December 20, 2021. www.aarp.org/home-family/friends-family/info-2021/failure-to-launch.html.

CHAPTER 7

1. Fink, J. L. W. "Your Kids Are More Competent Than You Think." *Building Boys*, March 19, 2017. https://buildingboys.net/your-kids-are-more-competent-than-you-think/.

2. Brenan, Megan. "Women Still Handle Main Household Tasks in U.S." Gallup, January 29, 2020. https://news.gallup.com/poll/283979/women-handle-main-household-tasks.aspx.

3. Brenan, Megan. "Women Still Handle Main Household Tasks in U.S." Gallup, January 29, 2020. https://news.gallup.com/poll/283979/women-handle-main-household-tasks.aspx.

4. Dernberger, Brittany N., and Joanna R. Pepin. "Gender Flexibility, but Not Equality: Young Adults' Division of Labor Preferences." *Sociological Science*, January 21, 2020. www.sociologicalscience.com/download/vol-7/january/SocSci_v7_36to56.pdf.

5. Goldscheider, Frances, and Sandra Hofferth. "Reflections on the Future of the Second Half of the Gender Revolution." Maryland Population Research Center, 2018. www.popcenter.umd.edu/news/news_1500574447256.

Livingston, Gretchen. "The Way U.S. Teens Spend Their Time Is Changing, but Differences between Boys and Girls Persist." Pew Research Center, February 20, 2019. www.pewresearch.org/fact-tank/2019/02/20/the-way-u-s-teens-spend-their-time-is-changing-but-differences-between-boys-and-girls-persist/.

Miller, Claire Cain. "A 'Generationally Perpetuated' Pattern: Daughters Do More Chores." *New York Times*, August 8, 2018. www.nytimes.com/2018/08/08/upshot/chores-girls-research-social-science.html.

6. Rees, Gwyther. "Children's Daily Activities: Age Variations between 8 and 12 Years Old across 16 Countries." *Journal of International and Comparative Social Policy*, March 27, 2017. www.tandfonline.com/doi/full/10.1080/21699763.2017.1307778?scroll=top&needAccess=true.

7. Hartley, Gemma. *Fed Up: Emotional Labor, Women, and the Way Forward*. New York: HarperOne, 2020.

8. Pinsker, J. "The Myth That Gets Men out of Doing Chores." *The Atlantic*, January 27, 2021. www.theatlantic.com/family/archive/2021/01/boys-men-messy-chores/617845/.

9. Tourjée, Diana. "Men Are Definitely Dirtier Than Women, According to Science." *Vice*, April 11, 2016. www.vice.com/en/article/nz88ad/men-are-definitely-dirtier-than-women-according-to-science.

10. Thébaud, Sarah, Sabino Kornrich, and Leah Ruppanner. "Good Housekeeping, Great Expectations: Gender and Housework Norms." *Sociological Methods & Research*, May 30, 2019. https://journals.sagepub.com/doi/10.1177/0049124119852395.

11. Al-Shawaf, Laith, David M.G. Lewis, and David M. Buss. "Sex Differences in Disgust: Why Are Women More Easily Disgusted Than Men?" *Emotion Review*, 2017. https://labs.la.utexas.edu/buss/files/2013/02/Why-Are-Women-More-Easily-Disgusted-than-Men.pdf.

12. Fjaeldstad, Alexander, Jens Sundbøll, Andreas Niklassen, and Therese Ovesen. "Odor Familiarity and Identification Abilities in Adolescents." *Chemical Senses* 42, no. 3 (March 2017): 239–46.

13. Thébaud, Sarah, Sabino Kornrich, and Leah Ruppanner. "Good Housekeeping, Great Expectations: Gender and Housework Norms." *Sociological Methods & Research*, May 30, 2019. https://journals.sagepub.com/doi/10.1177/0049124119852395.

14. Pinsker, Joe. "The Myth That Gets Men out of Doing Chores." *The Atlantic*, January 27, 2021. www.theatlantic.com/family/archive/2021/01/boys-men-messy-chores/617845/.

15. Gunnery, Mark. "Why Do Boys Get a Pass When It Comes to Household Chores? The Same Reasons Men Do." WAMU/American University Radio, May 31, 2019. https://wamu.org/story/19/05/31/why-do-boys-get-a-pass-when-it-comes-to-household-chores-the-same-reasons-men-do-2/.

16. Schulte, Brigid. "Providing Care Changes Men." New America, February 4, 2021. www.newamerica.org/better-life-lab/reports/providing-care-changes-men/.

17. College of Education & Human Development. "Involving Children in Household Tasks: Is It Worth the Effort?" Regents of the University of Minnesota, 2014. https://ghk.h-cdn.co/assets/cm/15/12/55071e0298a05_-_Involving-children-in-household-tasks-U-of-M.pdf.

The Center for Parenting Education. "Benefits of Chores." The Center for Parenting Education, 2006. https://centerforparentingeducation.org/library-of-articles/responsibility-and-chores/part-i-benefits-of-chores/.

18. Beresin, Eugene. "Why Chores Are Important for Kids." *Psychology Today*, August 7, 2019. www.psychologytoday.com/us/blog/inside-out-outside-in/201908/why-chores-are-important-kids.

19. Chen, Ying-Yeh, ZiYi Cai, Qingsong Chang, Silvia Sara Canetto, and Paul S. F. Yip. "Caregiving as Suicide-Prevention: An Ecological 20-Country Study of the Association between Men's Family Carework, Unemployment, and Suicide." *Social Psychiatry and Psychiatric Epidemiology*, May 5, 2021. https://link.springer.com/article/10.1007/s00127-021-02095-9.

20. Chen, Ying-Yeh, ZiYi Cai, Qingsong Chang, Silvia Sara Canetto, and Paul S. F. Yip. "Caregiving as Suicide-Prevention: An Ecological 20-Country Study of the Association between Men's Family Carework, Unemployment, and Suicide." *Social Psychiatry and Psychiatric Epidemiology*, May 5, 2021. https://link.springer.com/article/10.1007/s00127-021-02095-9.

21. Schulte, Brigid, Emily Hallgren, and Roselyn Miller. "Professional Caregiving Men Find Meaning and Pride in Their Work, but Face Stigma." New America, February 4, 2021. www.newamerica.org/better-life-lab/reports/professional-caregiving-men-find-meaning-and-pride-their-work-face-stigma/.

22. Carter, Christine, and Christina Vercelletto. "8 Ways to Motivate Kids to Do Chores." *Parents*, July 14, 2015. www.parents.com/kids/development/social/motivate-kids-to-do-chores/.

23. Koenig, Joan. *The Musical Child: Using the Power of Music to Raise Children Who Are Happy, Healthy, and Whole*. London: William Collins, 2021.

24. Carter, Christine, and Christina Vercelletto. "8 Ways to Motivate Kids to Do Chores." *Parents*, July 14, 2015. www.parents.com/kids/development/social/motivate-kids-to-do-chores/.

25. Strayed, Cheryl, and Steve Almond. "Save Me from This Domestic Drudgery!" *New York Times*, May 8, 2018. www.nytimes.com/2018/05/08/style/household-parenting-marriage-share-work.html.

26. Mae, Kristen. "Women Are Very Familiar with 'Weaponized Incompetence,' and We Are 100% over It." *Scary Mommy*, August 4, 2021. www.scarymommy.com/weaponized-incompetence-household-tasks.

27. Sitomer, Alan Lawrence, and Abby Carter. *Daddies Do It Different*. New York: Disney/Hyperion Books, 2012.

28. Holt, Hannah. *A Father's Love*. New York: Philomel Books, 2019.

29. Harvard Graduate School of Education. "Making Caring Common Project." Making Caring Common, 2014. https://static1.squarespace.com/static/5b7c56e255b02c683659fe43/t/5bae774424a694b5feb2b05f/1538160453604/report-children-raise.pdf.

30. The Harvard Graduate School of Education. "7 Tips for Raising Caring Kids." Making Caring Common Project, December 13, 2021. https://mcc.gse.harvard.edu/resources-for-families/7-tips-raising-caring-kids.

31. Jones, Clarence. "Girls in STEM 2021." NASA, March 30, 2021. www.nasa.gov/content/girls-in-stem-2021.

STEM Like a Girl, 2017. http://stemlikeagirl.org/.

32. American Association of University Women. "The STEM Gap: Women and Girls in Science, Technology, Engineering and Mathematics." AAUW, December 2, 2021. www.aauw.org/resources/research/the-stem-gap/.

33. Van Polanen, Marleen, Cristina Colonnesi, Ruben G. Fukkink, and Louis W. C. Tavecchio. "Is Caregiver Gender Important for Boys and Girls? Gender-Specific Child–Caregiver Interactions and Attachment Relationships." *Early Education and Development*, December 16, 2016. www.tandfonline.com/doi/full/10.1080/10409289.2016.1258928.

34. Kaufman, Scott Barry. "Why Don't People Care That More Men Don't Choose Caregiving Professions?" *Scientific American*, February 4, 2020. https://blogs.scientificamerican.com/beautiful-minds/why-dont-people-care-that-more-men-dont-choose-caregiving-professions/.

35. Kaufman, Scott Barry. "Why Don't People Care That More Men Don't Choose Caregiving Professions?" *Scientific American*, February 4, 2020. https://blogs.scientificamerican.com/beautiful-minds/why-dont-people-care-that-more-men-dont-choose-caregiving-professions/.

Schulte, Brigid. "Providing Care Changes Men." New America, February 4, 2021. www.newamerica.org/better-life-lab/reports/providing-care-changes-men/.

36. The American Association for Men in Nursing, 2021. www.aamn.org/.

CHAPTER 8

1. Watson, J. B. *Psychological Care of Infant and Child*. New York: W. W. Norton, 1928.

2. Duke, C., S. Fried, W. Pliley, and D. Walker. (1989). "Contributions to the History of Psychology: LIX. Rosalie Rayner Watson: The Mother of a Behaviorist's Sons." *Psychological Reports* 65, 1 (1989).

3. Duke, C., S. Fried, W. Pliley, and D. Walker. (1989). "Contributions to the History of Psychology: LIX. Rosalie Rayner Watson: The Mother of a Behaviorist's Sons." *Psychological Reports* 65, 1 (1989).

Smirle, Corinne. "Rosalie Rayner." Psychology's Feminist Voices, 2013. https://feministvoices.com/profiles/rosalie-rayner.

4. Smirle, Corinne. "Rosalie Rayner." Psychology's Feminist Voices, 2013. https://feministvoices.com/profiles/rosalie-rayner.

5. Reichert, Michael. *How to Raise a Boy: The Power of Connection to Build Good Men.* New York: TarcherPerigee, 2019.

6. Schore, Allan N. "All Our Sons: The Developmental Neurobiology and Neuroendocrinology of Boys at Risk." *Infant Mental Health Journal,* January 2, 2017. https://onlinelibrary.wiley.com/doi/10.1002/imhj.21616.

7. Cobb-Clark, Deborah A., and Erdal Tekin. "Fathers and Youth's Delinquent Behavior." National Bureau of Economic Research, October 13, 2011. www.nber.org/papers/w17507.

8. Plunkett, Scott W., Carolyn S. Henry, Linda C. Robinson, Andrew Behnke, and Pedro C. Falcon. "Adolescent Perceptions of Parental Behaviors, Adolescent Self-Esteem, and Adolescent Depressed Mood." *Journal of Child and Family Studies,* January 9, 2007. https://link.springer.com/article/10.1007/s10826-006-9123-0.

9. Fink, Jennifer L. W. "How to Raise a Boy with Michael C. Reichert." *On Boys* podcast, May 9, 2019. www.on-boys-podcast.com/how-to-raise-a-boy-with-michael-c-reichert/.

10. Lloyd, Katrina, and Paula Devine. "Parenting Practices in Northern Ireland: Evidence from the Northern Ireland Household Panel Survey." *Child Care in Practice,* November 29, 2006. www.tandfonline.com/doi/abs/10.1080/13575270600863275.

11. Fink, Jennifer L. W. "Hug Your Boys." *Building Boys,* May 29, 2009. https://buildingboys.net/hug-your-boys/.

12. Field, Tiffany. "Violence and Touch Deprivation in Adolescents." *The Free Library,* December 22, 2002. www.thefreelibrary.com/Violence+and+touch+deprivation+in+adolescents.-a097723210.

13. Feuerman, Marni. "How to Handle a Partner Who Is a 'Mama's Boy.'" Verywell Mind, April 12, 2021. www.verywellmind.com/ways-to-handle-mamas-boy-husband-4050817.

14. Currin, Grant. "Chimpanzee Moms Are Like Us: They Mourn, Dote, and Take 'Me' Time." *National Geographic,* May 5, 2021. www.nationalgeographic.com/animals/article/why-chimpanzee-moms-are-so-much-like-our-own.

15. Currin, Grant. "Chimpanzee Moms Are Like Us: They Mourn, Dote, and Take "Me" Time." *National Geographic,* May 5, 2021. www.nationalgeographic.com/animals/article/why-chimpanzee-moms-are-so-much-like-our-own.

16. Currin, Grant. "Chimpanzee Moms Are Like Us: They Mourn, Dote, and Take 'Me' Time." *National Geographic,* May 5, 2021. www.nationalgeographic.com/animals/article/why-chimpanzee-moms-are-so-much-like-our-own.

17. Moriba, Geraldine, and Jamila Paksima. "Proud Boys." Southern Poverty Law Center. *Sounds Like Hate* podcast, 2022. www.splcenter.org/fighting-hate/extremist-files/group/proud-boys.

18. Pearson, Catherine. "How to Raise Boys Who Aren't Afraid to Be Vulnerable." HuffPost, March 5, 2021. www.huffpost.com/entry/how-to-raise-boys-who-arent-afraid-to-be-vulnerable_l_60413b06c5b6429d08320c8f?ncid=tweetlnkushpmg00000067.

19. Pearson, Catherine. "How to Raise Boys Who Aren't Afraid to Be Vulnerable." HuffPost, March 5, 2021. www.huffpost.com/entry/how-to-raise-boys-who-arent-afraid-to-be-vulnerable_l_60413b06c5b6429d08320c8f?ncid=tweetlnkushpmg00000067.

20. Dent, Maggie. "Teen Boys Are Hungry for Fathers Who Can Care and Connect." Maggie Dent (blog), May 28, 2021. www.maggiedent.com/blog/teen-boys-are-hungry-for-fathers-who-can-care-and-connect/.

21. Allison, Janet, and Jennifer L. W. Fink. "Charlie Capen on Fatherhood and Raising Boys." *On Boys* podcast, October 29, 2019. www.on-boys-podcast.com/charlie-capen-on-fatherhood-and-raising-boys/.

22. Chesler, Caren. "The Model of a Mother and Son Project." Next Avenue, May 12, 2022. www.nextavenue.org/the-model-of-a-mother-and-son-pron/?fbclid=IwAR2a3-78Xeu4CImaQ4auGd0bfVNAUYrPRTNW4VEjuC-WPNxWPoPCnxtvY3cI.

23. Chesler, Caren. "The Model of a Mother and Son Project." Next Avenue, May 12, 2022. www.nextavenue.org/the-model-of-a-mother-and-son-pron/?fbclid=IwAR2a3-78Xeu4CImaQ4auGd0bfVNAUYrPRTNW4VEjuC-WPNxWPoPCnxtvY3cI.

24. Kris, Deborah Farmer. "Listen and Connect: How Parents Can Support Teens' Mental Health Right Now." KQED, December 14, 2020. www.kqed.org/mindshift/57108/listen-and-connect-how-parents-can-support-teens-mental-health-right-now.

25. Kris, Deborah Farmer. "Listen and Connect: How Parents Can Support Teens' Mental Health Right Now." KQED, December 14, 2020. www.kqed.org/mindshift/57108/listen-and-connect-how-parents-can-support-teens-mental-health-right-now.

26. Shaw, Kristin. "The 4 Words That Inspire My Son to Dream." *Today*, January 15, 2020. https://community.today.com/parentingteam/post/the-four-words-that-inspire-my-son-to-dream?cid=sm_npd_td_fb_ma&fbclid=IwAR1nTn6e8RPAXifNehABAyox0YHfhqMUYWx4wgyu6xIbeE_pdE5l-4gMwTAM.

27. Dent, Maggie. "Teen Boys Are Hungry for Fathers Who Can Care and Connect." Maggie Dent (blog), May 28, 2021. www.maggiedent.com/blog/teen-boys-are-hungry-for-fathers-who-can-care-and-connect/.

28. Kin Parents, "Parenting Performance Reviews." YouTube, February 21, 2012. www.youtube.com/watch?v=2P8xB-_0-UY&t=36s.

29. Abdullah, Maryam. "When Do Teens Feel Loved by Their Parents?" *Greater Good Magazine*, September 28, 2020. https://greatergood.berkeley.edu/article/item/when_do_teens_feel_loved_by_their_parents.

30. Joyce, Amy. "'The Power of Showing Up': How to Be a Better, Not Perfect, Parent." *Washington Post*, January 24, 2020. www.washingtonpost. com/lifestyle/2020/01/24/power-showing-up-how-be-better-not-perfect-parent/?utm_campaign=on_parenting&utm_medium=Email&utm_source=Newsletter&wpisrc=nl_parent&wpmm=1.

31. Lester, Leanne, Jacinth Watson, Stacey Waters, and Donna Cross. "The Association of Fly-in Fly-out Employment, Family Connectedness, Parental Presence and Adolescent Wellbeing." *Journal of Child and Family Studies*, August 19, 2016. https://link.springer.com/article/10.1007/s10826-016-0512-8.

Resnick, Michael D., Peter S. Bearman, Robert Blum, Karl E. Bauman, Kathleen M. Harris, Jo Jones, Joyce Tabor, Trish Beuhring, Renee E. Sieving, Marcia Shew, Marjorie Ireland, Linda H. Bearinger, and J. Richard Udry. "Protecting Adolescents from Harm: Findings from the National Longitudinal Study on Adolescent Health." *The Journal of the American Medical Association*, September 1997. www.researchgate.net/profile/Karl-Bauman/publication/13927256_Protecting_Adolescents_From_HarmFindings_From_the_National_Longitudinal_Study_on_Adolescent_Health/links/0deec52deaaea3255b000000/Protecting-Adolescents-From-Harm-Findings-From-the-National-Longitudinal-Study-on-Adolescent-Health.pdf.

32. Damour, Lisa. "What Do Teenagers Want? Potted Plant Parents." *New York Times*, December 14, 2016. www.nytimes.com/2016/12/14/well/family/what-do-teenagers-want-potted-plant-parents.html.

33. Joyce, Amy. "'The Power of Showing Up': How to Be a Better, Not Perfect, Parent." *Washington Post*, January 24, 2020. www.washingtonpost. com/lifestyle/2020/01/24/power-showing-up-how-be-better-not-perfect-parent/?utm_campaign=on_parenting&utm_medium=Email&utm_source=Newsletter&wpisrc=nl_parent&wpmm=1.

CHAPTER 9

1. Lister, Josephine. "Connecting Children to the Outside World Benefits Everyone, Here's Why." HundrED, December 12, 2018. https://hundred.org/en/articles/connecting-children-to-the-outside-world-benefits-everyone-here-s-why.

2. Gurian, Michael. "What We Must Do to Stop the Killing." Gurian Institute, June 2, 2022. https://gurianinstitute.com/what-we-must-do-to-stop-the-killing/.

3. Reichert, Michael C., and Joseph Derrick Nelson. "The State of America's Boys: An Urgent Case for a More Connected Boyhood." Promundo Global, 2020. https://promundoglobal.org/wp-content/uploads/2020/06/GDIGM-Promundo-Masculinity-Research-2020-Final.pdf.

4. Allison, Janet, and Jennifer L. W. Fink, "Cracking the Boy Code with Dr. Adam Cox." *On Boys* podcast, December 17, 2020. www.on-boys-pod-cast.com/cracking-the-boy-code-with-dr-adam-cox/.

5. Ackerly, Rick. "How Can We Help Boys Succeed?" *Building Boys*, December 6, 2016. https://buildingboys.net/how-can-we-help-boys-suc-ceed/.

6. Ackerly, Rick. "How Can We Help Boys Succeed?" *Building Boys*, December 6, 2016. https://buildingboys.net/how-can-we-help-boys-suc-ceed/.

7. Wage and Hour Division. "Child Labor." US Department of Labor. Accessed June 18, 2022. www.dol.gov/agencies/whd/child-labor.

8. ASCD. "What Is the Purpose of Education?" ASCD, 2012. https://files.ascd.org/staticfiles/ascd/pdf/journals/ed_update/eu201207_info-graphic.pdf.

9. ASCD. "What Is the Purpose of Education?" ASCD, 2012. https://files.ascd.org/staticfiles/ascd/pdf/journals/ed_update/eu201207_info-graphic.pdf.

10. Achieve. "College and Career Readiness." Achieve.org, March 29, 2017. www.achieve.org/college-and-career-readiness.

11. Hobson, Thomas. "How Children Take Ownership of Their Lives." *Teacher Tom* (blog), June 9, 2021. https://teachertoms-blog.blogspot.com/2021/06/how-children-take-ownership-of-their.html?fbclid=IwAR2EKpsQKSvd8KZJ-IV2Y2zEFz3QOeC6xqT-NgaQYN-0WNw-Q2uITGJGxSgM#.YMDFNlZsZRw.facebook.

12. Hobson, Thomas. "How Children Take Ownership of Their Lives." *Teacher Tom* (blog), June 9, 2021. https://teachertoms-blog.blogspot.com/2021/06/how-children-take-ownership-of-their.html?fbclid=IwAR2EKpsQKSvd8KZJ-IV2Y2zEFz3QOeC6xqT-NgaQYN-0WNw-Q2uITGJGxSgM#.YMDFNlZsZRw.facebook.

13. "The Cooperative Human." *Nature Human Behavior*, July 9, 2018. www.nature.com/articles/s41562-018-0389-1.

14. Burns, Jane, Philippa Collin, Michelle Blanchard, Natasha De-Freitas, and Sian Lloyd. "Preventing Youth Disengagement and Promoting Engage-ment." Australian Research Alliance for Children and Youth, August 2008. www.aracy.org.au/publications-resources/command/download_file/id/120/filename/.

Hancock, Kirsten J., and Stephen R. Zubrick. "Children and Young People at Risk of Disengagement from School: Literature Review." Com-missioner for Children and Young People Western Australia, August 2015. www.researchgate.net/publication/281257513_Children_and_young_peo-ple_at_risk_of_disengagement_from_school_literature_review.

15. Kutner, Samantha. "Swiping Right: The Allure of Hyper Masculinity and Cryptofascism for Men Who Join the Proud Boys." International Centre for Counter-Terrorism, May 2020. https://icct.edu.ph/.

"Similarities and Differences between Gangs and Violent Extremist Groups." Step Together, 2020. https://steptogether.nsw.gov.au/step-to-gether-home/blog/2020/similarities-and-differences-between-gangs-and-violent-extremist.html.

16. Thrush, Glenn, and Matt Richtel. "A Disturbing New Pattern in Mass Shootings: Young Assailants." *New York Times*, June 2, 2022. www.nytimes.com/2022/06/02/us/politics/mass-shootings-young-men-guns.html?smid=tw-share.

17. Hancock, Kirsten J., and Stephen R. Zubrick. "Children and Young People at Risk of Disengagement from School: Literature Review." Commissioner for Children and Young People Western Australia, August 2015. www.researchgate.net/publication/281257513_Children_and_young_people_at_risk_of_disengagement_from_school_literature_review.

18. Allison, Janet, and Jennifer L. W. Fink. "Cracking the Boy Code with Dr. Adam Cox." *On Boys* podcast, December 17, 2020. www.on-boys-podcast.com/cracking-the-boy-code-with-dr-adam-cox/.

19. Coleman, Patrick A. "It's Time for Americans to Stop Fearing Teenagers." Fatherly.com, August 17, 2017. www.fatherly.com/health-science/why-are-teenagers-scary-cnn-super-predators.

20. Coleman, Patrick A. "It's Time for Americans to Stop Fearing Teenagers." Fatherly.com, August 17, 2017. www.fatherly.com/health-science/why-are-teenagers-scary-cnn-super-predators.

21. Byron, Tanya. "We See Children as Pestilent." *Guardian*, March 16, 2009. www.theguardian.com/education/2009/mar/17/ephebiphobia-young-people-mosquito.

22. Robinson, Susan, and Jenny Cooke. "Engaging Youth in Community Decision Making." YouthREX, 2007. https://youthrex.com/.

23. Godsil, Rachel D., and Alexis McGill Johnson. "Transforming Perception: Black Men and Boys." Perception.org, March 2013. http://perception.org/wp-content/uploads/2014/11/Transforming-Perception.pdf.

24. Taylor, Matthew. "Are Male Babysitters Safe? (Facts & Stats You Should Know)." Kidsit.com, February 1, 2019. https://kidsit.com/are-male-babysitters-safe.

25. Brendtro, Larry K. "The Vision of Urie Bronfenbrenner: Adults Who Are Crazy about Kids." CYC-Net, November 2010. https://cyc-net.org/cyc-online/cyconline-nov2010-brendtro.html.

26. Unger, Layla, and Anna V. Fisher. "Rapid, Experience-Related Changes in the Organization of Children's Semantic Knowledge." *Journal of Experimental Child Psychology* 179 (2019): 1. doi: 10.1016/j.jecp.2018.10.007.

27. Burns, Jane, Philippa Collin, Michelle Blanchard, Natasha De-Freitas, and Sian Lloyd. "Preventing Youth Disengagement and Promoting Engagement." Australian Research Alliance for Children and Youth, August 2008. www.aracy.org.au/publications-resources/command/download_file/id/120/filename/.

28. "Age Requirements." U.S. Department of Labor. Accessed June 18, 2022. www.dol.gov/general/topic/youthlabor/agerequirements#:~:text=As%20a%20general%20rule%2C%20the,under%20the%20age%20of%2016.

29. Miller, Dianna. "Teen Employment Has Many Benefits." Youth First, July 4, 2017. https://youthfirstinc.org/teen-employment-many-benefits/.

30. Jenkins, Henry. "'Cultural Acupuncture': Fan Activism and the Harry Potter Alliance." Transformative Works and Cultures. TWC, June 15, 2012. https://journal.transformativeworks.org/index.php/twc/article/view/305/259.

31. Hollier, Emma, Janae Phillips, Marcella Raphael, Becca Simpson, and Camille Talag. "Avatar: The Last Toolkit." Fandom Forward, 2021. https://static1.squarespace.com/static/5bb7c102aadd3458f7d0aca2/t/60ba8a174a556e560d5308ff/1622837790898/avatar_toolkit.pdf.

32. "Youth Volunteering." Dane County Humane Society, 2022. www.giveshelter.org/how-to-help/volunteer/volunteer-positions/youth.

33. Associated Press. "Ukraine's Teen Drone Hero 'Happy That We Destroyed Someone.'" *Politico*, June 12, 2022. www.politico.com/news/2022/06/12/teen-drones-ukraine-russia-war-00039006.

Bell, Stewart, and Jeff Semple. "Exclusive: How a 15-Year-Old Ukrainian Drone Pilot Helped Destroy a Russian Army Column." *Global News*, June 6, 2022. https://globalnews.ca/news/8893672/15-year-old-ukrainian-drone-pilot-russian-column/.

34. Zook, Chris. "What Are the California CTE Career Pathways?" AES, January 27, 2022. www.aeseducation.com/blog/california-career-pathways.

35. Cardona, Miguel. "Statement by Secretary of Education Miguel Cardona on the President's Fiscal Year 2023 Budget." US Department of Education, March 28, 2022. www.ed.gov/news/press-releases/statement-secretary-education-miguel-cardona-presidents-fiscal-year-2023-budget.

CHAPTER 10

1. Putnick, Diane L., Marc H. Bornstein, Jennifer E. Lansford, Lei Chang, Kirby Deater-Deckard, Laura Di Giunta, Kenneth A. Dodge, Patrick S. Malone, Paul Oburu, Concetta Pastorelli, Ann T. Skinner, Emma Sorbring, Sombat Tapanya, Liliana Maria Uribe Tirado, Arnaldo Zelli, Liane Peña Alampay, Suha M. Al-Hassan, Dario Bacchini, and Anna Silvia Bombi. "Parental Acceptance-Rejection and Child Prosocial Behavior: Developmental Transactions across the Transition to Adolescence in Nine Countries, Mothers and Fathers, and Girls and Boys." *Developmental Psychology*, October 2018. www.ncbi.nlm.nih.gov/pmc/articles/PMC6152837/.

2. Carrasco, Miguel Angel, Begoña Delgado, and Francisco Pablo Holgado-Tello. "Parental Acceptance and Children's Psychological Adjustment: The Moderating Effects of Interpersonal Power and Prestige across Age." *PLOS ONE*, April 11, 2019. https://journals.plos.org/plosone/article?id=10.1371%2Fjournal.pone.0215325.

3. Carrasco, Miguel Angel, Begoña Delgado, and Francisco Pablo Holgado-Tello. "Parental Acceptance and Children's Psychological Adjustment: The Moderating Effects of Interpersonal Power and Prestige across Age." *PLOS ONE*, April 11, 2019. https://journals.plos.org/plosone/article?id=10.1371%2Fjournal.pone.0215325.

Mendo-Lázaro, Santiago, Benito León-Del-Barco, María-Isabel Polo-Del-Río, Rocío Yuste-Tosina, and Víctor-María López-Ramos. "The Role of Parental Acceptance–Rejection in Emotional Instability during Adolescence." International Journal of Environmental Research and Public Health, April 3, 2019. www.ncbi.nlm.nih.gov/pmc/articles/PMC6480184/.

Putnick, Diane L., Marc H. Bornstein, Jennifer E. Lansford, Lei Chang, Kirby Deater-Deckard, Laura Di Giunta, Kenneth A. Dodge, Patrick S. Malone, Paul Oburu, Concetta Pastorelli, Ann T. Skinner, Emma Sorbring, Sombat Tapanya, Liliana Maria Uribe Tirado, Arnaldo Zelli, Liane Peña Alampay, Suha M. Al-Hassan, Dario Bacchini, and Anna Silvia Bombi. " Parental Acceptance-Rejection and Child Prosocial Behavior: Developmental Transactions across the Transition to Adolescence in Nine Countries, Mothers and Fathers, and Girls and Boys." *Developmental Psychology*, October 2018. www.ncbi.nlm.nih.gov/pmc/articles/PMC6152837/.

Rohner, Ronald P. "Introduction to Interpersonal Acceptance-Rejection Theory (Ipartheory), Methods, Evidence, and Implications." University of Connecticut, October 6, 2015. https://csiar.uconn.edu/wp-content/uploads/sites/494/2014/02/Interpersonal-ACCEPTANCE-for-web-10-07-15.pdf.

4. Rohner, Ronald P. "Introduction to Interpersonal Acceptance-Rejection Theory (Ipartheory), Methods, Evidence, and Implications." University of Connecticut, October 6, 2015. https://csiar.uconn.edu/wp-content/uploads/sites/494/2014/02/Interpersonal-ACCEPTANCE-for-web-10-07-15.pdf.

5. Rohner, Ronald P. "Introduction to Interpersonal Acceptance-Rejection Theory (Ipartheory), Methods, Evidence, and Implications." University of Connecticut, October 6, 2015. https://csiar.uconn.edu/wp-content/uploads/sites/494/2014/02/Interpersonal-ACCEPTANCE-for-web-10-07-15.pdf.

6. Rohner, Ronald P. "Introduction to Interpersonal Acceptance-Rejection Theory (Ipartheory), Methods, Evidence, and Implications." University of Connecticut, October 6, 2015. https://csiar.uconn.edu/wp-content/uploads/sites/494/2014/02/Interpersonal-ACCEPTANCE-for-web-10-07-15.pdf.

7. *Mother Love*. Regensburg, Germany: Frederick Pustet Co., 1926.

8. Gordon, Thomas. *Parent Effectiveness Training: The Proven Program for Raising Responsible Children*. New York: Three Rivers Press, 2000.

9. Reichert, Michael. *How to Raise a Boy: The Power of Connection to Build Good Men*. New York: TarcherPerigee, 2020.

10. Kohn, Alfie. "When a Parent's 'I Love You' Means 'Do as I Say.'" *New York Times*, September 14, 2009. www.nytimes.com/2009/09/15/health/15mind.html.

11. Mendo-Lázaro, Santiago, Benito León-Del-Barco, María-Isabel Polo-Del-Río, Rocío Yuste-Tosina, and Víctor-María López-Ramos. "The Role of Parental Acceptance–Rejection in Emotional Instability during Adolescence." International Journal of Environmental Research and Public Health, April 3, 2019. www.ncbi.nlm.nih.gov/pmc/articles/PMC6480184/.

12. Reber, Deborah. "Stop Fighting Your Child's Neurodiversity: A Step-by-Step Plan for Parents in Diagnosis Denial." *ADDitude*, July 15, 2020. www.additudemag.com/neurodivergent-diagnosis-adhd-autism-learning/.

13. Gresko, Brian. "Boys in Dresses and the Differences That Define Us." Quiet Revolution, November 13, 2016. https://quietrev.com/boys-in-dresses-and-the-differences-that-define-us/#.YiY0NZQlP5M.twitter.

14. Deitcher, Jay. "I Wanted My Son to Reject Masculine Stereotypes. Then He Fell in Love with Tractors." *Today*, April 21, 2022. www.today.com/parents/essay/man-boxes-stereotypes-tractors-rcna25364.

15. Deitcher, Jay. "I Wanted My Son to Reject Masculine Stereotypes. Then He Fell in Love with Tractors." *Today*, April 21, 2022. www.today.com/parents/essay/man-boxes-stereotypes-tractors-rcna25364.

16. Ketteler, Judi, "Call Me by My Name." *Cincinnati Magazine*, January 24, 2022. www.cincinnatimagazine.com/article/call-me-by-my-name/.

17. Bell, Braden. "If Teens Know You Love and Trust Them They Will Do All They Can to Return That (Part 1)." *Parent-Teacher Conference: A Teacher-Dad on Parenting Teens*. April 3, 2022. https://bradenbellphd.substack.com/p/if-teens-know-you-love-and-trust?s=r.

18. Nagata, Jason M., Kirsten Bibbins-Domingo, Andrea K. Garber, Scott Griffiths, Eric Vittinghoff, and Stuart B. Murray. "Boys, Bulk, and Body Ideals: Sex Differences in Weight-Gain Attempts among Adolescents in the United States." *Journal of Adolescent Health*, October 25, 2018. www.jahonline.org/article/S1054-139X(18)30417-8/fulltext.

19. Eisenberg, Marla E., Melanie Wall, and Dianne Neumark-Sztainer. "Muscle-Enhancing Behaviors among Adolescent Girls and Boys." American Academy of Pediatrics, December 1, 2012. https://publications.aap.org/pediatrics/article-abstract/130/6/1019/30280/Muscle-enhancing-Behaviors-Among-Adolescent-Girls?redirectedFrom=fulltext.

20. Nagata, Jason M., Stuart B. Murray, Kirsten Bibbins-Domingo, Andrea K. Garber, Deborah Mitchison, and Scott Griffiths. "Predictors of

Muscularity-Oriented Disordered Eating Behaviors in U.S. Young Adults: A Prospective Cohort Study." *International Journal of Eating Disorders*, June 20, 2019. https://onlinelibrary.wiley.com/doi/full/10.1002/eat.23094.

21. Rozin, Paul, and Edward Poyzman. "Why Is the News Always So Depressing?" The Decision Lab, 2022. https://thedecisionlab.com/biases/negativity-bias.

22. Kohn, Alfie. "When a Parent's 'I Love You' Means 'Do as I Say.'" *New York Times*, September 14, 2009. www.nytimes.com/2009/09/15/health/15mind.html.

23. Gordon, Thomas. *Parent Effectiveness Training: The Proven Program for Raising Responsible Children*. New York: Three Rivers Press, 2000.

24. Reichert, Michael. *How to Raise a Boy: The Power of Connection to Build Good Men*. New York: TarcherPerigee, 2020.

Index

About the Author

Jennifer L. W. Fink is the creator of BuildingBoys.net and cohost of the podcast *On Boys: Real Talk about Parenting, Teaching, & Reaching Tomorrow's Men*. She's a freelance journalist whose work has been published by the *New York Times, Washington Post, U.S. News and World Report,* Fox News, *Parents,* and *Parade*. Fink is also the author of *The First-Time Mom's Guide to Raising Boys: Practical Advice for Your Son's Formative Years*. She lives in rural Wisconsin and is the proud mother of four sons.